Epilogue 50>> December 6th



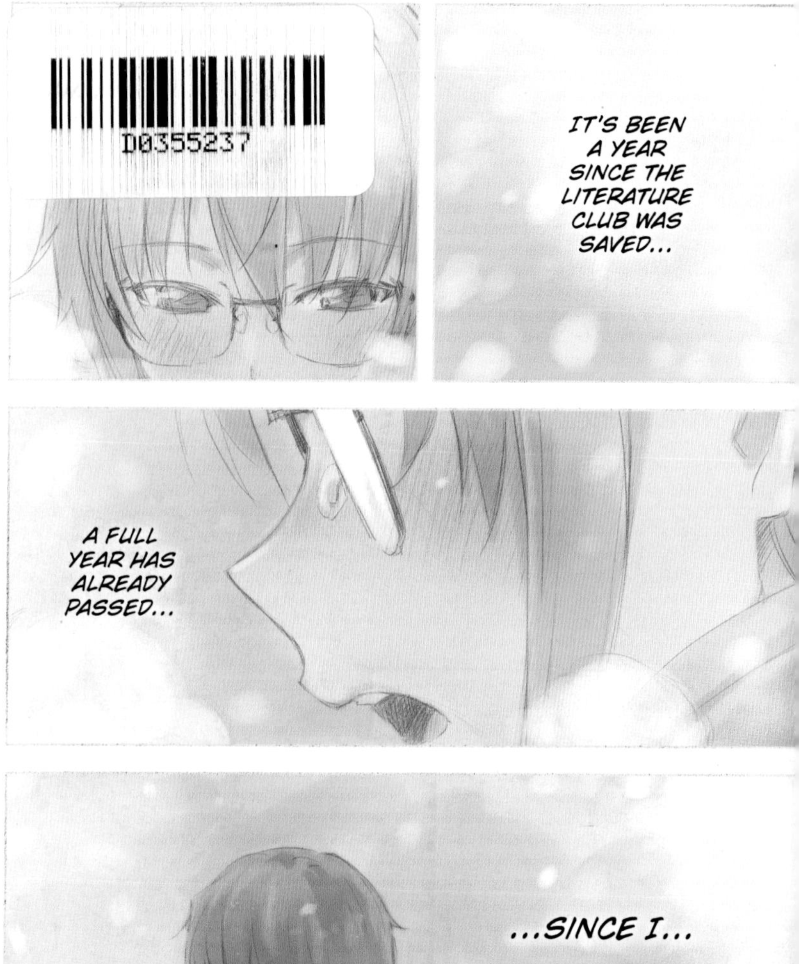
IT'S BEEN A YEAR SINCE THE LITERATURE CLUB WAS SAVED...
A FULL YEAR HAS ALREADY PASSED...
...SINCE I...

...FELL IN LOVE WITH HIM.

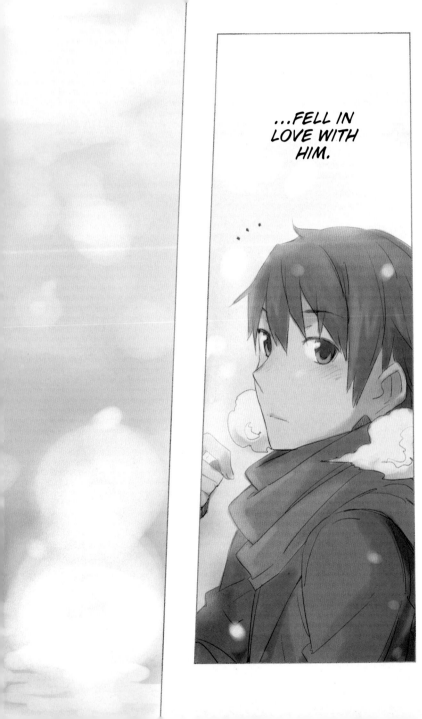

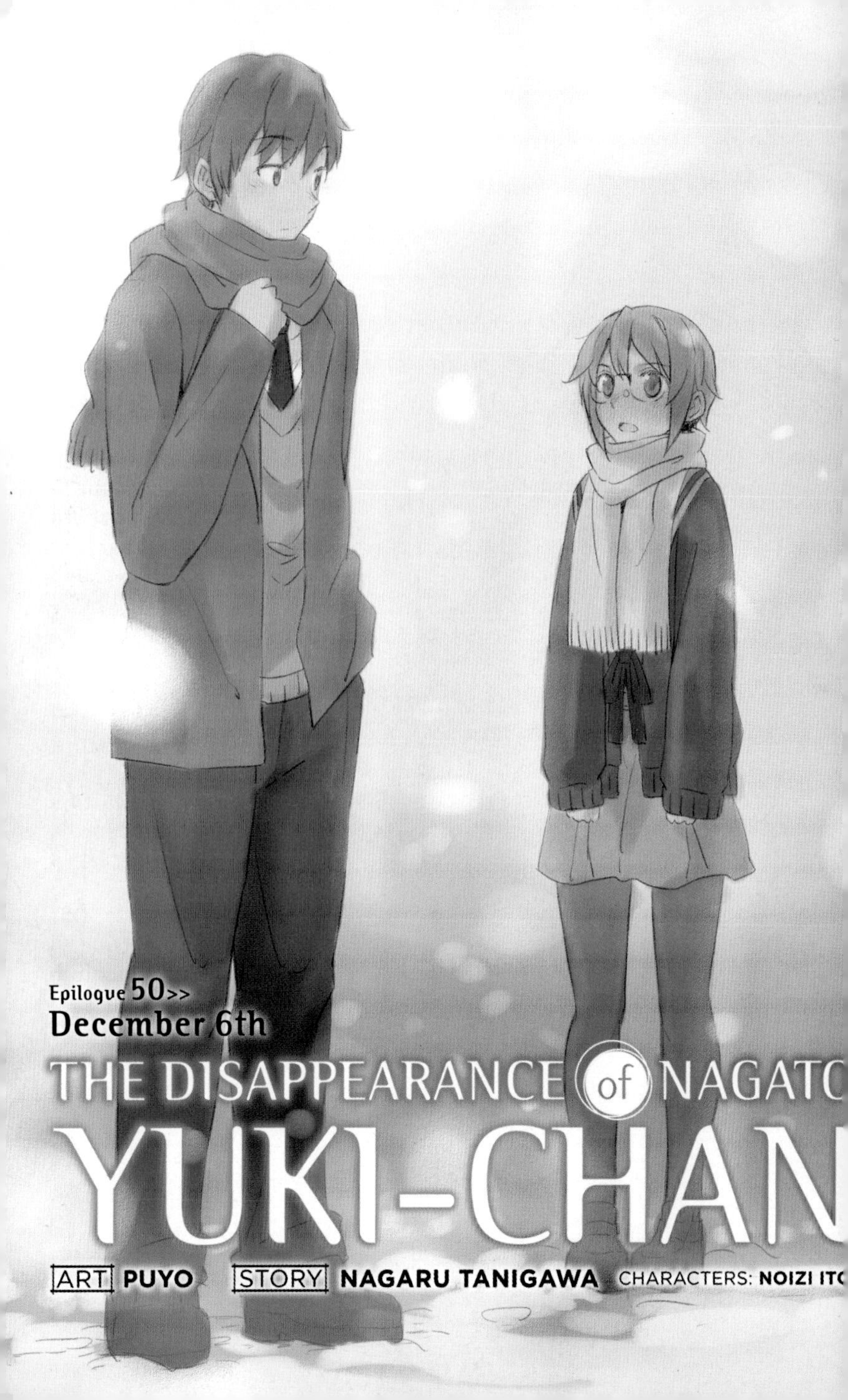
Epilogue 50>>
December 6th
THE DISAPPEARANCE of NAGATO
YUKI-CHAN
ART PUYO
STORY NAGARU TANIGAWA
CHARACTERS: NOIZI ITO

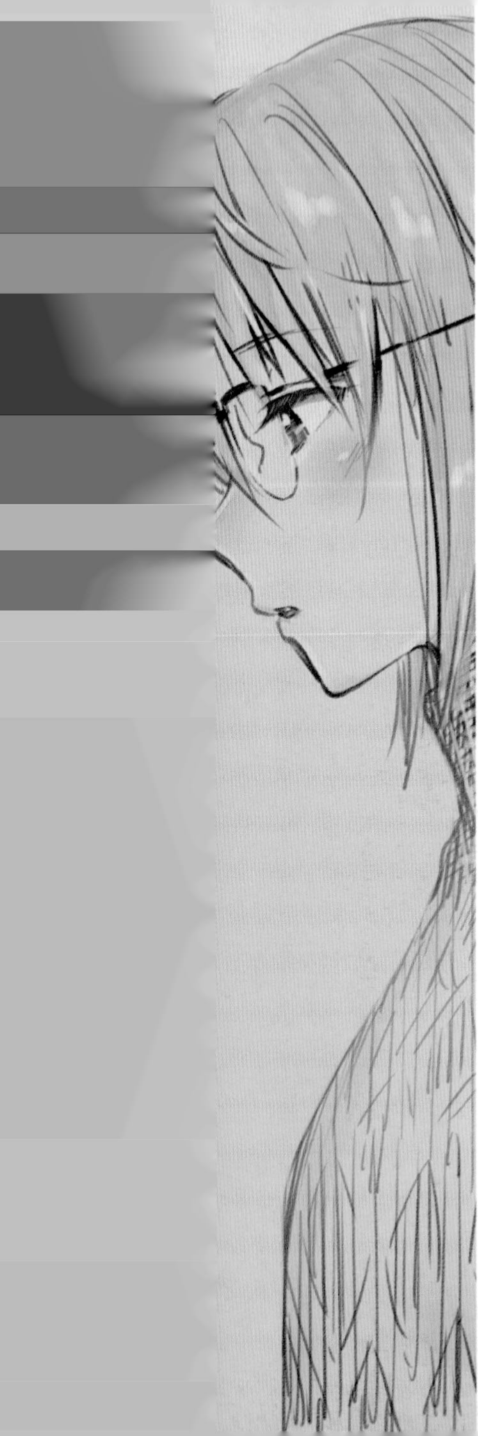

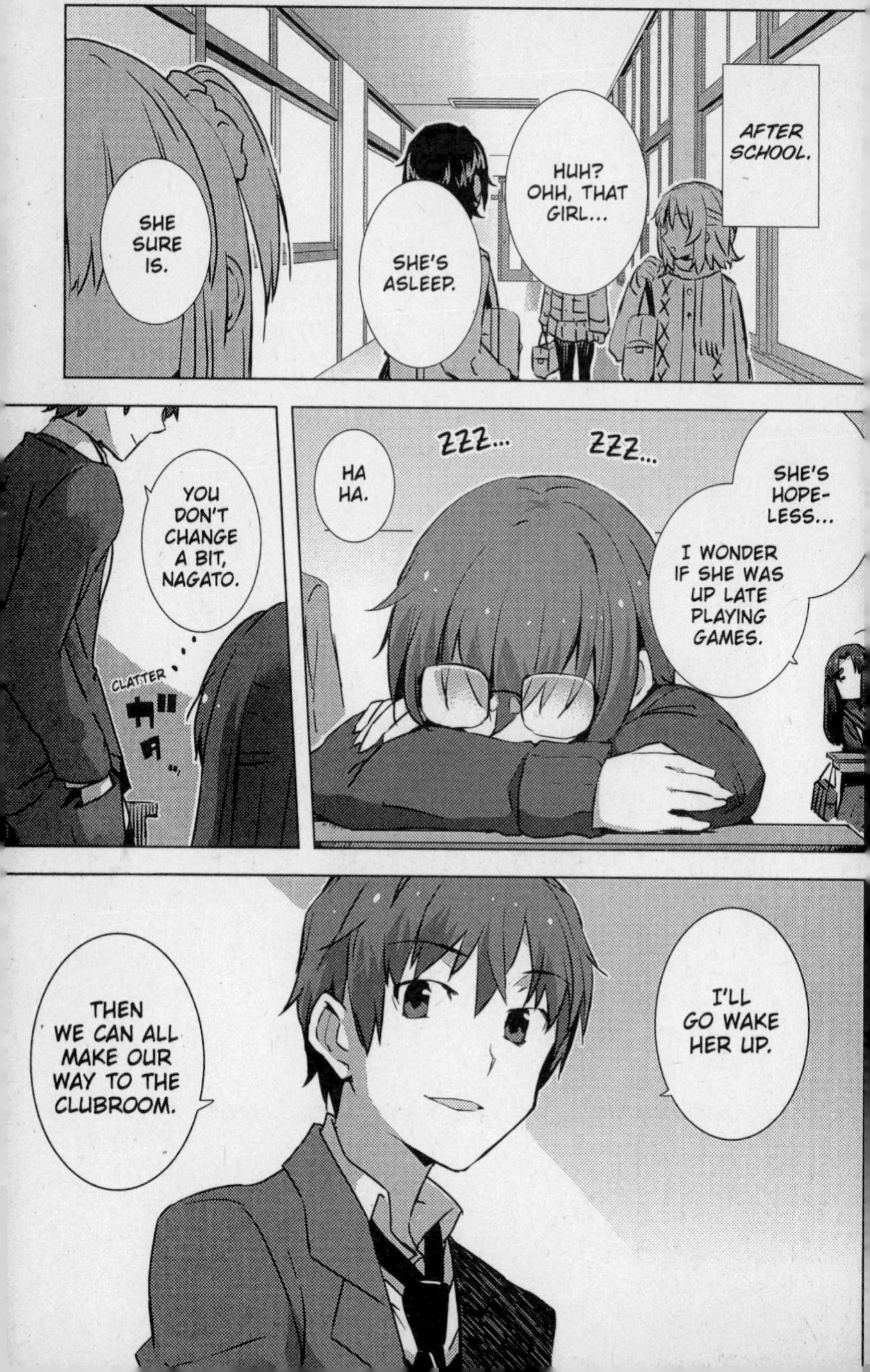
AFTER SCHOOL.
HUH? OHH, THAT GIRL...
SHE'S ASLEEP.
SHE SURE IS.
ZZZ...
ZZZ...
SHE'S HOPE-LESS...
I WONDER IF SHE WAS UP LATE PLAYING GAMES.
HA HA.
YOU DON'T CHANGE A BIT, NAGATO.
CLATTER
I'LL GO WAKE HER UP.
THEN WE CAN ALL MAKE OUR WAY TO THE CLUBROOM.

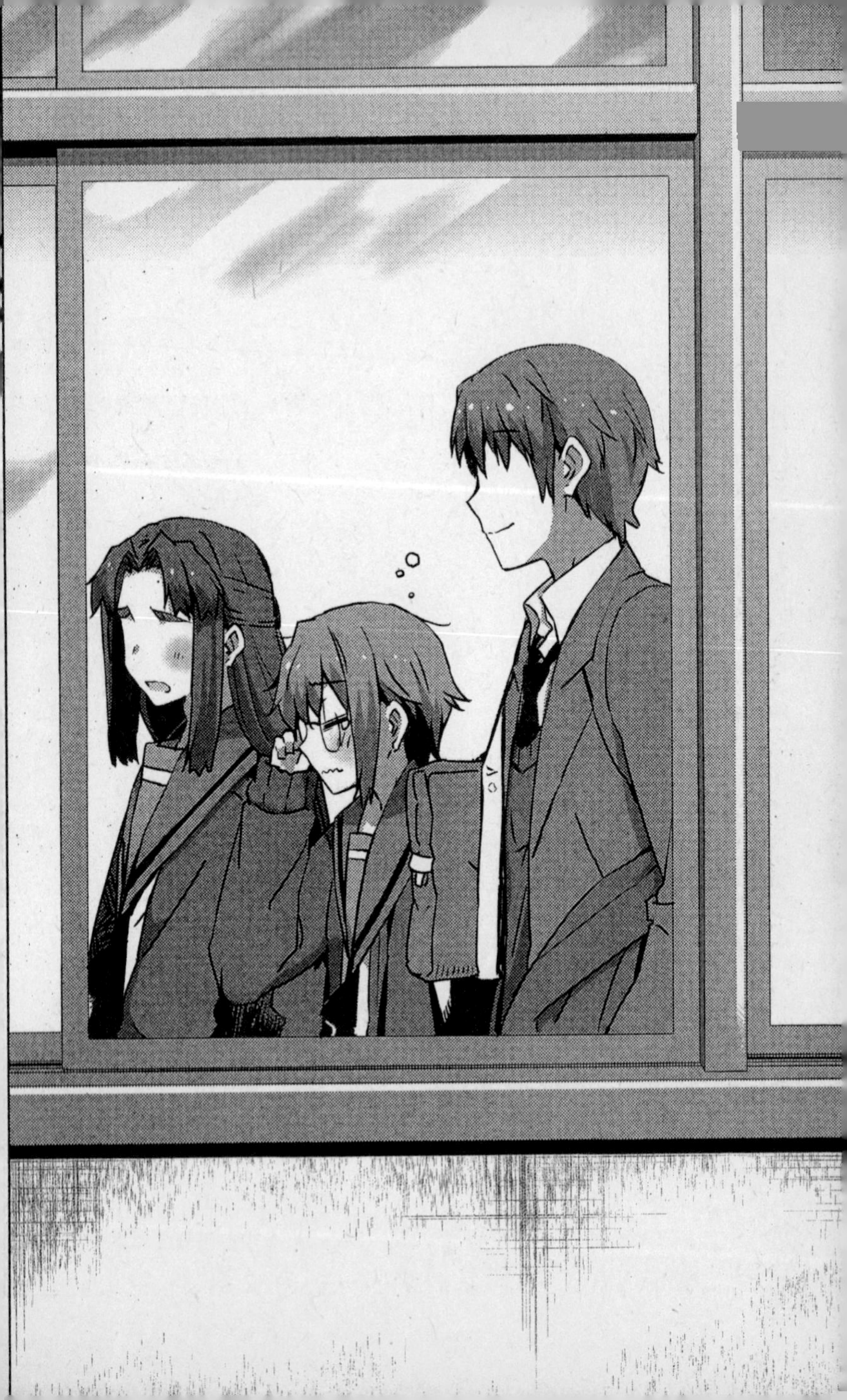

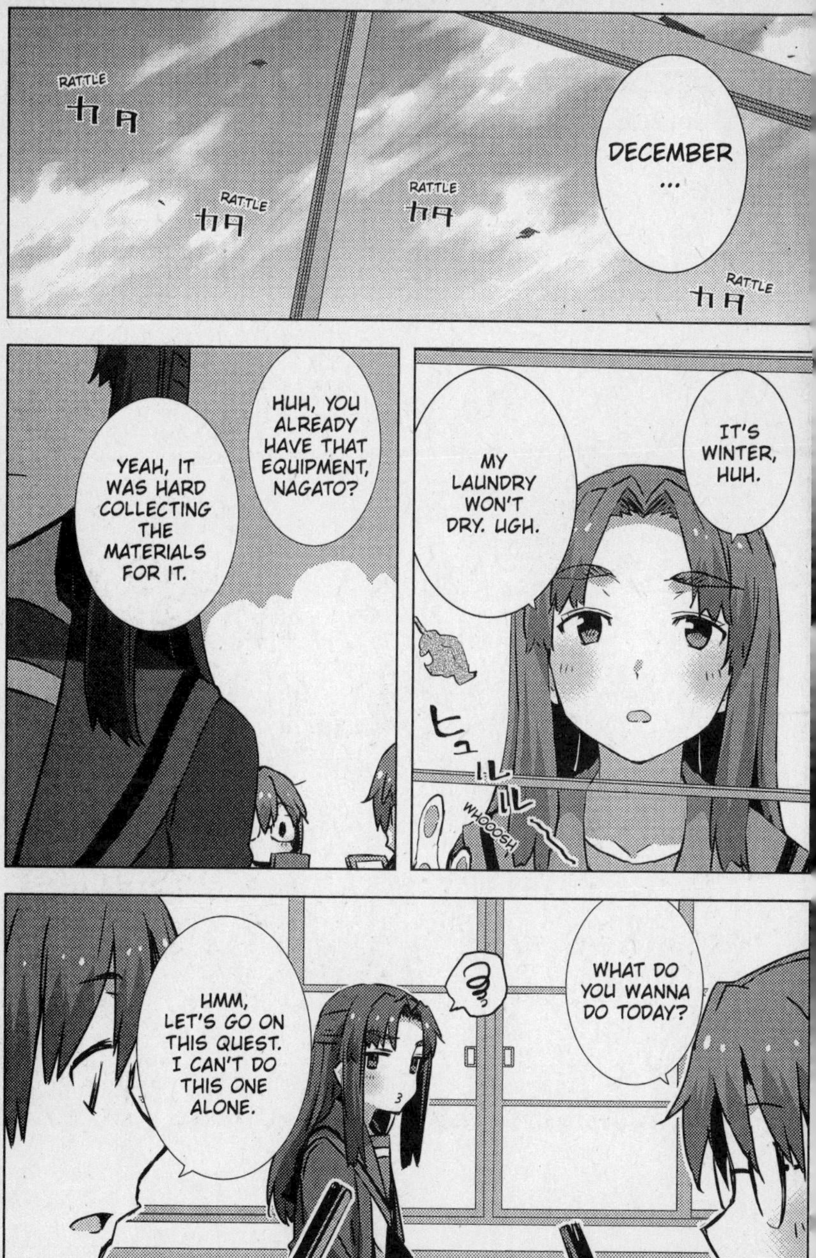
DECEMBER ...
RATTLE
カタ
RATTLE
カタ
RATTLE
カタ
RATTLE
カタ
IT'S WINTER, HUH.
MY LAUNDRY WON'T DRY. UGH.
ヒュルル～
WHOOOSH
HUH, YOU ALREADY HAVE THAT EQUIPMENT, NAGATO?
YEAH, IT WAS HARD COLLECTING THE MATERIALS FOR IT.
WHAT DO YOU WANNA DO TODAY?
HMM, LET'S GO ON THIS QUEST. I CAN'T DO THIS ONE ALONE.

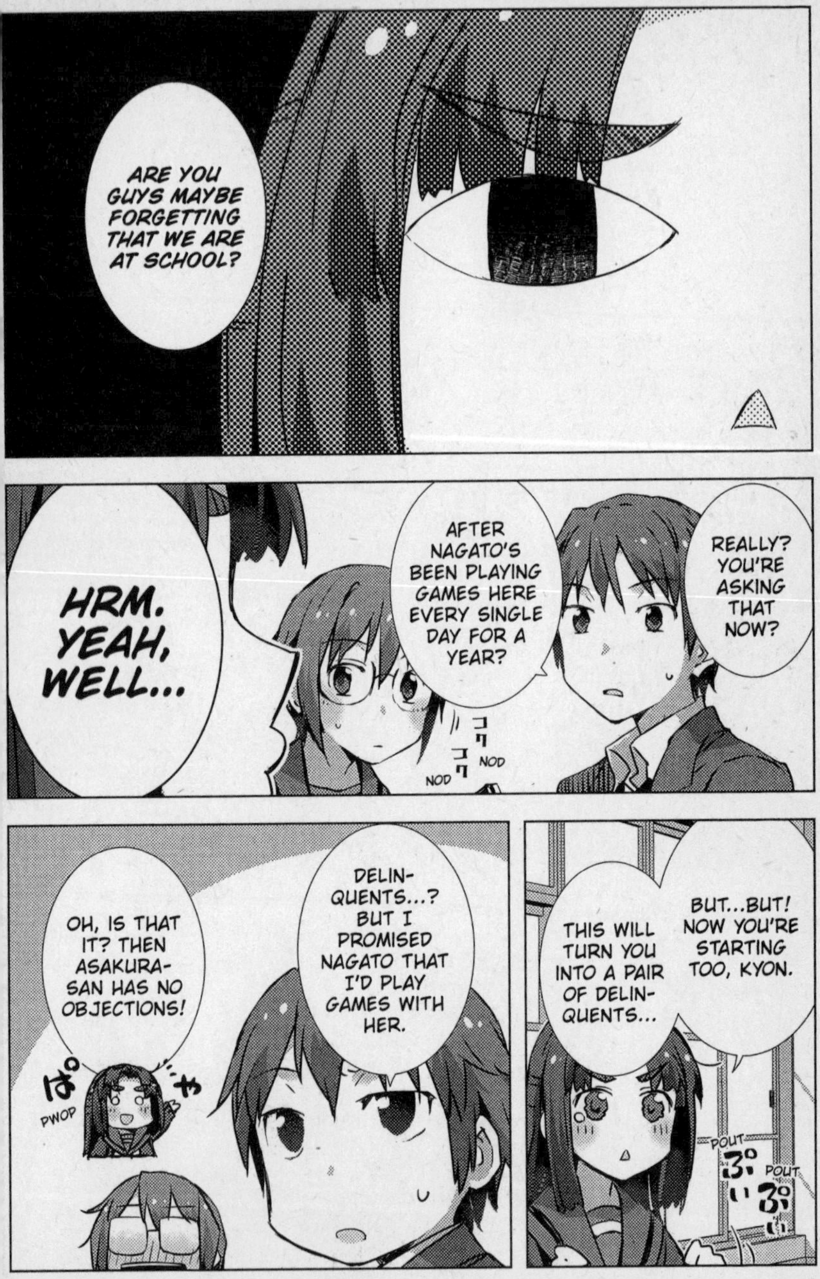
ARE YOU GUYS MAYBE FORGETTING THAT WE ARE AT SCHOOL?
REALLY? YOU'RE ASKING THAT NOW?
AFTER NAGATO'S BEEN PLAYING GAMES HERE EVERY SINGLE DAY FOR A YEAR?
NOD
NOD
HRM. YEAH, WELL...
BUT...BUT! NOW YOU'RE STARTING TOO, KYON.
THIS WILL TURN YOU INTO A PAIR OF DELIN-QUENTS...
POUT
POUT
DELIN-QUENTS...? BUT I PROMISED NAGATO THAT I'D PLAY GAMES WITH HER.
OH, IS THAT IT? THEN ASAKURA-SAN HAS NO OBJECTIONS!
PWOP

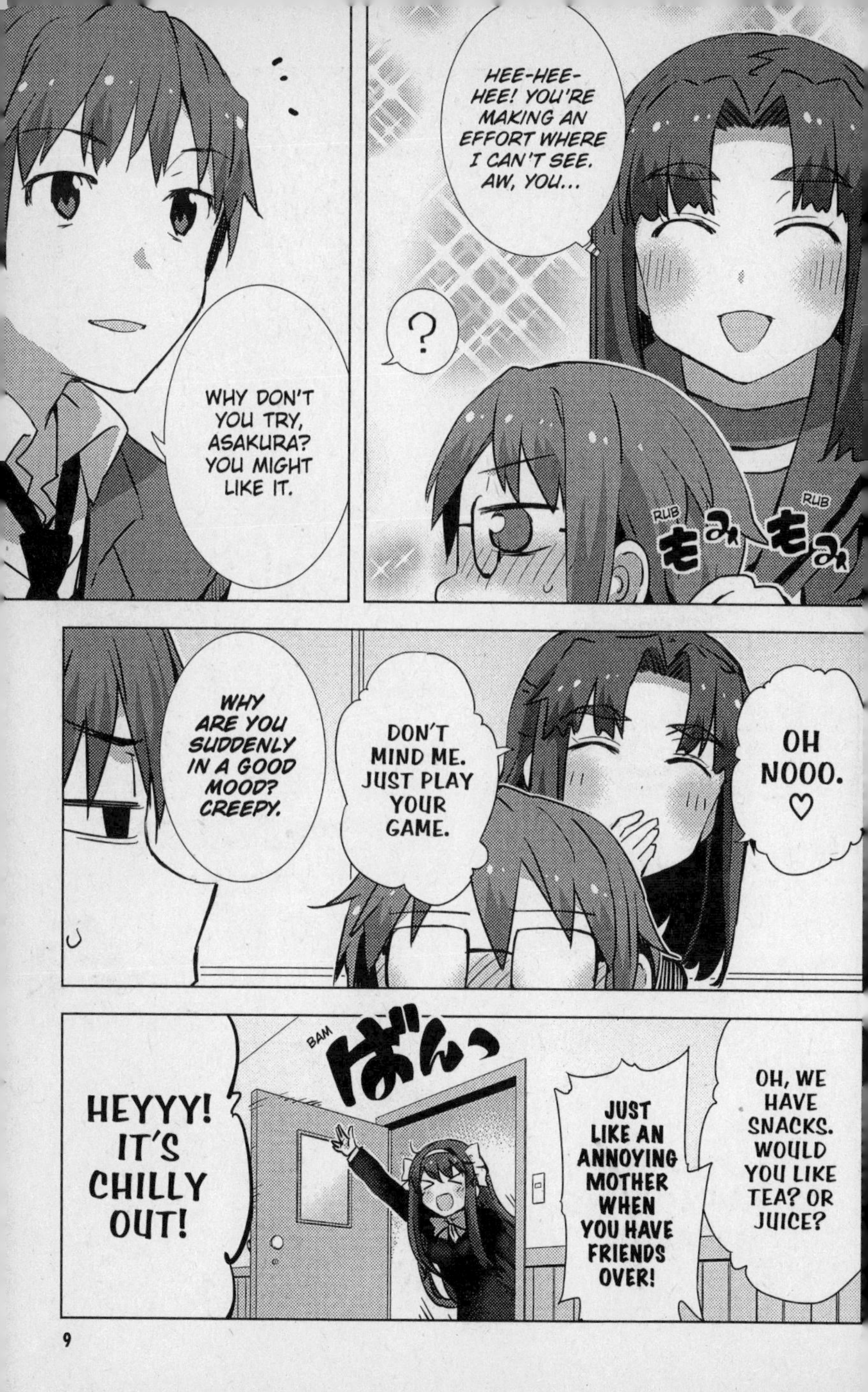
HEE-HEE-HEE! YOU'RE MAKING AN EFFORT WHERE I CAN'T SEE. AW, YOU...
?
RUB RUB
もみもみ
...
WHY DON'T YOU TRY, ASAKURA? YOU MIGHT LIKE IT.
OH NOOO. ♡
DON'T MIND ME. JUST PLAY YOUR GAME.
WHY ARE YOU SUDDENLY IN A GOOD MOOD? CREEPY.
OH, WE HAVE SNACKS. WOULD YOU LIKE TEA? OR JUICE?
JUST LIKE AN ANNOYING MOTHER WHEN YOU HAVE FRIENDS OVER!
BAM
ばんっ
HEYYY! IT'S CHILLY OUT!

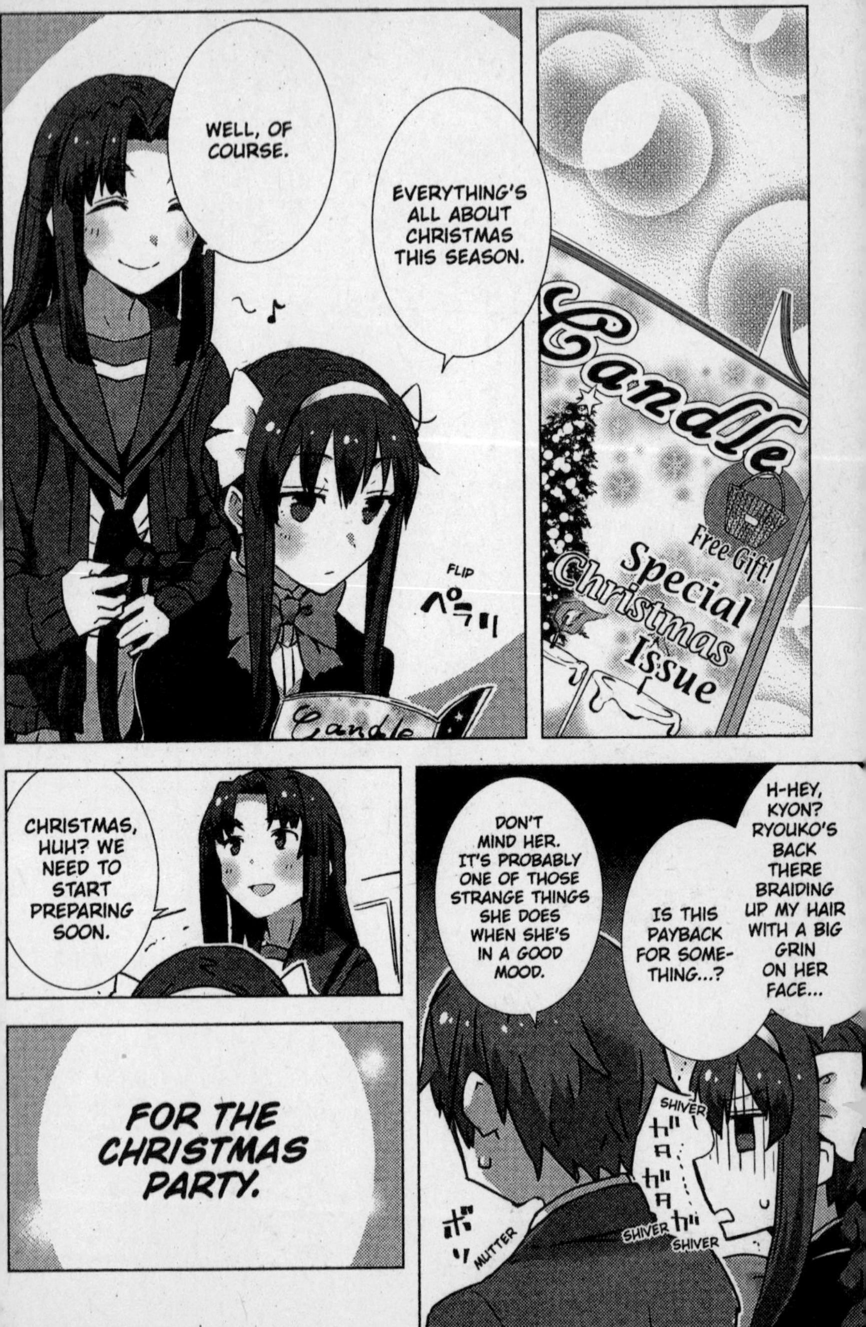
Candle
Free Gift!
Special Christmas Issue
WELL, OF COURSE.
EVERYTHING'S ALL ABOUT CHRISTMAS THIS SEASON.
FLIP
ペラり
Candle
H-HEY, KYON? RYOUKO'S BACK THERE BRAIDING UP MY HAIR WITH A BIG GRIN ON HER FACE...
IS THIS PAYBACK FOR SOME-THING...?
DON'T MIND HER. IT'S PROBABLY ONE OF THOSE STRANGE THINGS SHE DOES WHEN SHE'S IN A GOOD MOOD.
SHIVER SHIVER SHIVER
MUTTER
CHRISTMAS, HUH? WE NEED TO START PREPARING SOON.
FOR THE CHRISTMAS PARTY.

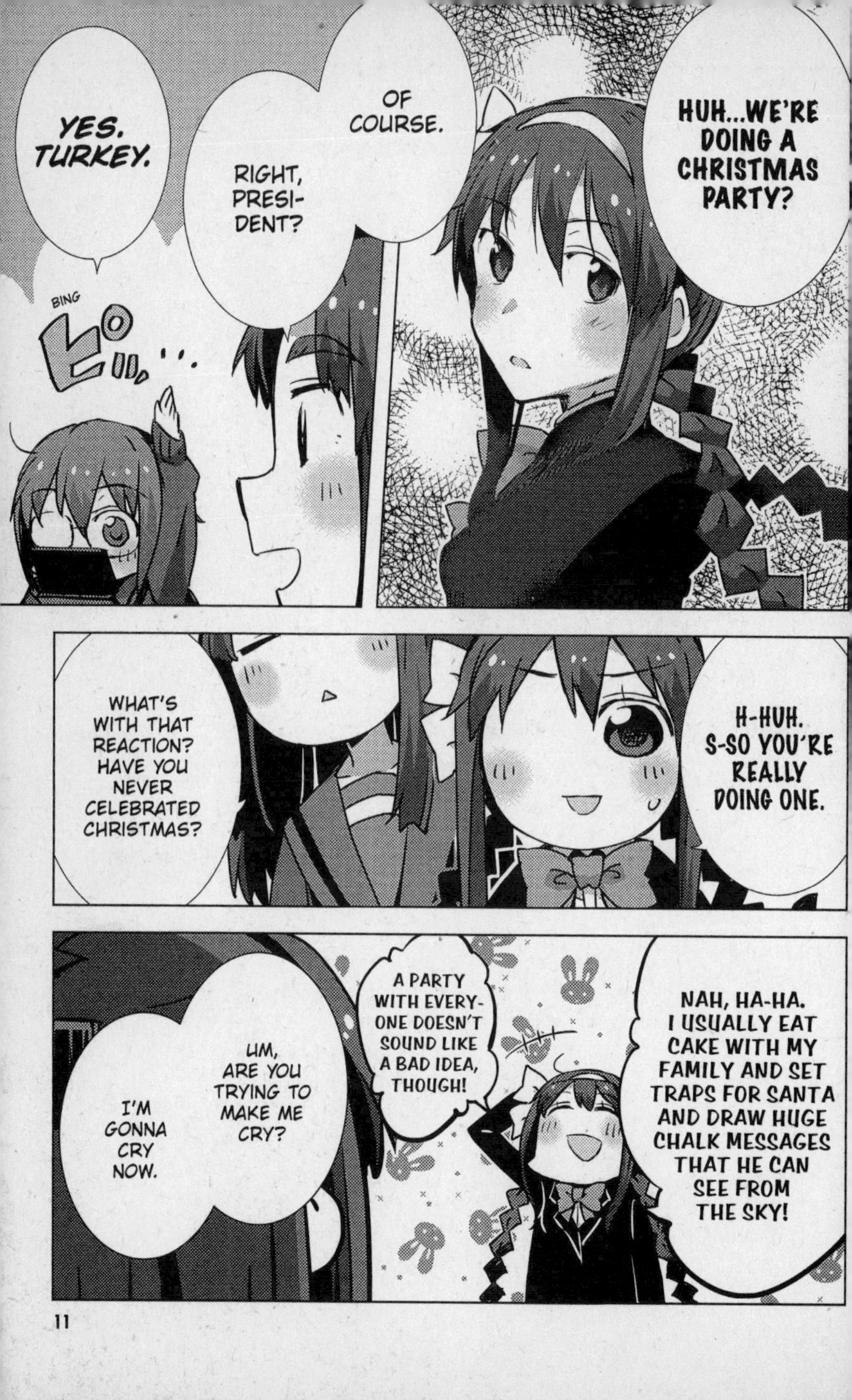

HUH...WE'RE DOING A CHRISTMAS PARTY?
OF COURSE.
RIGHT, PRESIDENT?
YES. TURKEY.
BING
H-HUH. S-SO YOU'RE REALLY DOING ONE.
WHAT'S WITH THAT REACTION? HAVE YOU NEVER CELEBRATED CHRISTMAS?
NAH, HA-HA. I USUALLY EAT CAKE WITH MY FAMILY AND SET TRAPS FOR SANTA AND DRAW HUGE CHALK MESSAGES THAT HE CAN SEE FROM THE SKY!
A PARTY WITH EVERYONE DOESN'T SOUND LIKE A BAD IDEA, THOUGH!
UM, ARE YOU TRYING TO MAKE ME CRY?
I'M GONNA CRY NOW.

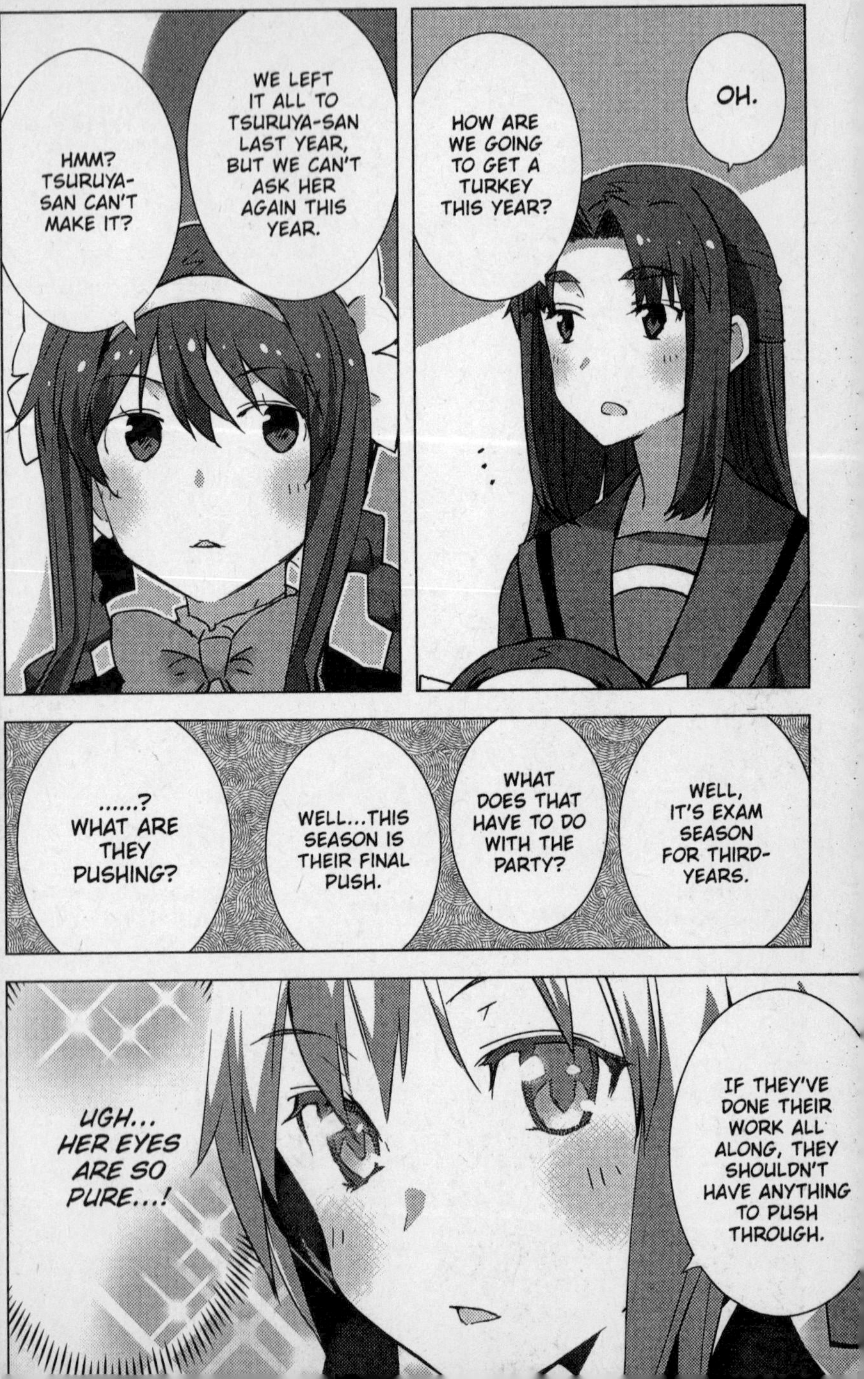
OH.
HOW ARE WE GOING TO GET A TURKEY THIS YEAR?
WE LEFT IT ALL TO TSURUYA-SAN LAST YEAR, BUT WE CAN'T ASK HER AGAIN THIS YEAR.
HMM? TSURUYA-SAN CAN'T MAKE IT?
WELL, IT'S EXAM SEASON FOR THIRD-YEARS.
WHAT DOES THAT HAVE TO DO WITH THE PARTY?
WELL...THIS SEASON IS THEIR FINAL PUSH.
......? WHAT ARE THEY PUSHING?
IF THEY'VE DONE THEIR WORK ALL ALONG, THEY SHOULDN'T HAVE ANYTHING TO PUSH THROUGH.
UGH... HER EYES ARE SO PURE...!

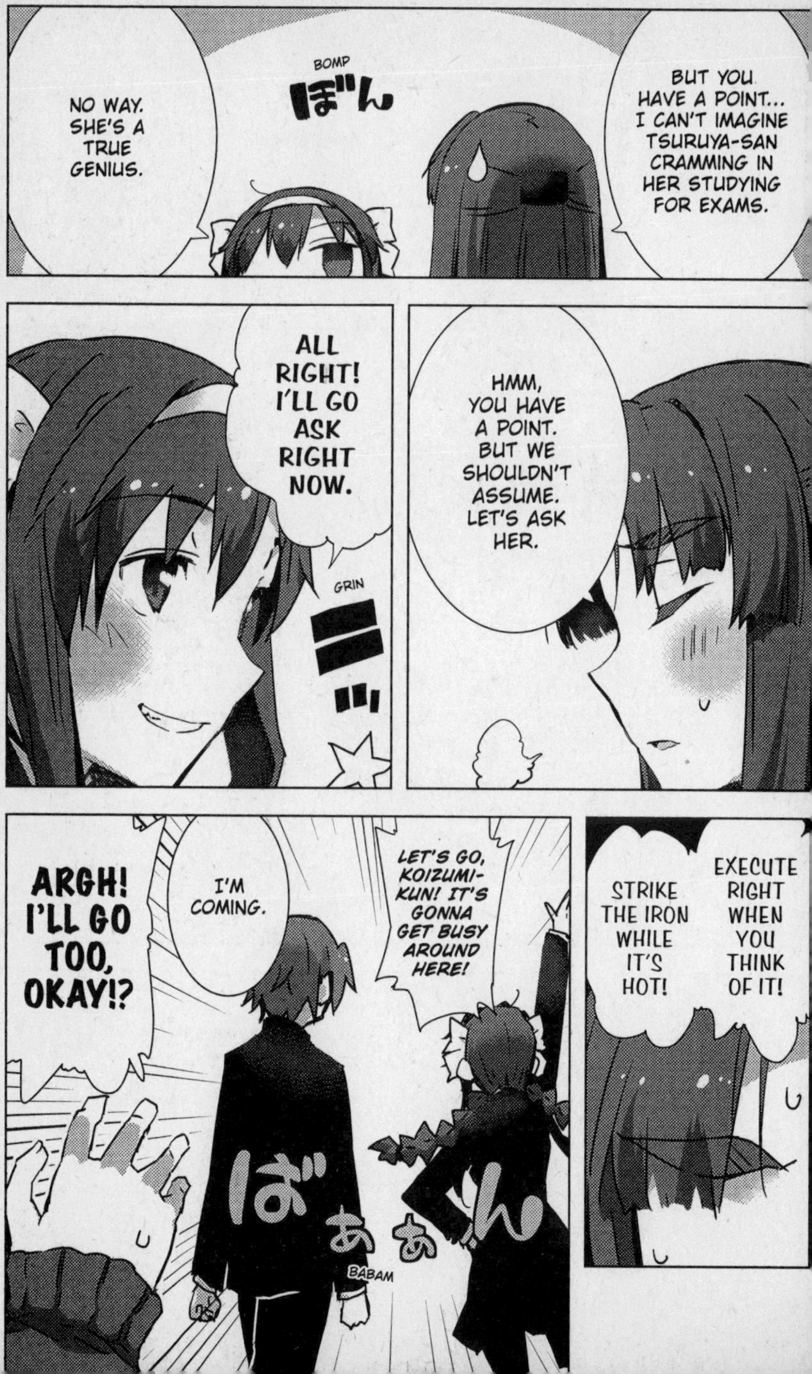
BUT YOU HAVE A POINT... I CAN'T IMAGINE TSURUYA-SAN CRAMMING IN HER STUDYING FOR EXAMS.
BOMP
ぼん
NO WAY. SHE'S A TRUE GENIUS.
HMM, YOU HAVE A POINT. BUT WE SHOULDN'T ASSUME. LET'S ASK HER.
ALL RIGHT! I'LL GO ASK RIGHT NOW.
GRIN
EXECUTE RIGHT WHEN YOU THINK OF IT!
STRIKE THE IRON WHILE IT'S HOT!
LET'S GO, KOIZUMI-KUN! IT'S GONNA GET BUSY AROUND HERE!
I'M COMING.
ARGH! I'LL GO TOO, OKAY!?
ばぁぁん
BABAM

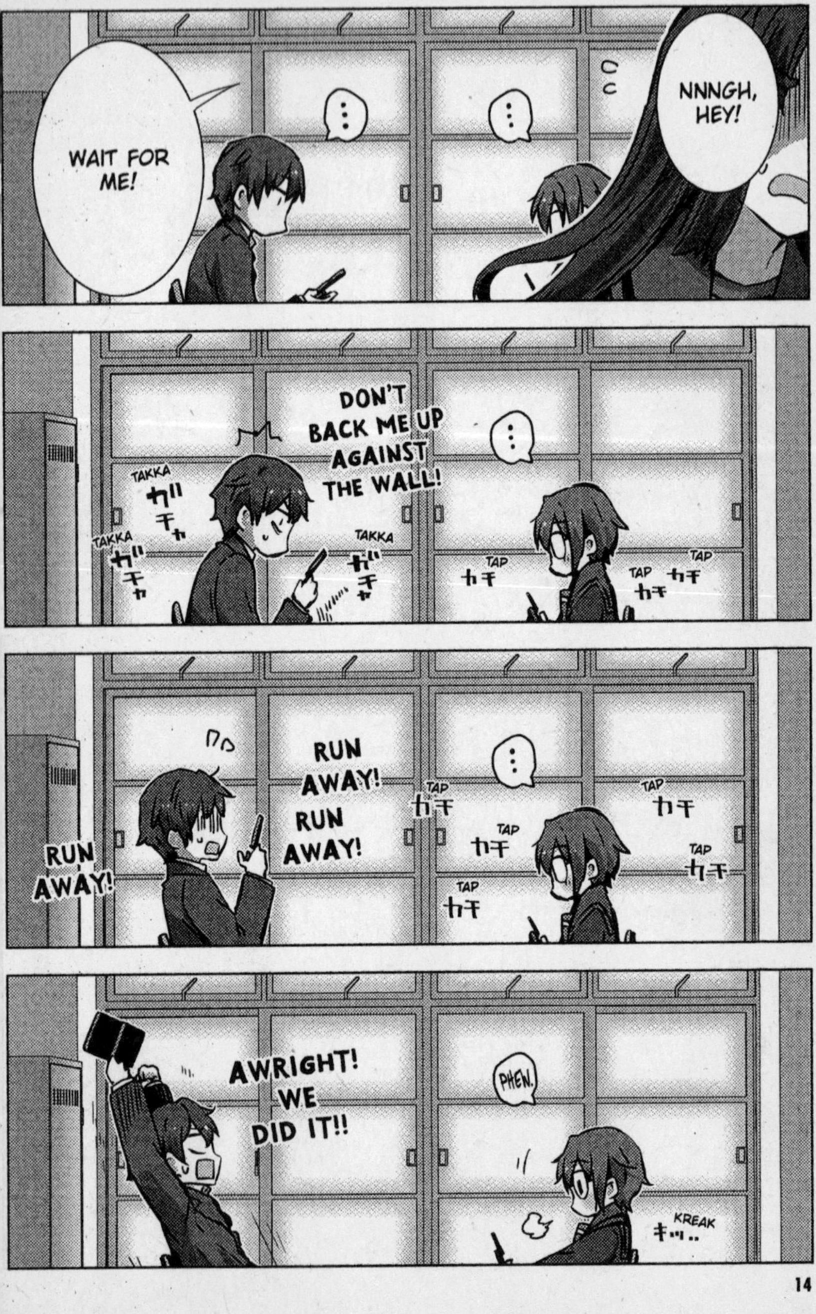
NNNGH, HEY!
…
…
WAIT FOR ME!
TAP カチ
TAP カチ
TAP カチ
…
DON'T BACK ME UP AGAINST THE WALL!
TAKKA ガチャ
TAKKA ガチャ
TAKKA ガチャ
TAP カチ
TAP カチ
…
TAP カチ
RUN AWAY!
RUN AWAY!
TAP カチ
RUN AWAY!
PHEW.
KREAK キッ..
AWRIGHT! WE DID IT!!

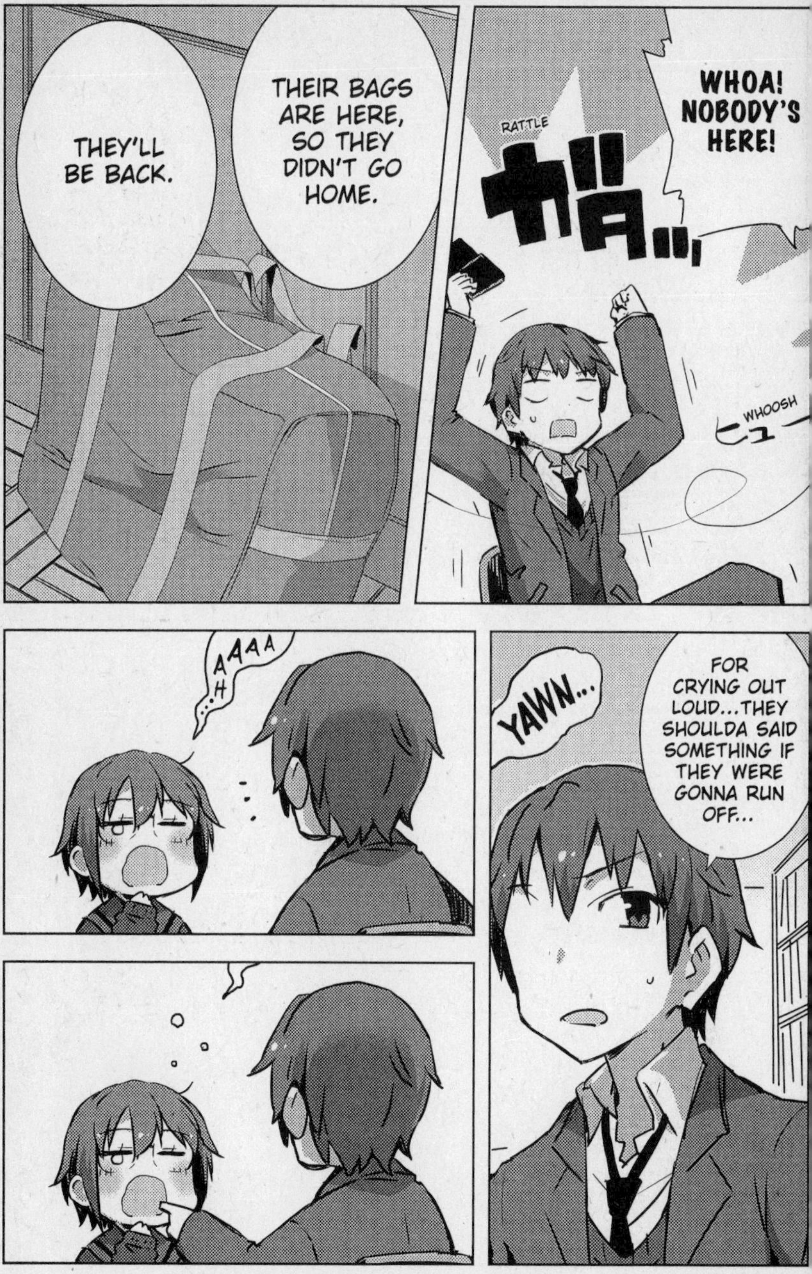
WHOA! NOBODY'S HERE!
RATTLE
WHOOSH
THEIR BAGS ARE HERE, SO THEY DIDN'T GO HOME.
THEY'LL BE BACK.
FOR CRYING OUT LOUD...THEY SHOULDA SAID SOMETHING IF THEY WERE GONNA RUN OFF...
YAWN...
AAAAH

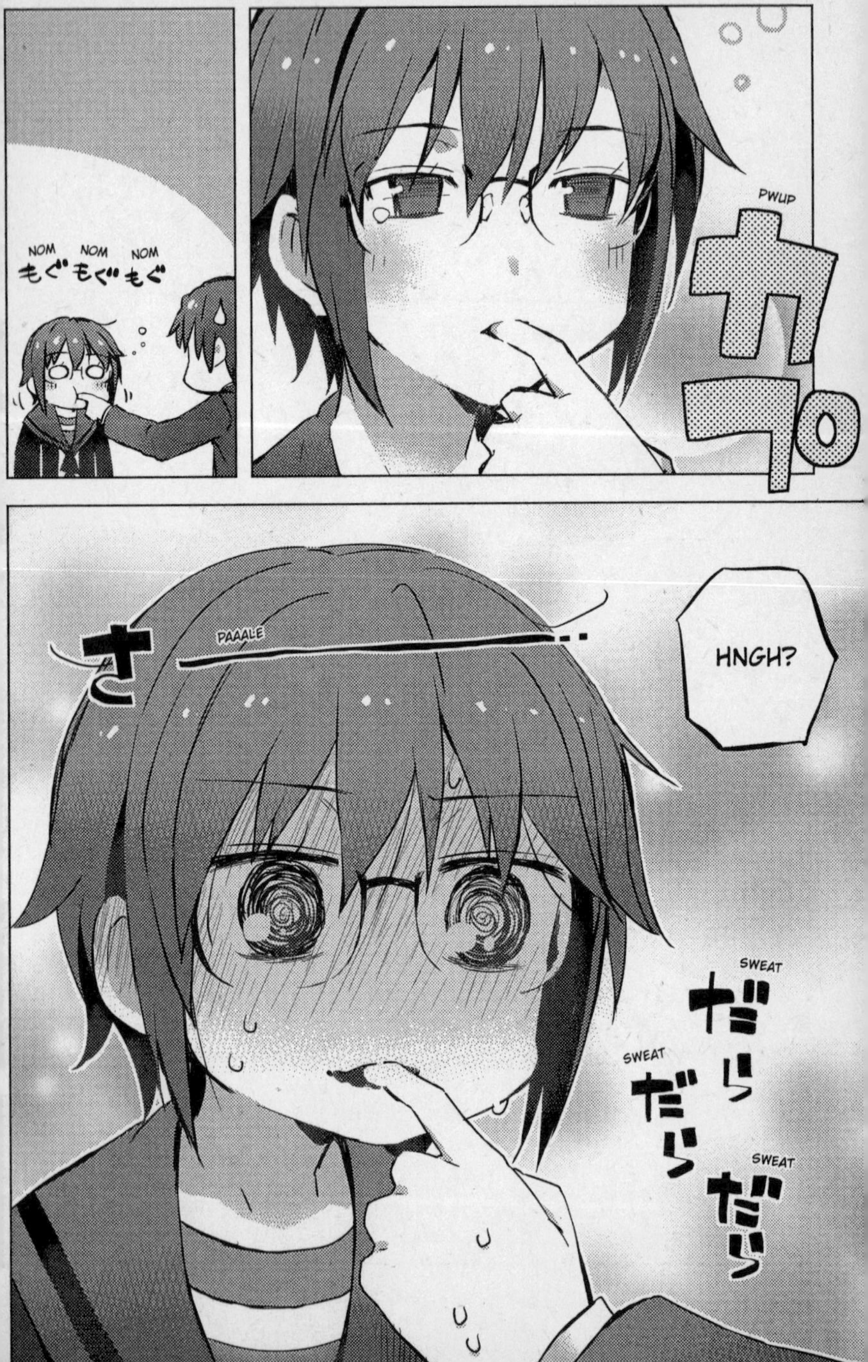
PWUP
カプ
NOM NOM NOM
もぐもぐもぐ
HNGH?
PAAALE
さーー…
SWEAT SWEAT SWEAT
だらだらだらだら

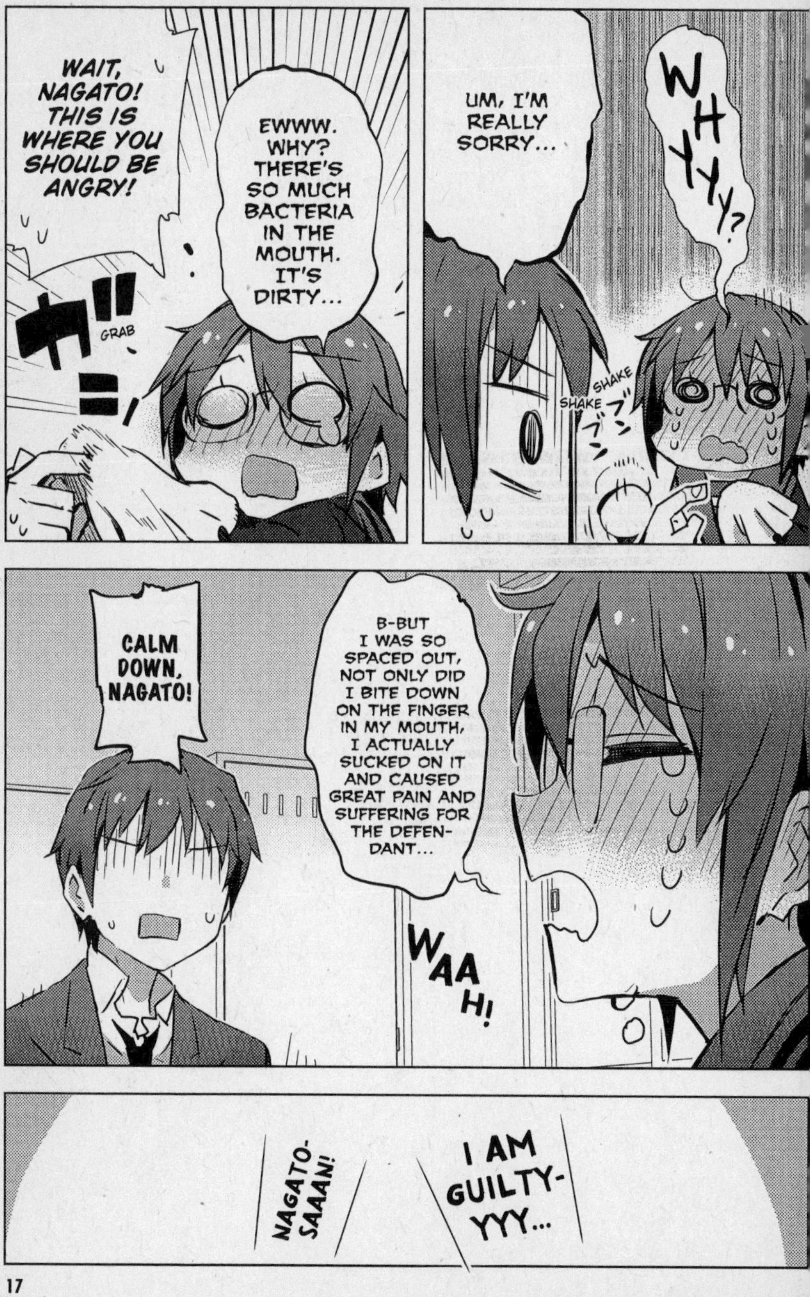
WHYYYY?
UM, I'M REALLY SORRY...
SHAKE
SHAKE
EWWW. WHY? THERE'S SO MUCH BACTERIA IN THE MOUTH. IT'S DIRTY...
WAIT, NAGATO! THIS IS WHERE YOU SHOULD BE ANGRY!
GRAB
B-BUT I WAS SO SPACED OUT, NOT ONLY DID I BITE DOWN ON THE FINGER IN MY MOUTH, I ACTUALLY SUCKED ON IT AND CAUSED GREAT PAIN AND SUFFERING FOR THE DEFEN-DANT...
WAAH!
CALM DOWN, NAGATO!
I AM GUILTY-YYY...
NAGATO-SAAAN!

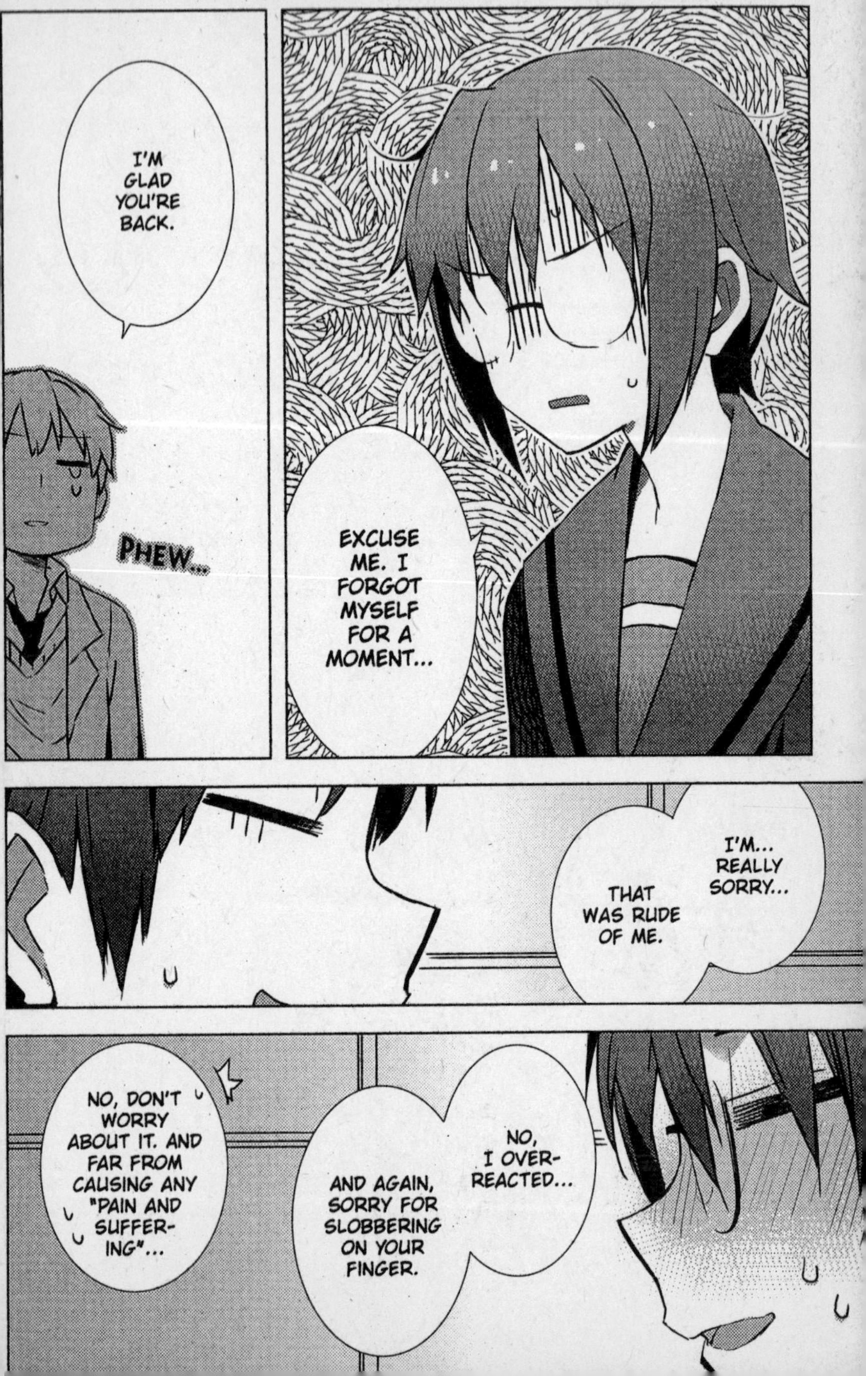
EXCUSE ME. I FORGOT MYSELF FOR A MOMENT...
I'M GLAD YOU'RE BACK.
PHEW...
I'M... REALLY SORRY...
THAT WAS RUDE OF ME.
NO, I OVER-REACTED...
AND AGAIN, SORRY FOR SLOBBERING ON YOUR FINGER.
NO, DON'T WORRY ABOUT IT. AND FAR FROM CAUSING ANY "PAIN AND SUFFER-ING"...

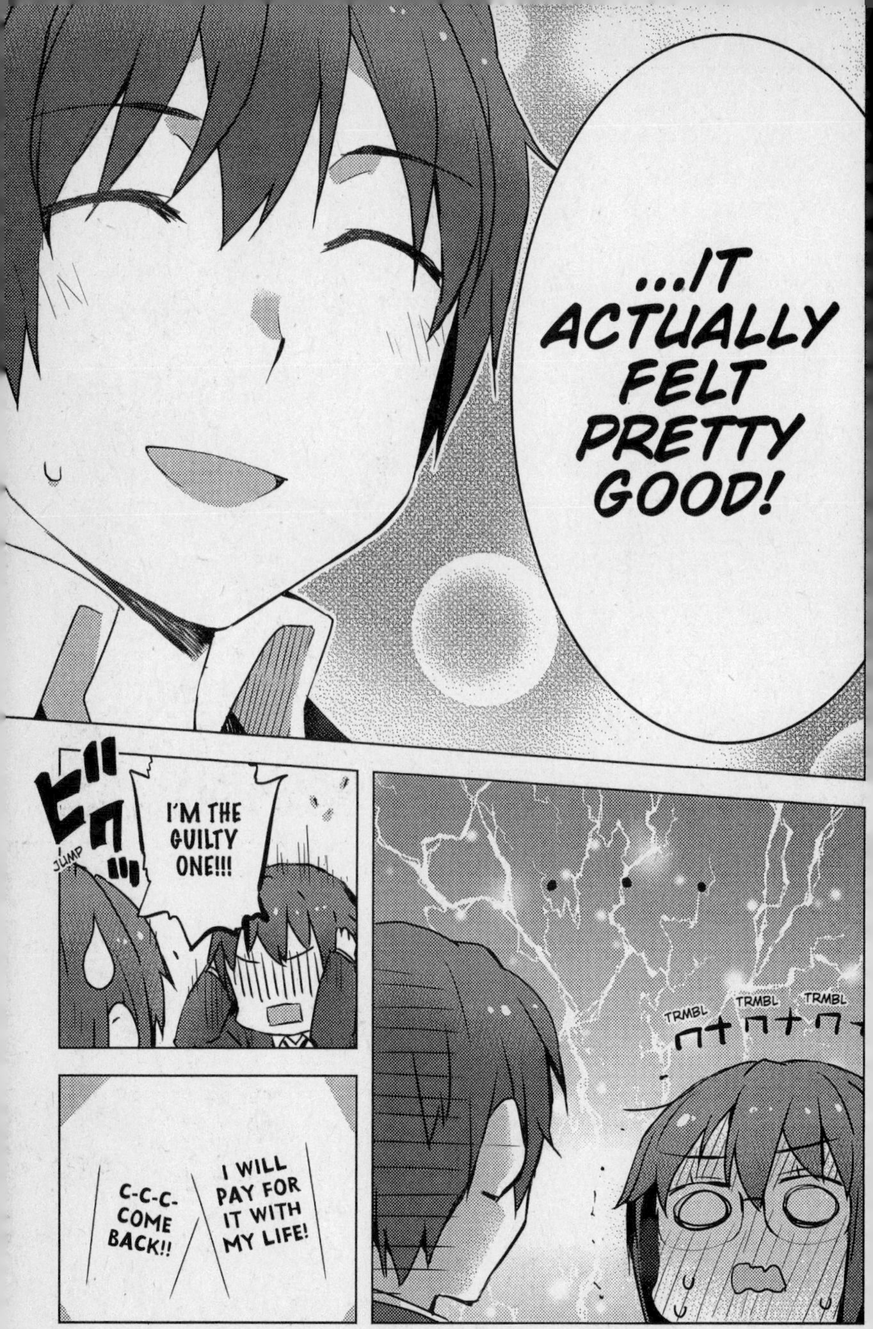
...IT ACTUALLY FELT PRETTY GOOD!
TRMBL TRMBL TRMBL
JUMP
I'M THE GUILTY ONE!!!
I WILL PAY FOR IT WITH MY LIFE!
C-C-C-COME BACK!!

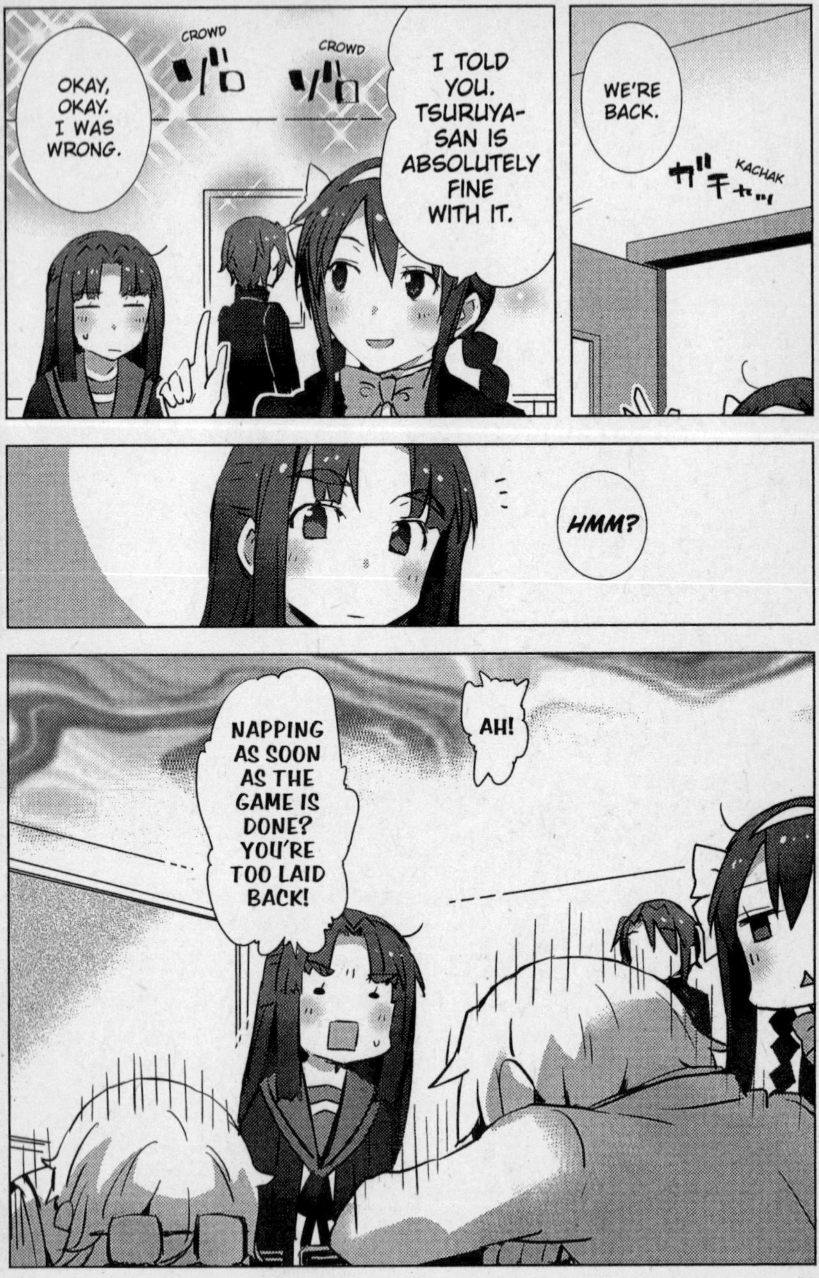
WE'RE BACK.
KACHAK
I TOLD YOU. TSURUYA-SAN IS ABSOLUTELY FINE WITH IT.
CROWD
CROWD
OKAY, OKAY. I WAS WRONG.
HMM?
AH!
NAPPING AS SOON AS THE GAME IS DONE? YOU'RE TOO LAID BACK!

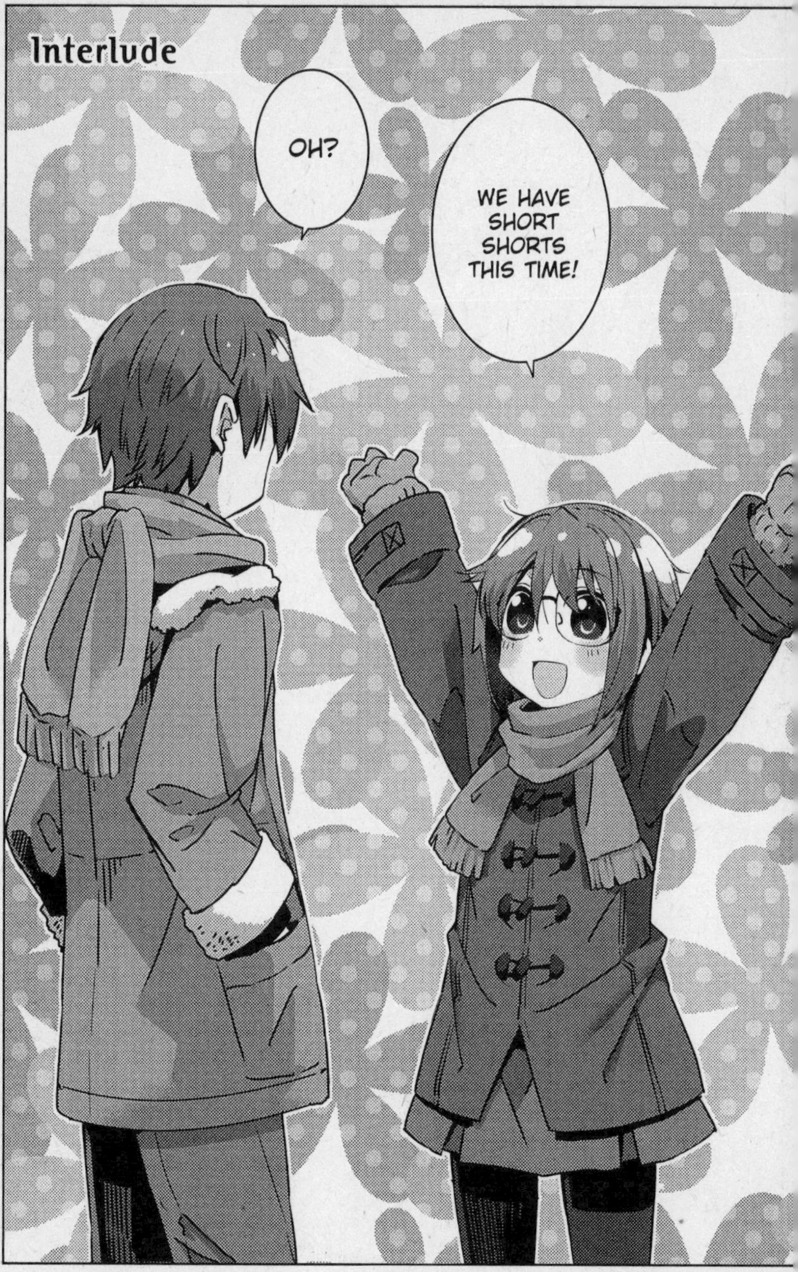
Interlude
WE HAVE SHORT SHORTS THIS TIME!
OH?

## Cultural Festival: Invitation to Form a Band

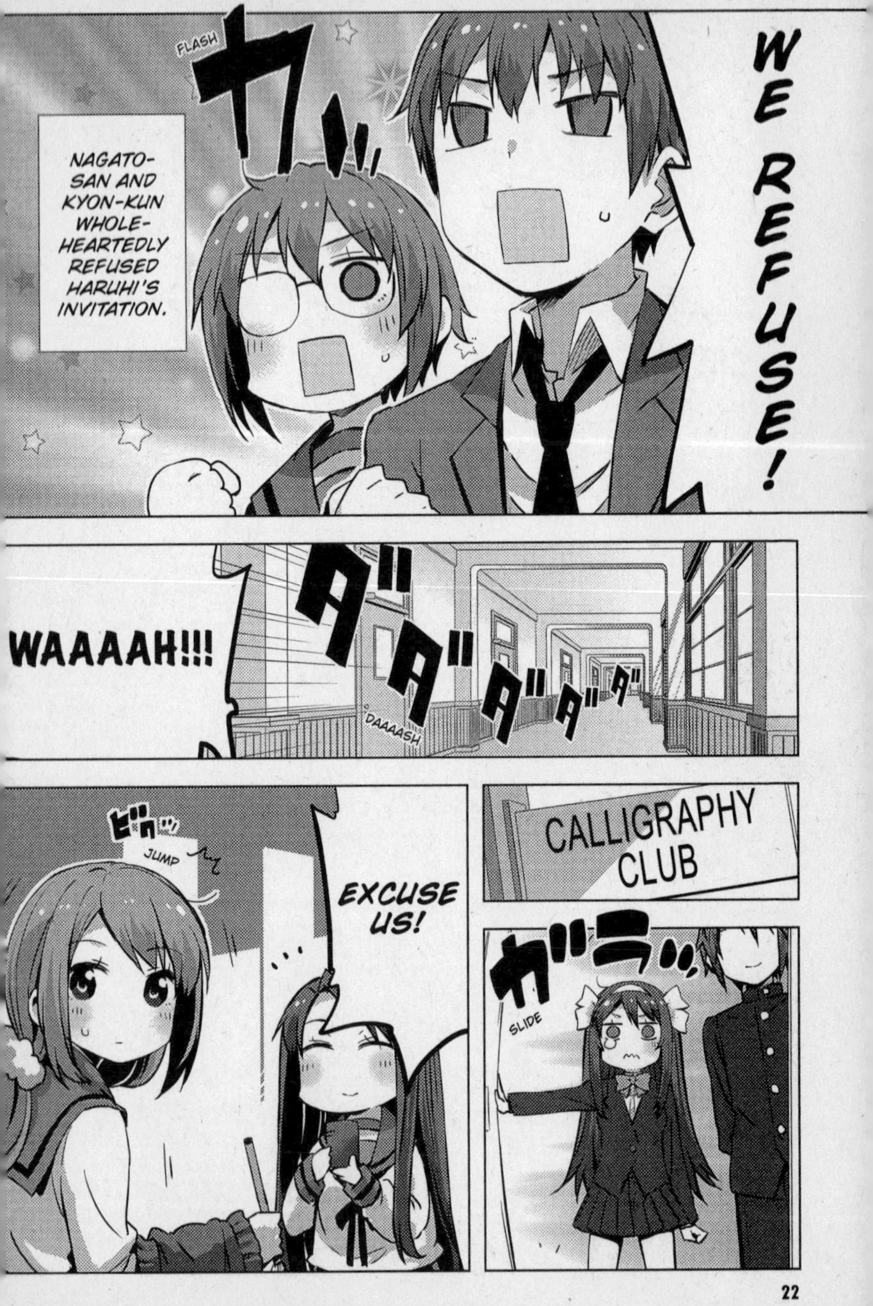
WE REFUSE!
FLASH
NAGATO-SAN AND KYON-KUN WHOLE-HEARTEDLY REFUSED HARUHI'S INVITATION.
DAAAASH
WAAAAH!!!
CALLIGRAPHY CLUB
SLIDE
EXCUSE US!
...
JUMP

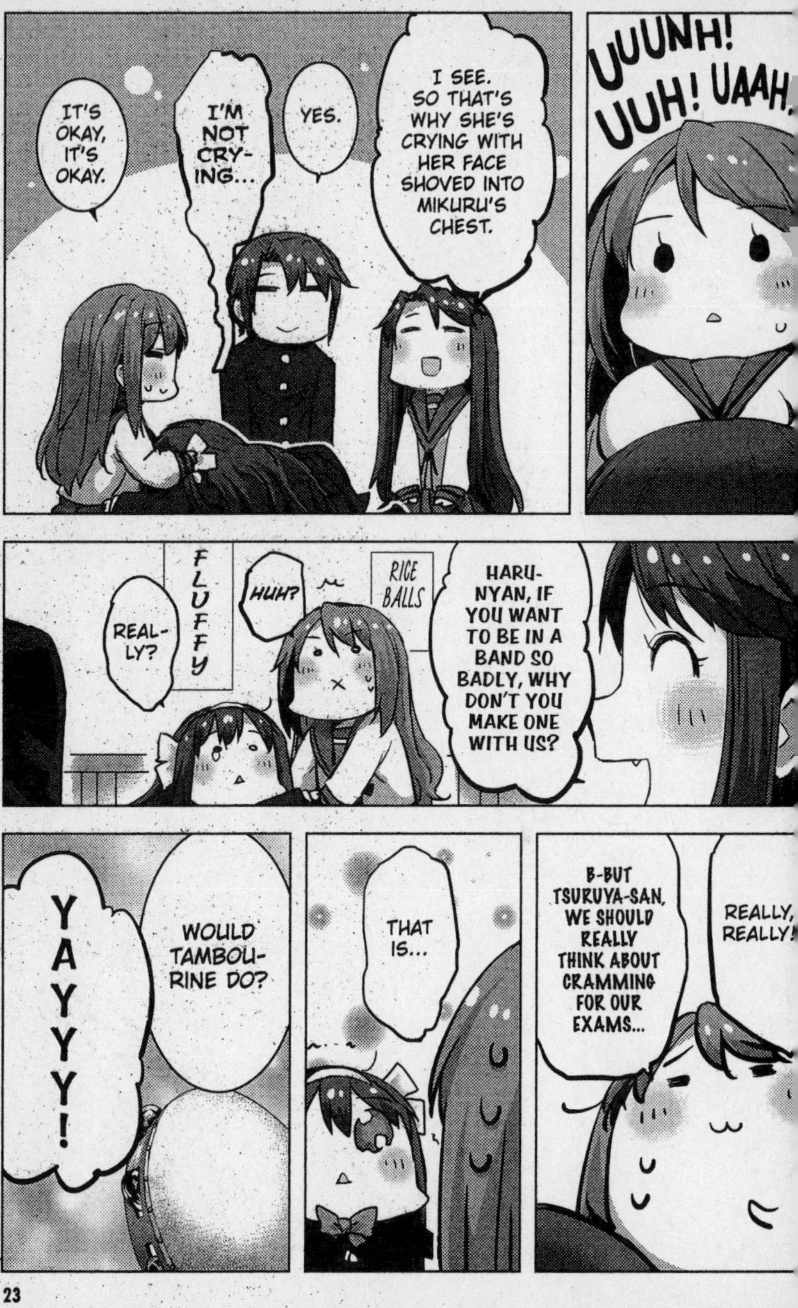
UUUNH! UUH! UAAH.
I SEE. SO THAT'S WHY SHE'S CRYING WITH HER FACE SHOVED INTO MIKURU'S CHEST.
YES.
I'M NOT CRY-ING...
IT'S OKAY, IT'S OKAY.
HARU-NYAN, IF YOU WANT TO BE IN A BAND SO BADLY, WHY DON'T YOU MAKE ONE WITH US?
RICE BALLS
HUH?
FLUFFY
REAL-LY?
REALLY, REALLY!
B-BUT TSURUYA-SAN, WE SHOULD REALLY THINK ABOUT CRAMMING FOR OUR EXAMS...
THAT IS...
WOULD TAMBOU-RINE DO?
YAYYY!

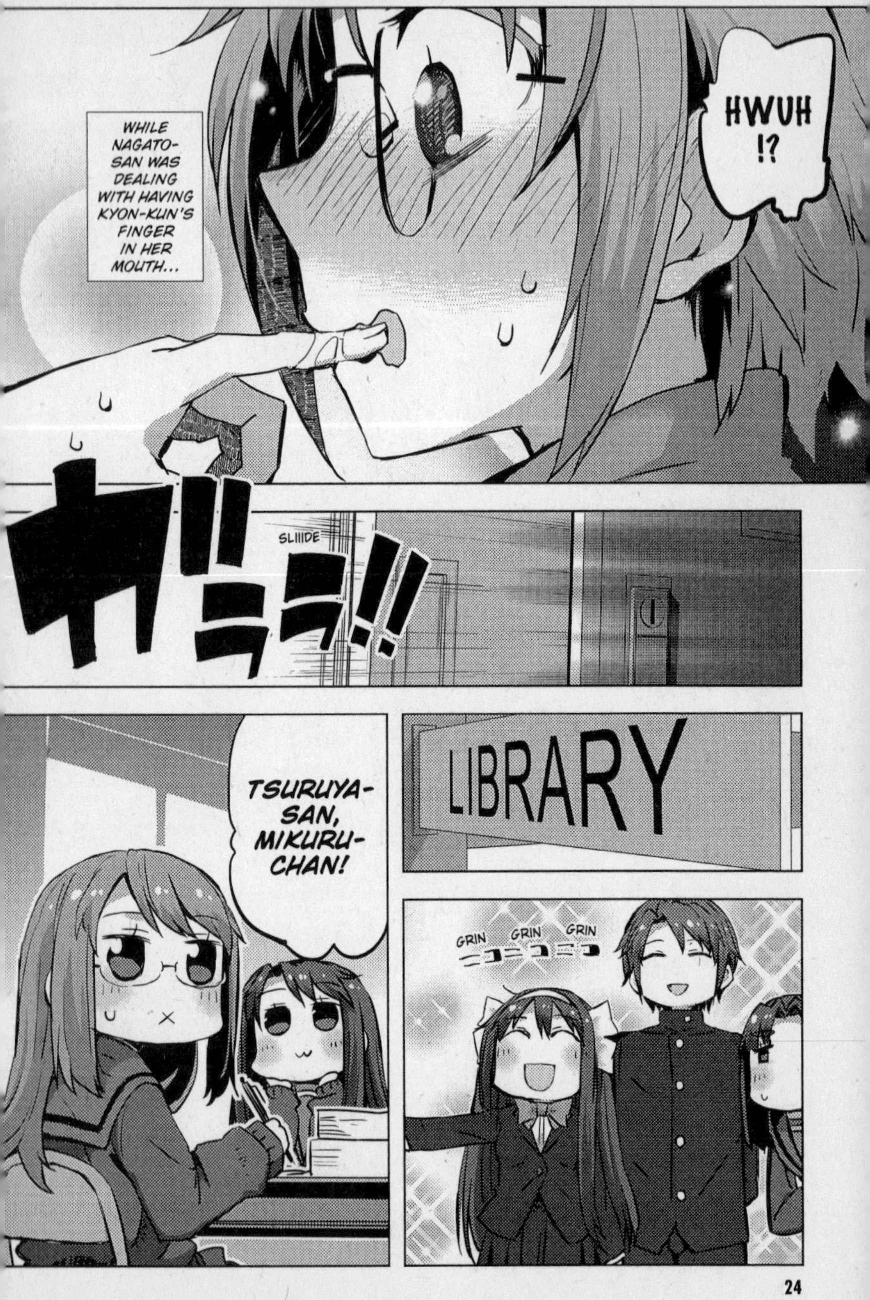
HWUH !?
WHILE NAGATO-SAN WAS DEALING WITH HAVING KYON-KUN'S FINGER IN HER MOUTH...
SLIIIDE
ガララ!!
LIBRARY
GRIN GRIN GRIN
ニコニコニコ
TSURUYA-SAN, MIKURU-CHAN!

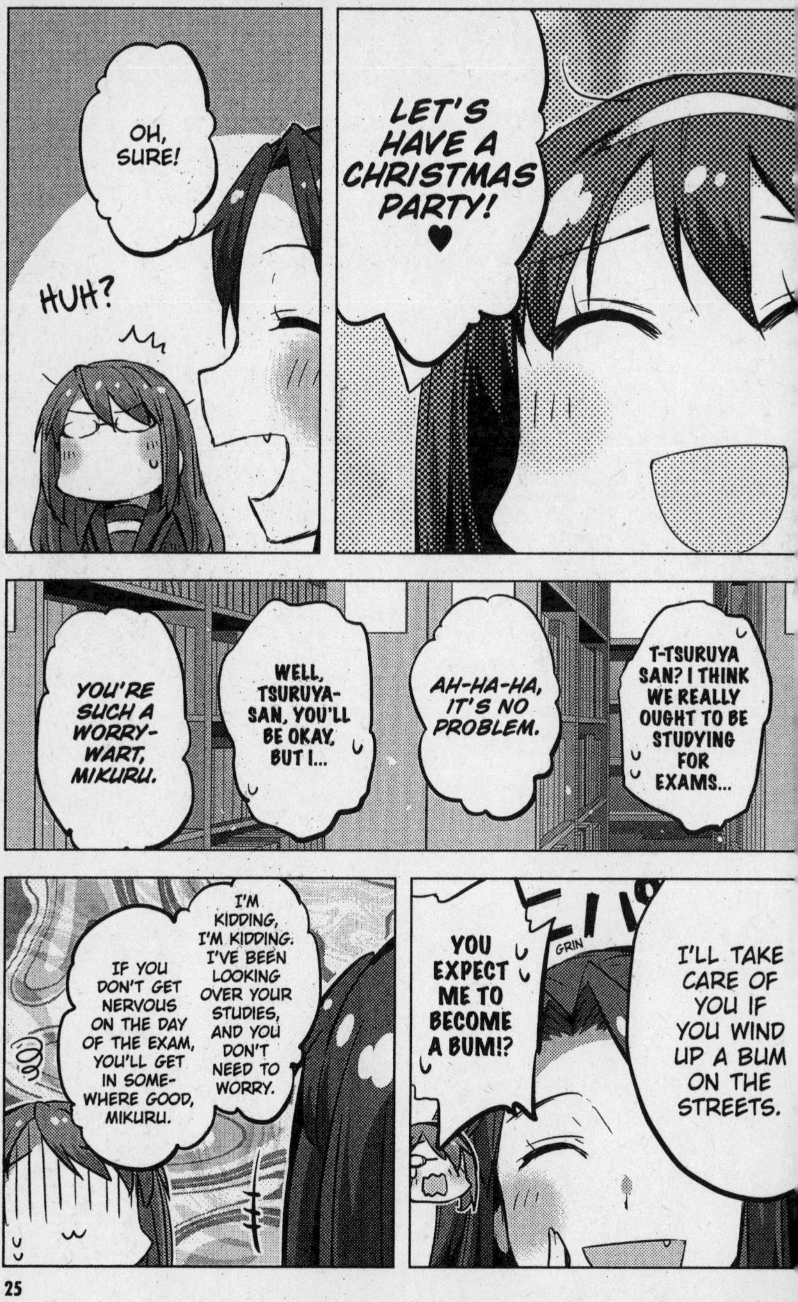
LET'S HAVE A CHRISTMAS PARTY! ♥
OH, SURE!
HUH?
T-TSURUYA SAN? I THINK WE REALLY OUGHT TO BE STUDYING FOR EXAMS...
AH-HA-HA, IT'S NO PROBLEM.
WELL, TSURUYA-SAN, YOU'LL BE OKAY, BUT I...
YOU'RE SUCH A WORRY-WART, MIKURU.
I'LL TAKE CARE OF YOU IF YOU WIND UP A BUM ON THE STREETS.
GRIN
YOU EXPECT ME TO BECOME A BUM!?
I'M KIDDING, I'M KIDDING. I'VE BEEN LOOKING OVER YOUR STUDIES, AND YOU DON'T NEED TO WORRY.
IF YOU DON'T GET NERVOUS ON THE DAY OF THE EXAM, YOU'LL GET IN SOME-WHERE GOOD, MIKURU.

# Video Game Promise

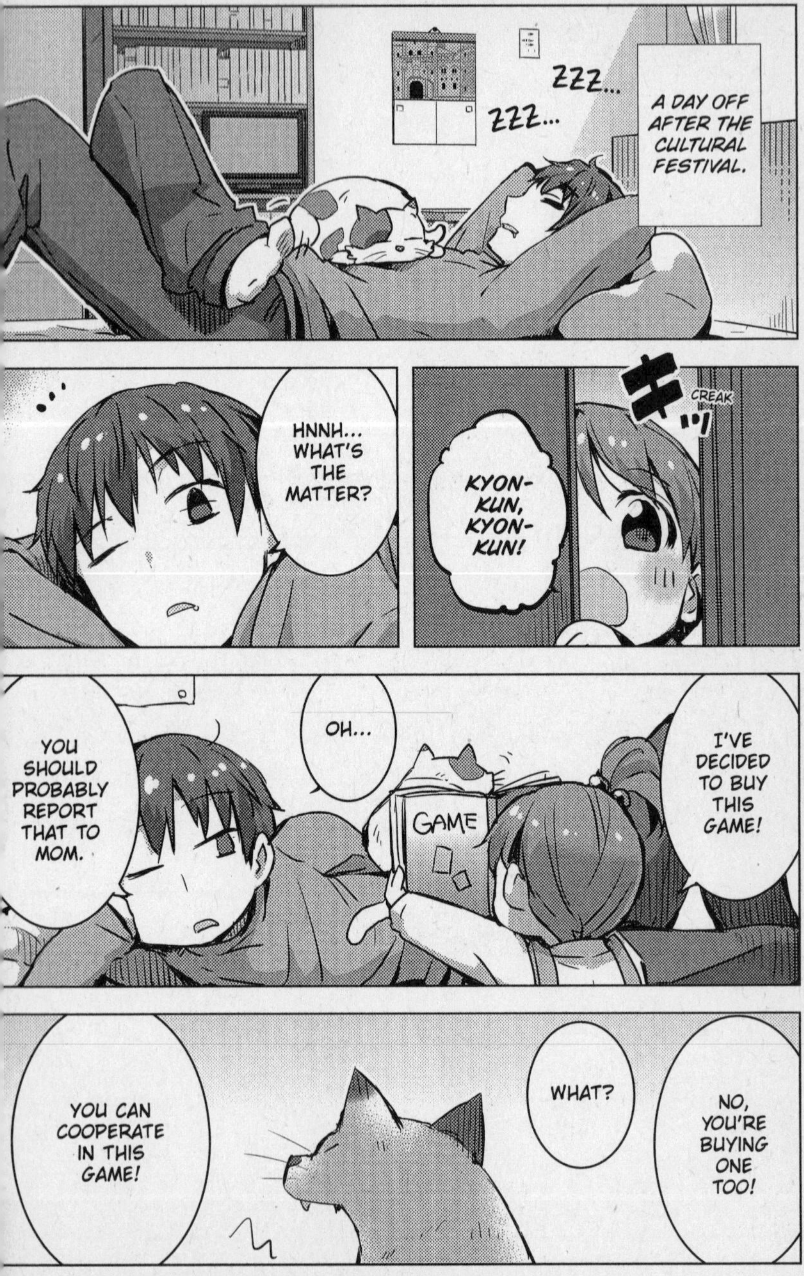
A DAY OFF AFTER THE CULTURAL FESTIVAL.
ZZZ...
ZZZ...
CREAK
KYON-KUN, KYON-KUN!
HNNH... WHAT'S THE MATTER?
I'VE DECIDED TO BUY THIS GAME!
GAME
OH...
YOU SHOULD PROBABLY REPORT THAT TO MOM.
NO, YOU'RE BUYING ONE TOO!
WHAT?
YOU CAN COOPERATE IN THIS GAME!

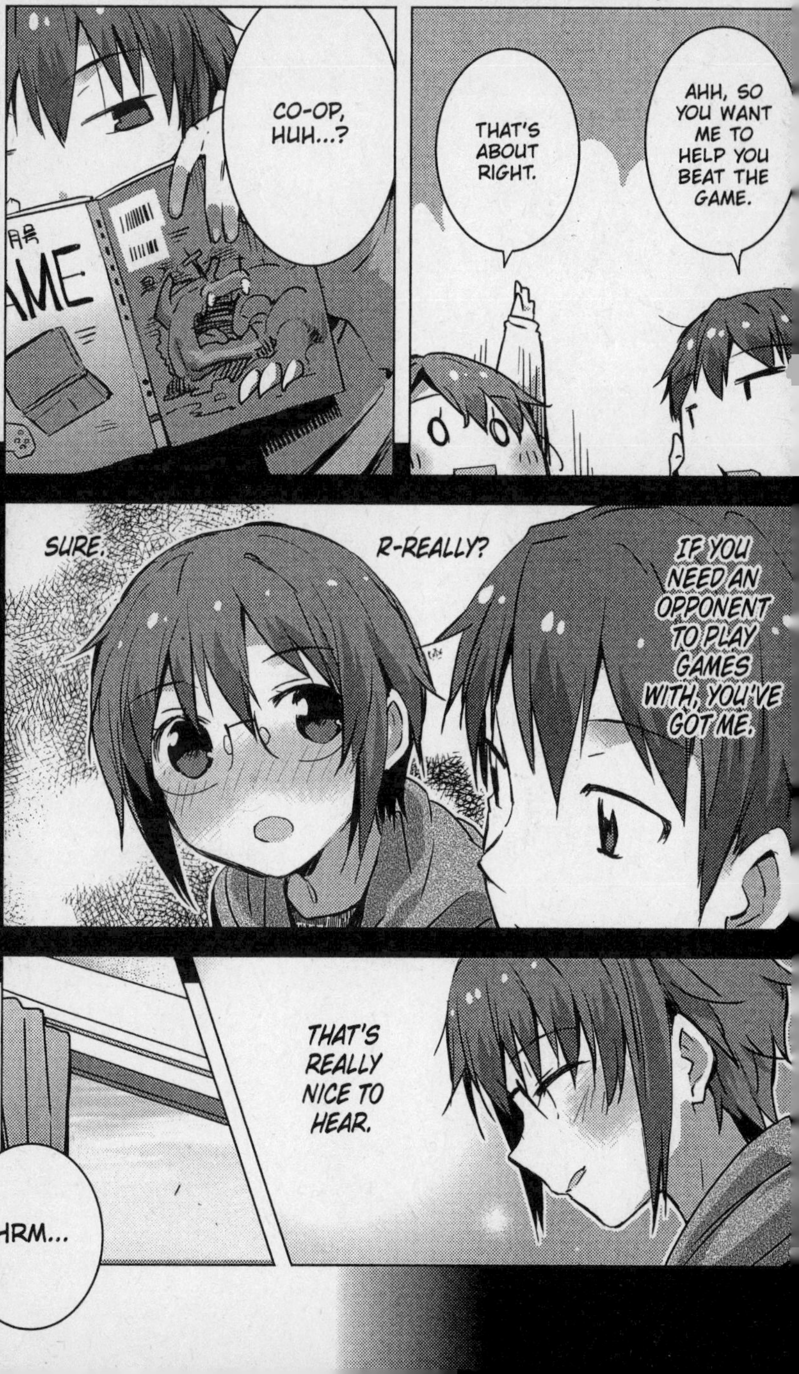
AHH, SO YOU WANT ME TO HELP YOU BEAT THE GAME.
THAT'S ABOUT RIGHT.
CO-OP, HUH...?
IF YOU NEED AN OPPONENT TO PLAY GAMES WITH, YOU'VE GOT ME.
R-REALLY?
SURE.
THAT'S REALLY NICE TO HEAR.
HRM...

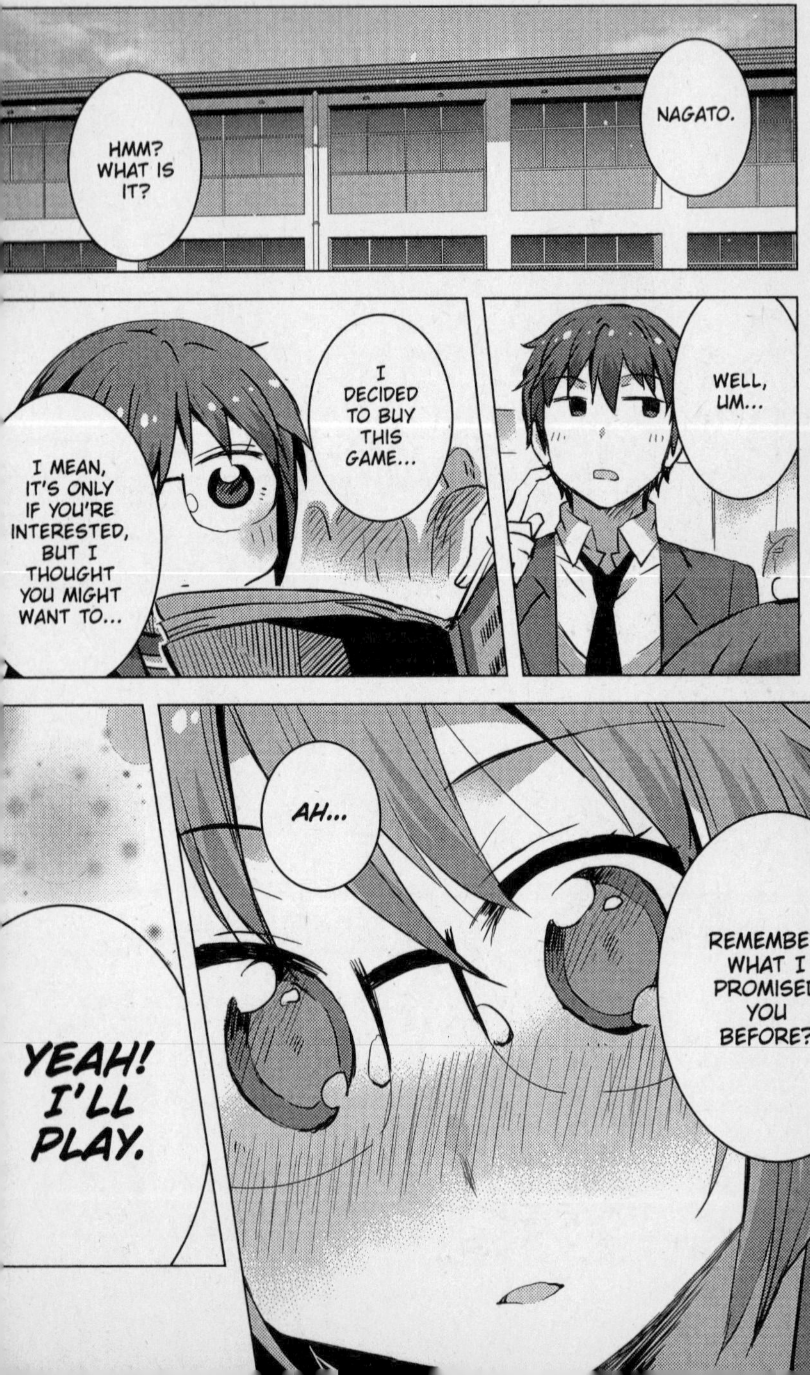
NAGATO.
HMM? WHAT IS IT?
WELL, UM...
I DECIDED TO BUY THIS GAME...
I MEAN, IT'S ONLY IF YOU'RE INTERESTED, BUT I THOUGHT YOU MIGHT WANT TO...
REMEMBER WHAT I PROMISED YOU BEFORE?
AH...
YEAH! I'LL PLAY.

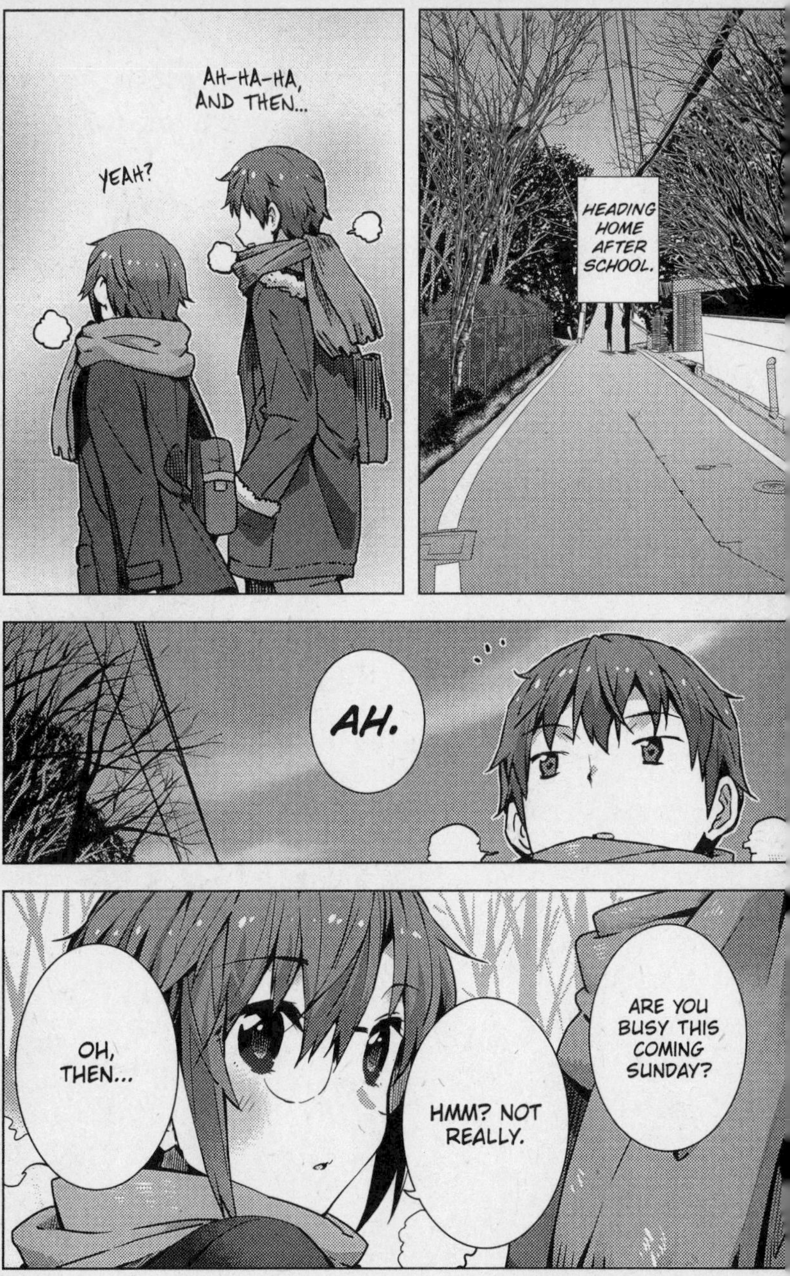
HEADING HOME AFTER SCHOOL.
AH-HA-HA, AND THEN...
YEAH?
AH.
ARE YOU BUSY THIS COMING SUNDAY?
HMM? NOT REALLY.
OH, THEN...

Epilogue 51>> December 8th

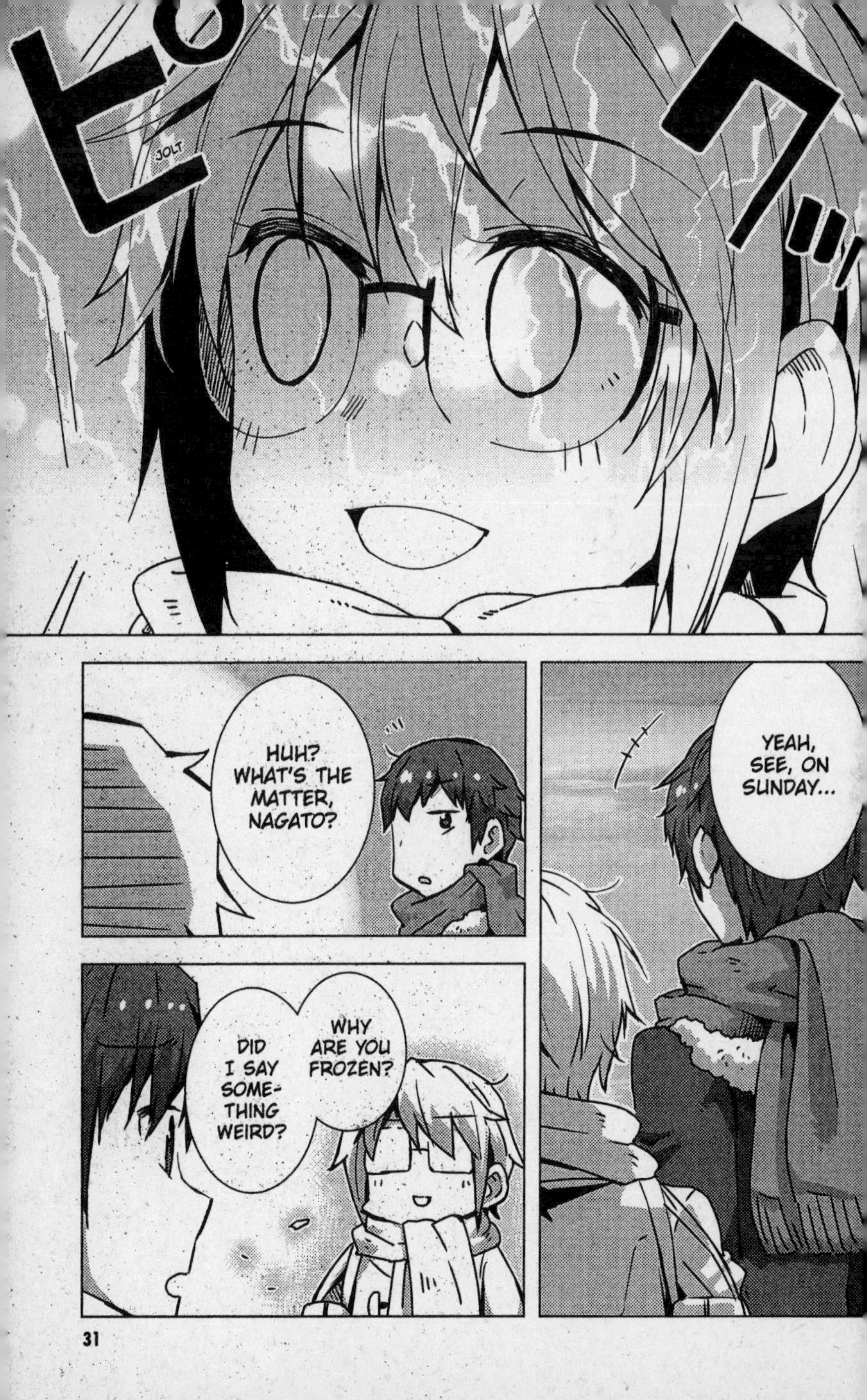
JOLT
YEAH, SEE, ON SUNDAY...
HUH? WHAT'S THE MATTER, NAGATO?
WHY ARE YOU FROZEN?
DID I SAY SOME-THING WEIRD?

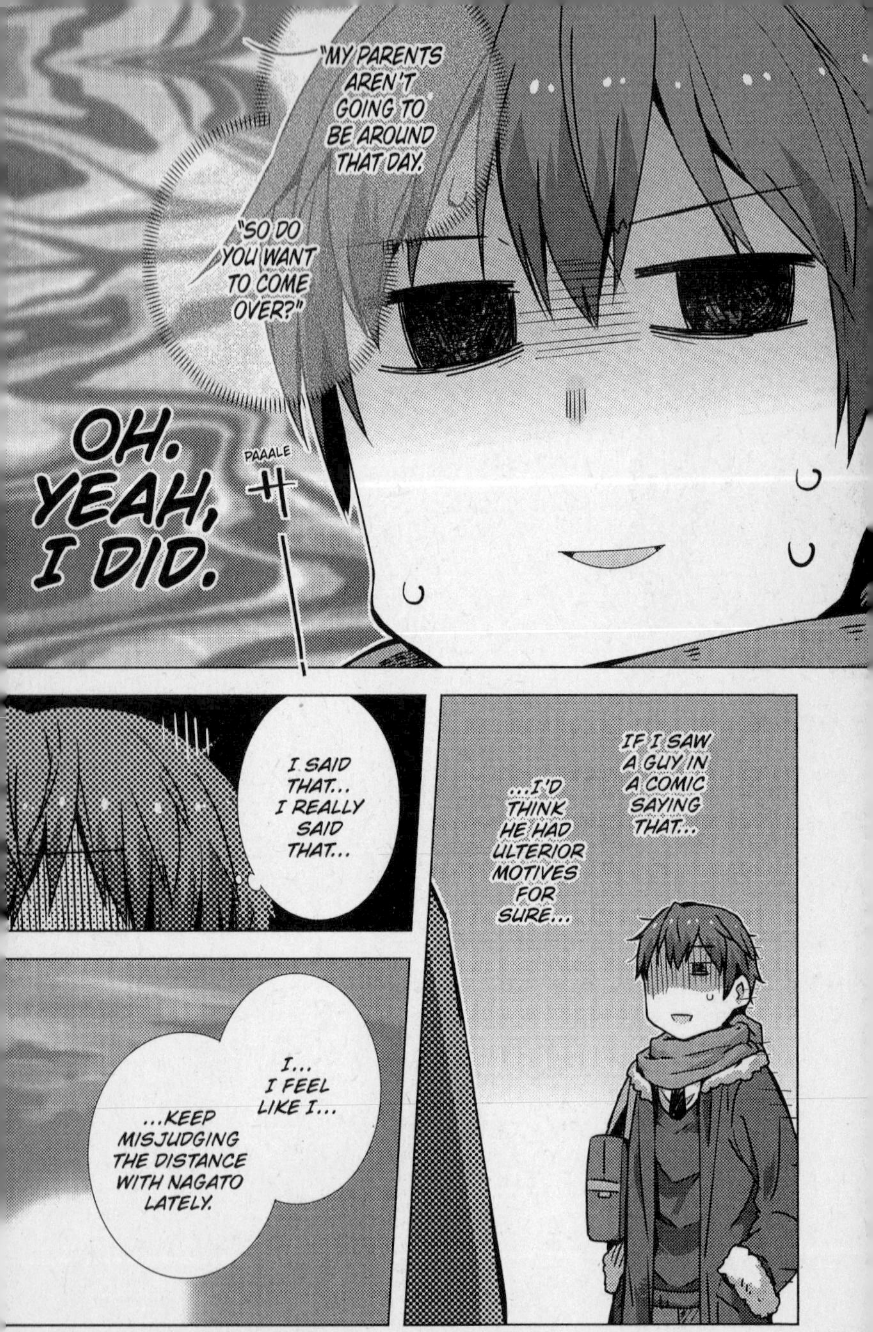
"MY PARENTS AREN'T GOING TO BE AROUND THAT DAY.
"SO DO YOU WANT TO COME OVER?"
PAAALE
OH. YEAH, I DID.
IF I SAW A GUY IN A COMIC SAYING THAT...
...I'D THINK HE HAD ULTERIOR MOTIVES FOR SURE...
I SAID THAT... I REALLY SAID THAT...
I... I FEEL LIKE I...
...KEEP MISJUDGING THE DISTANCE WITH NAGATO LATELY.

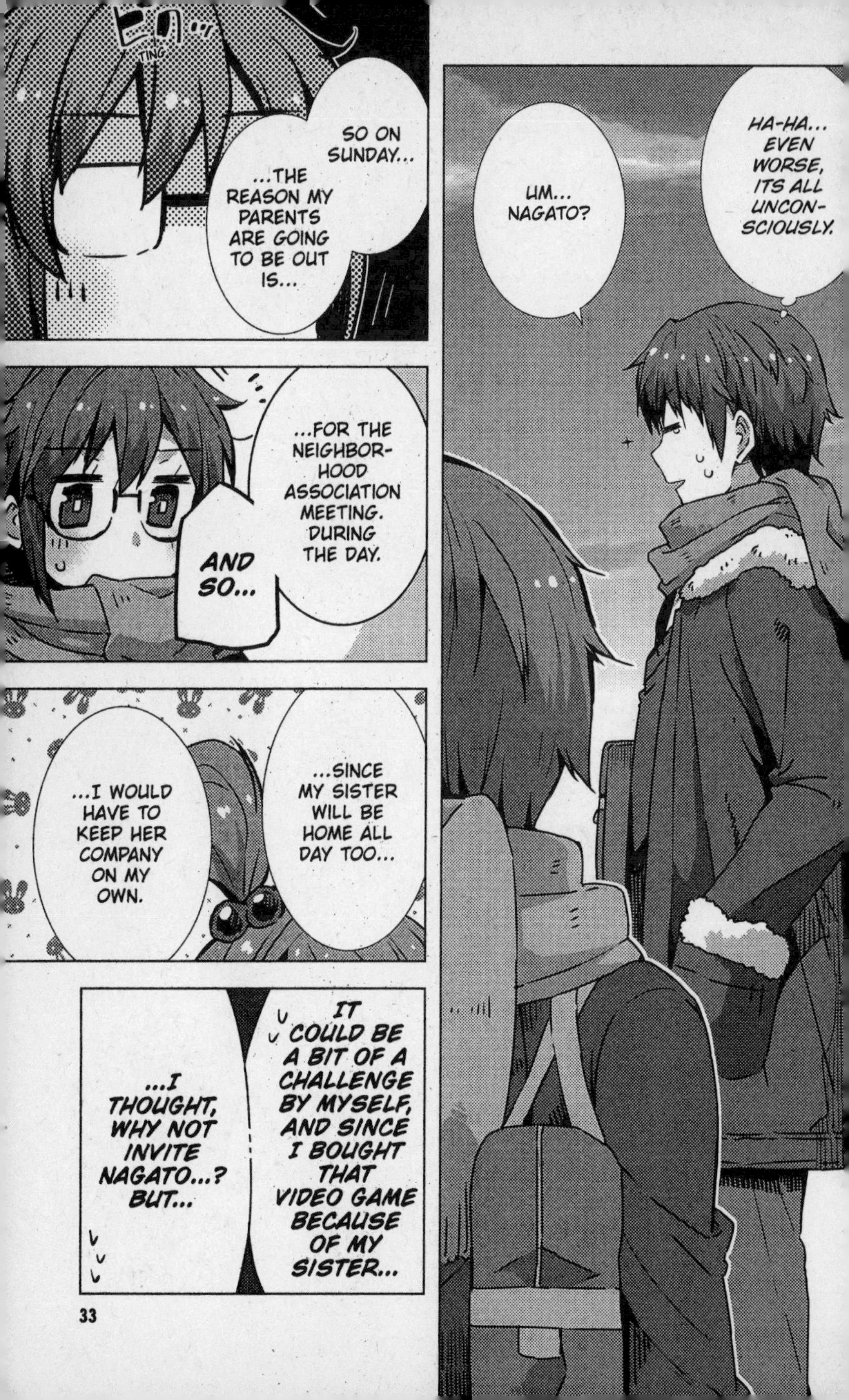
UM... NAGATO?
HA-HA... EVEN WORSE, ITS ALL UNCON-SCIOUSLY.
TING
SO ON SUNDAY...
...THE REASON MY PARENTS ARE GOING TO BE OUT IS...
...FOR THE NEIGHBOR-HOOD ASSOCIATION MEETING. DURING THE DAY.
AND SO...
...SINCE MY SISTER WILL BE HOME ALL DAY TOO...
...I WOULD HAVE TO KEEP HER COMPANY ON MY OWN.
IT COULD BE A BIT OF A CHALLENGE BY MYSELF, AND SINCE I BOUGHT THAT VIDEO GAME BECAUSE OF MY SISTER...
...I THOUGHT, WHY NOT INVITE NAGATO...? BUT...

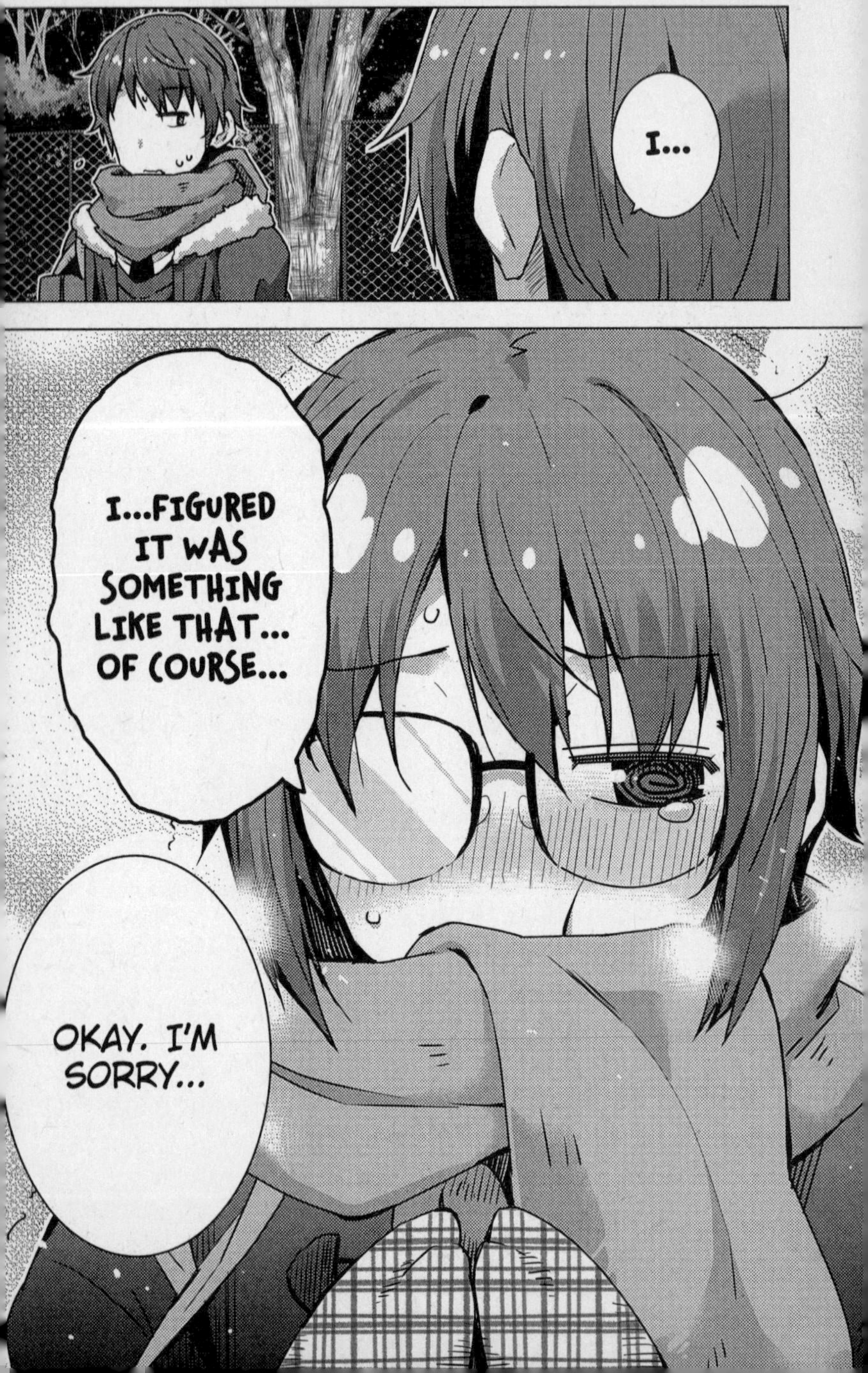
I...
I...FIGURED IT WAS SOMETHING LIKE THAT... OF COURSE...
OKAY. I'M SORRY...

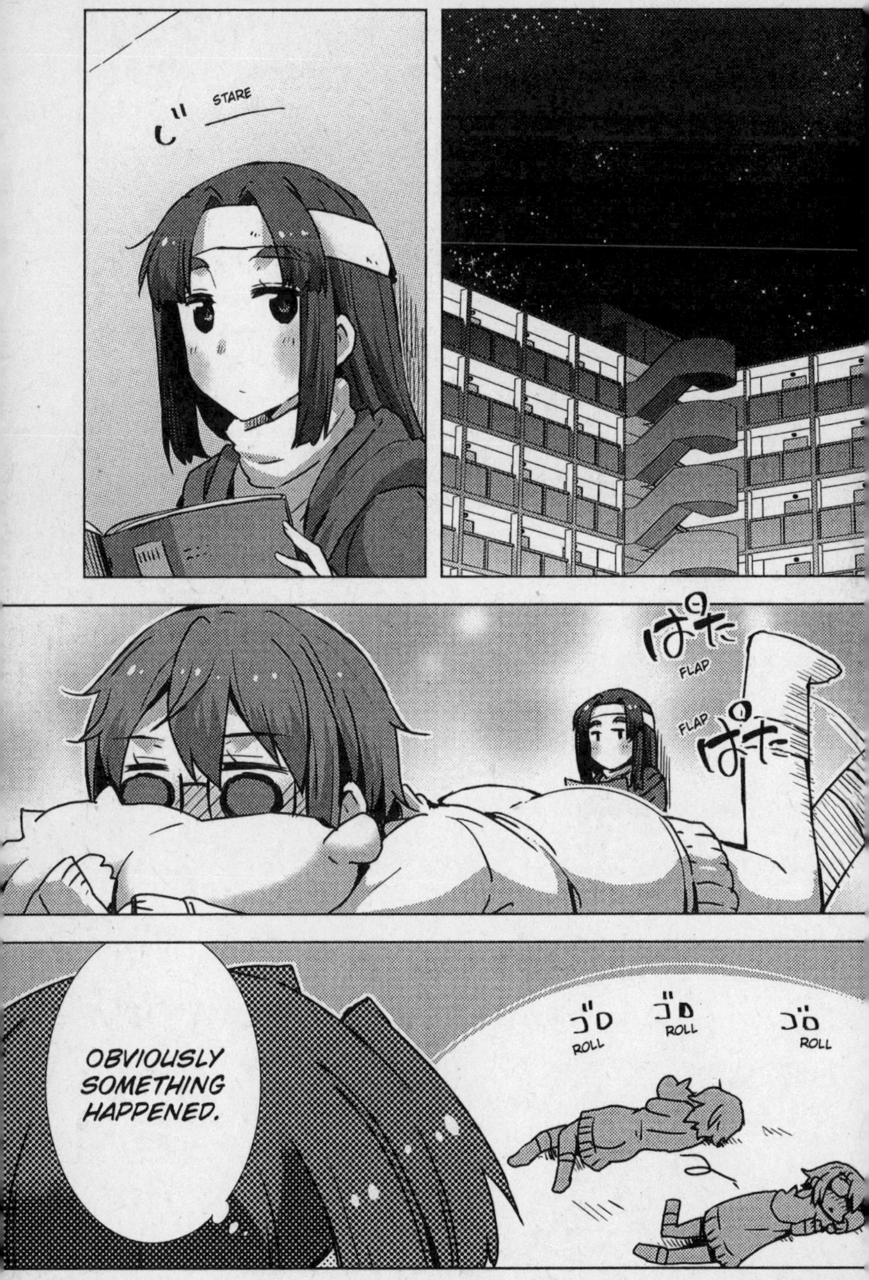
じー
STARE
ぱた
FLAP
ぱた
FLAP
ゴロ
ROLL
ゴロ
ROLL
ゴロ
ROLL
OBVIOUSLY SOMETHING HAPPENED.

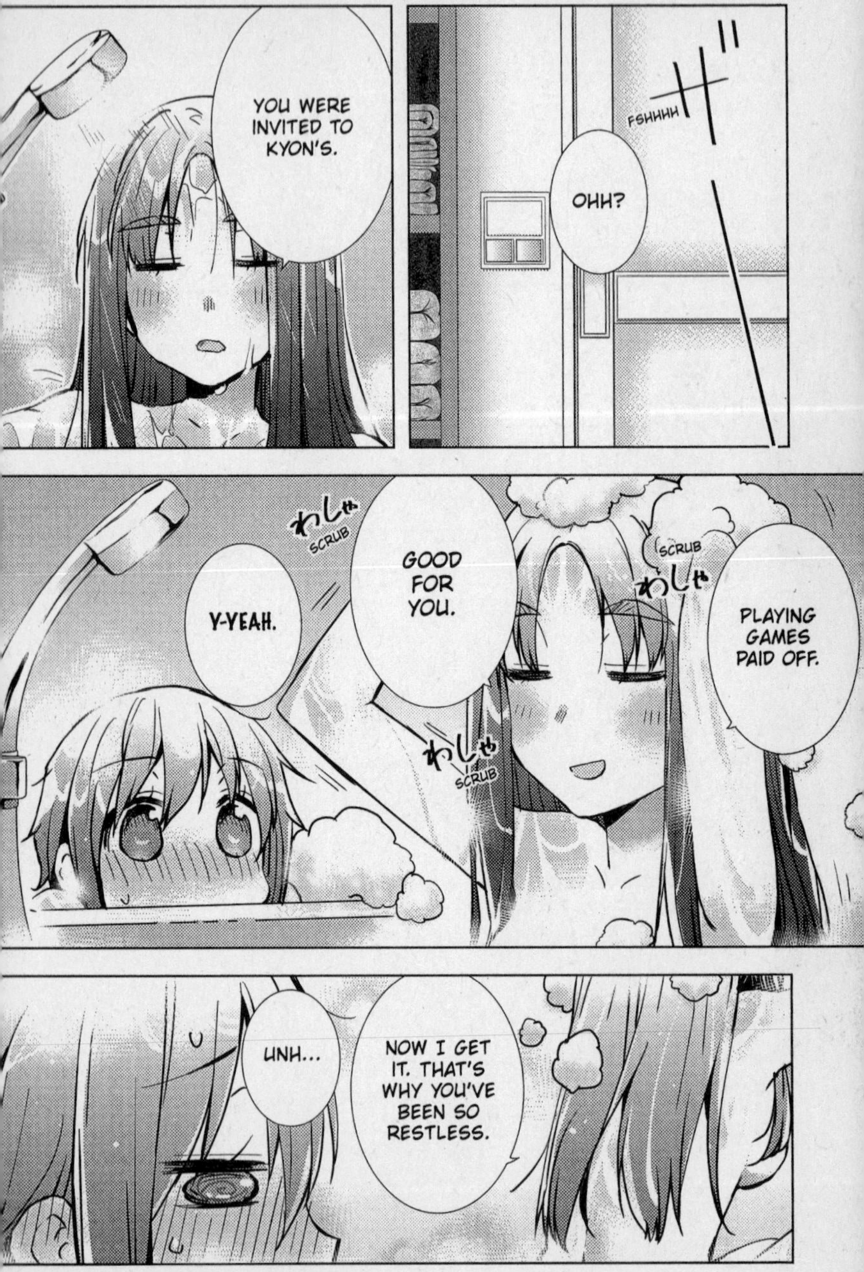
FSHHHH
OHH?
YOU WERE INVITED TO KYON'S.
PLAYING GAMES PAID OFF.
わしゃ
SCRUB
GOOD FOR YOU.
わしゃ
SCRUB
わしゃ
SCRUB
Y-YEAH.
NOW I GET IT. THAT'S WHY YOU'VE BEEN SO RESTLESS.
UNH...

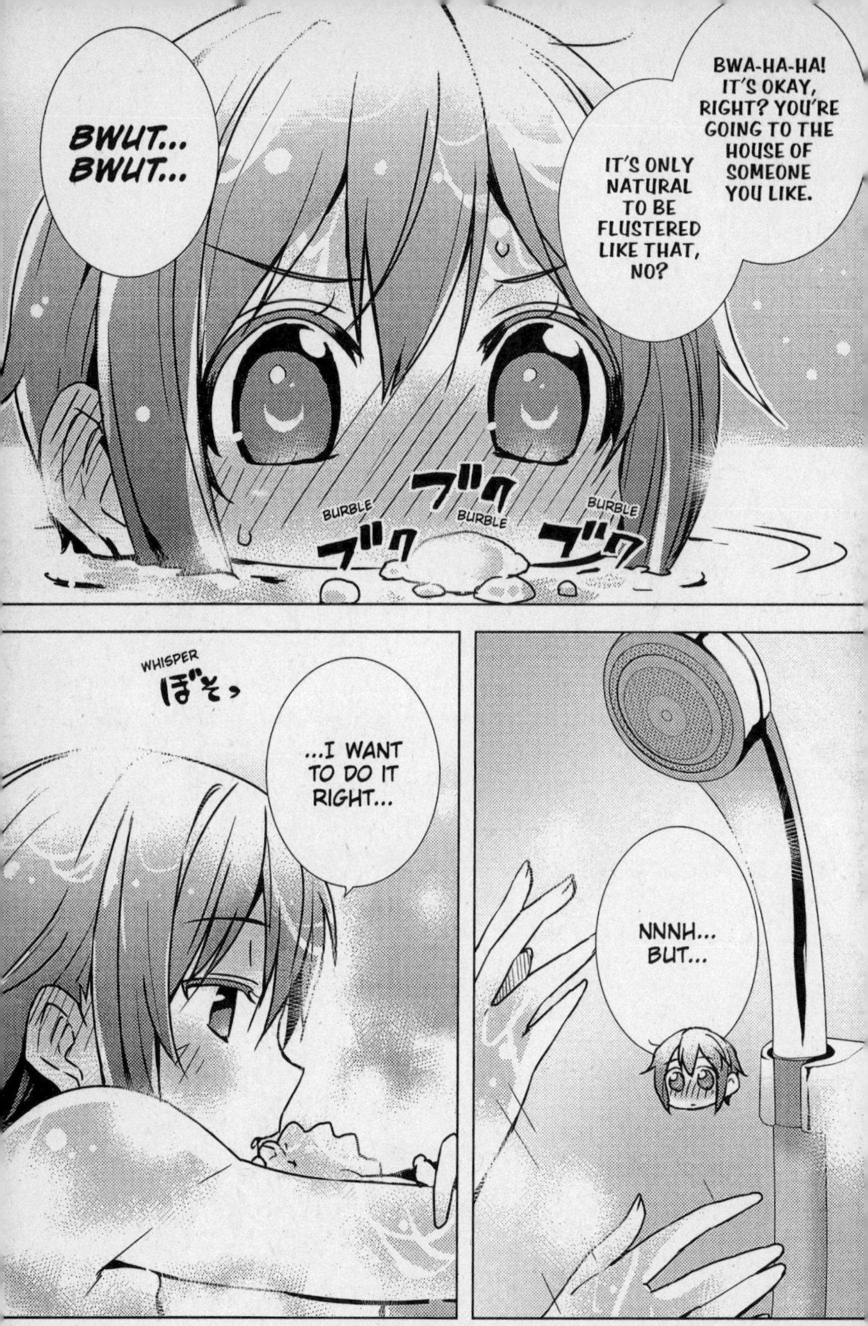
BWA-HA-HA! IT'S OKAY, RIGHT? YOU'RE GOING TO THE HOUSE OF SOMEONE YOU LIKE.
IT'S ONLY NATURAL TO BE FLUSTERED LIKE THAT, NO?
BWUT... BWUT...
ブク BURBLE
BURBLE
ブク BURBLE
NNNH... BUT...
ぼそっ WHISPER
...I WANT TO DO IT RIGHT...

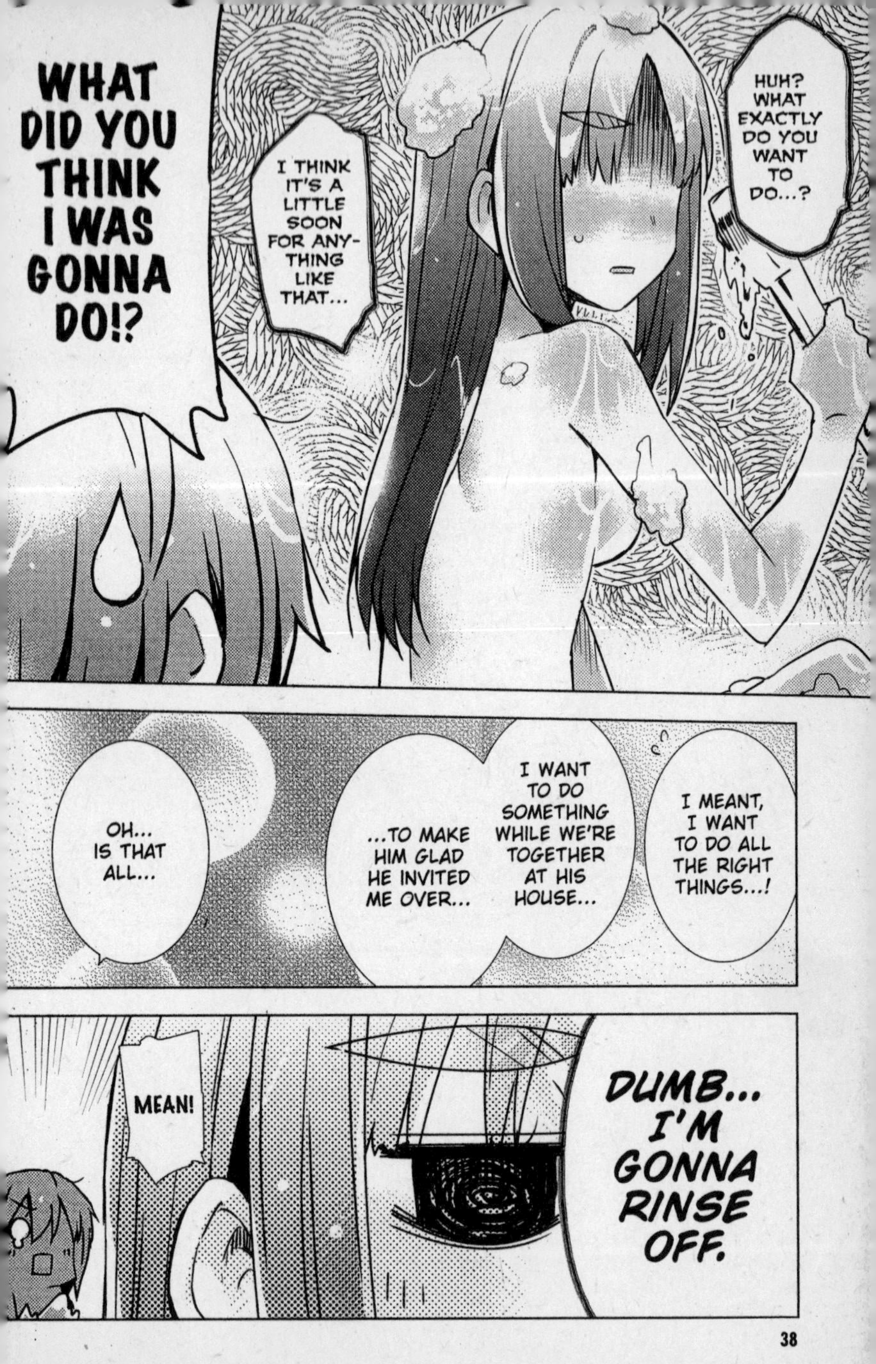
HUH? WHAT EXACTLY DO YOU WANT TO DO...?
I THINK IT'S A LITTLE SOON FOR ANY-THING LIKE THAT...
WHAT DID YOU THINK I WAS GONNA DO!?
I MEANT, I WANT TO DO ALL THE RIGHT THINGS...!
I WANT TO DO SOMETHING WHILE WE'RE TOGETHER AT HIS HOUSE...
...TO MAKE HIM GLAD HE INVITED ME OVER...
OH... IS THAT ALL...
DUMB... I'M GONNA RINSE OFF.
MEAN!

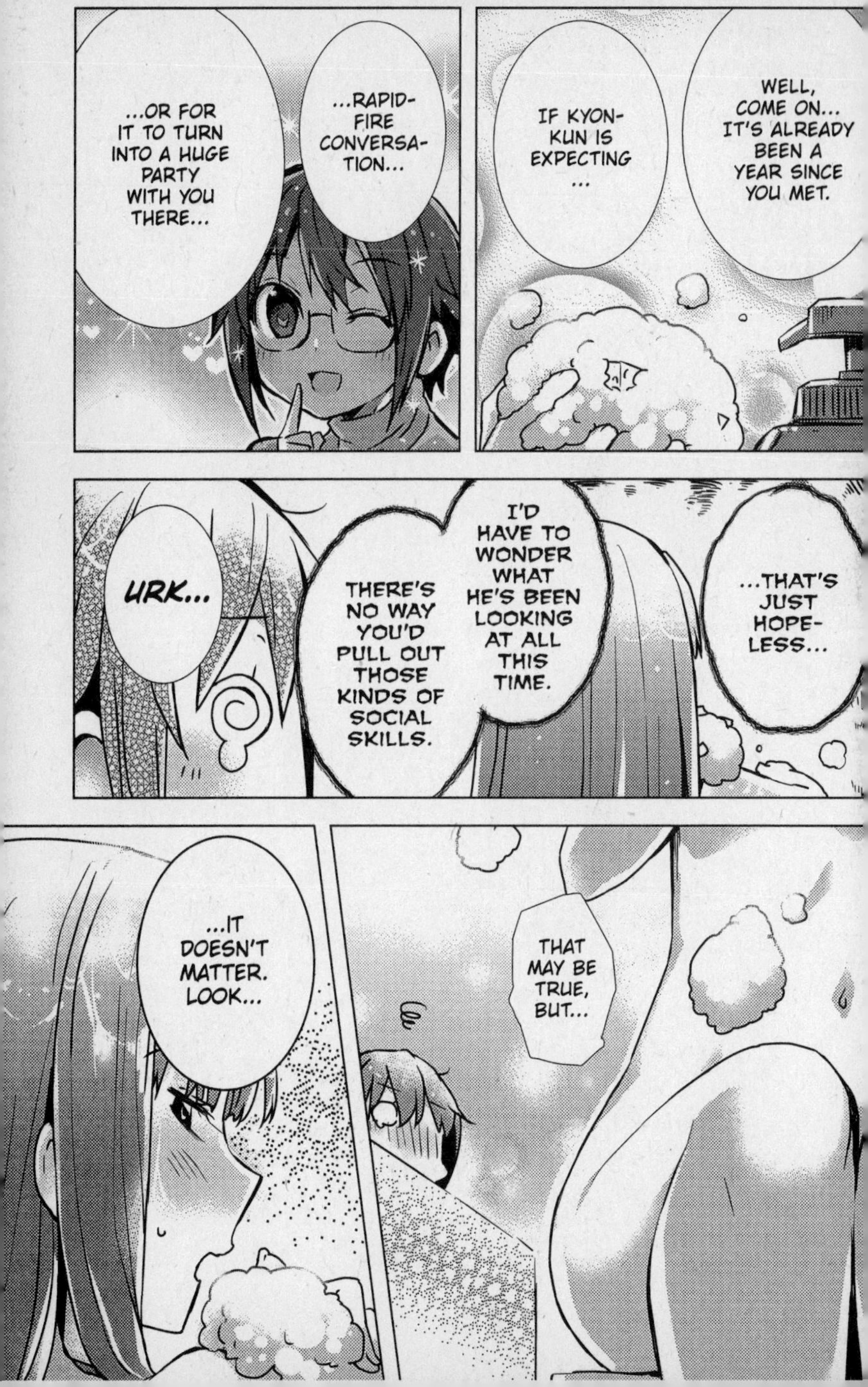
WELL, COME ON... IT'S ALREADY BEEN A YEAR SINCE YOU MET.
IF KYON-KUN IS EXPECTING...
...RAPID-FIRE CONVERSA-TION...
...OR FOR IT TO TURN INTO A HUGE PARTY WITH YOU THERE...
...THAT'S JUST HOPE-LESS...
I'D HAVE TO WONDER WHAT HE'S BEEN LOOKING AT ALL THIS TIME.
THERE'S NO WAY YOU'D PULL OUT THOSE KINDS OF SOCIAL SKILLS.
URK...
THAT MAY BE TRUE, BUT...
...IT DOESN'T MATTER. LOOK...

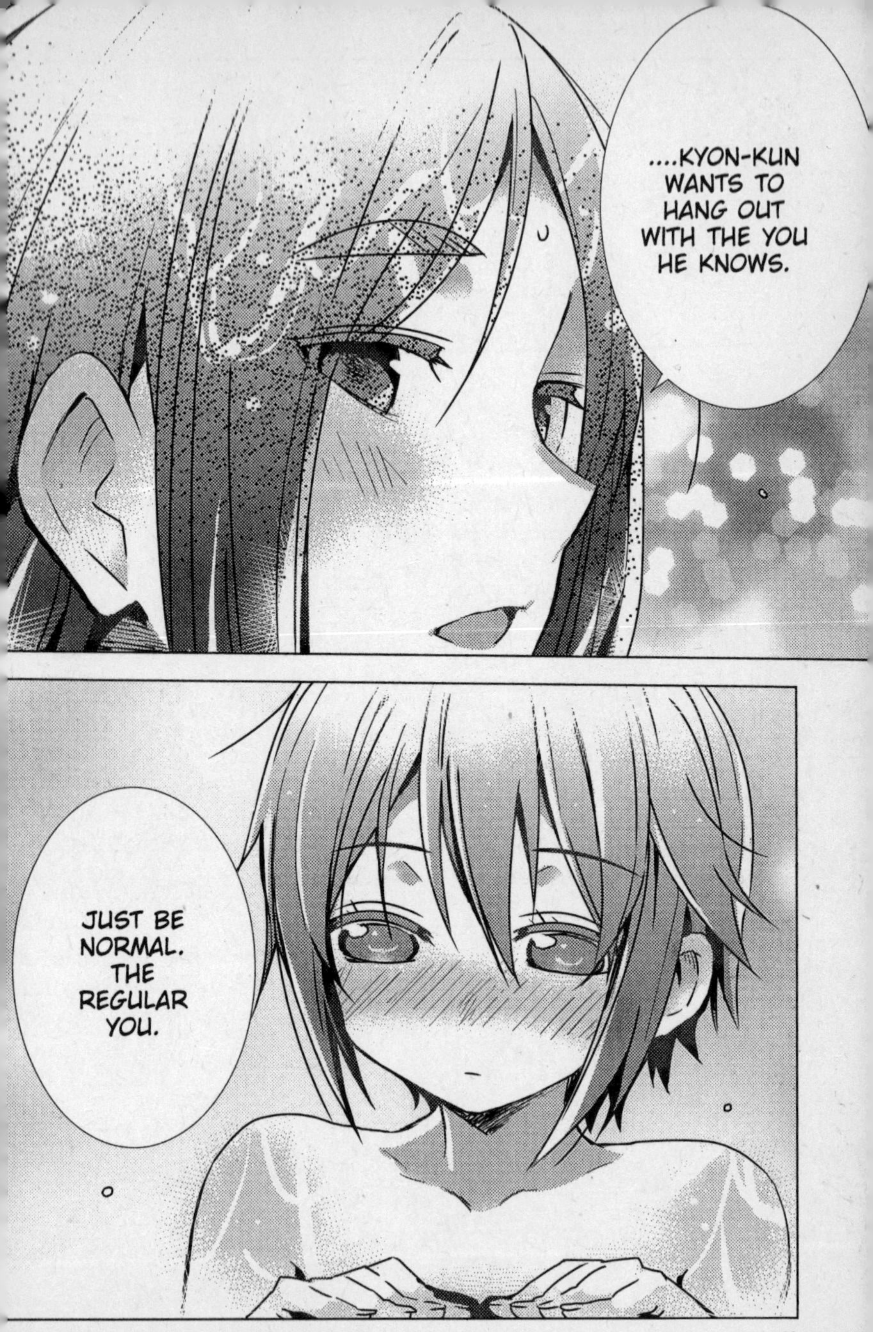
....KYON-KUN WANTS TO HANG OUT WITH THE YOU HE KNOWS.
JUST BE NORMAL. THE REGULAR YOU.

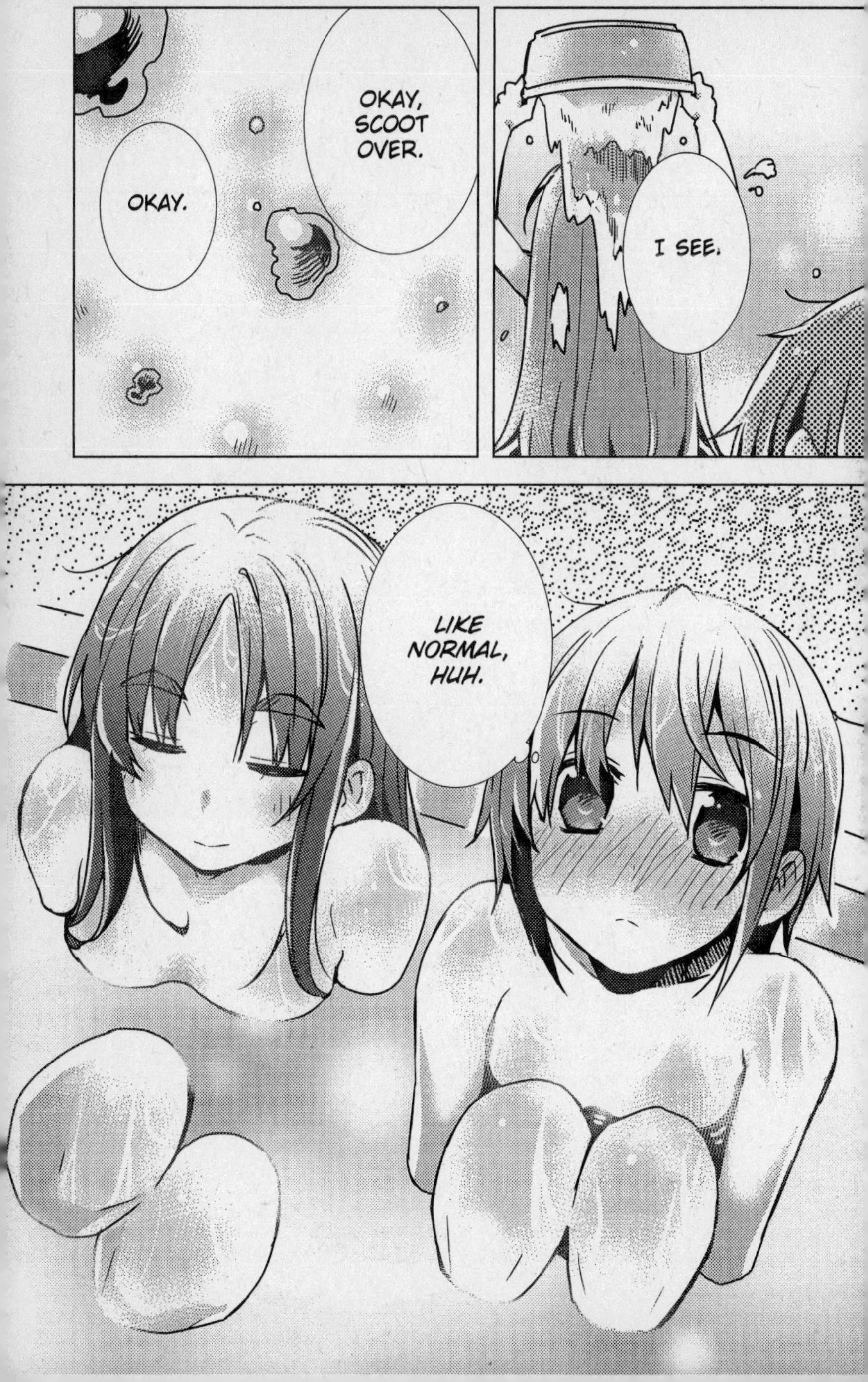
I SEE.
OKAY, SCOOT OVER.
OKAY.
LIKE NORMAL, HUH.

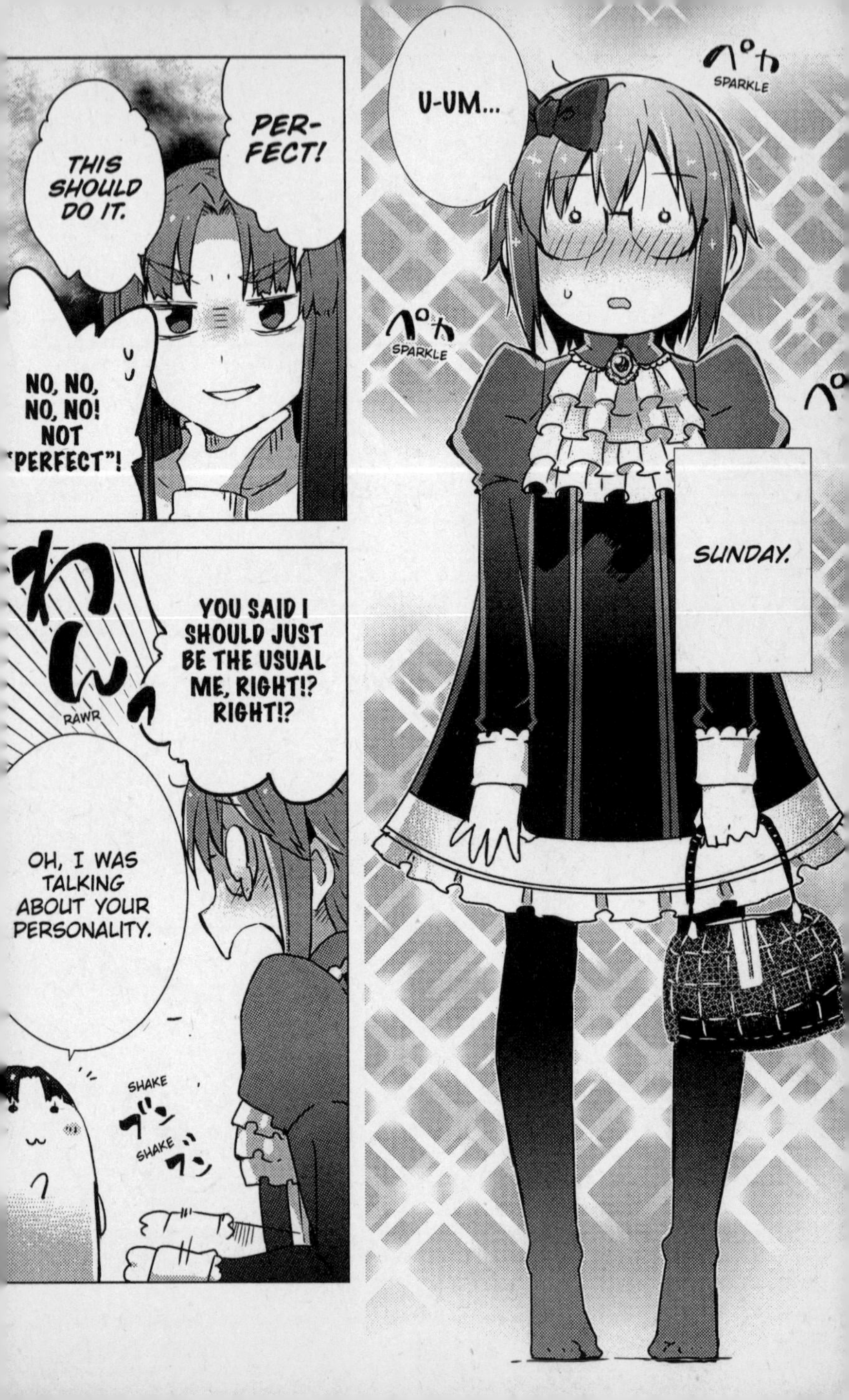
ぺか
SPARKLE
U-UM...
ぺか
SPARKLE
SUNDAY.
PER-FECT!
THIS SHOULD DO IT.
NO, NO, NO, NO! NOT "PERFECT"!
わん
RAWR
YOU SAID I SHOULD JUST BE THE USUAL ME, RIGHT!? RIGHT!?
OH, I WAS TALKING ABOUT YOUR PERSONALITY.
ブン
SHAKE
ブン
SHAKE

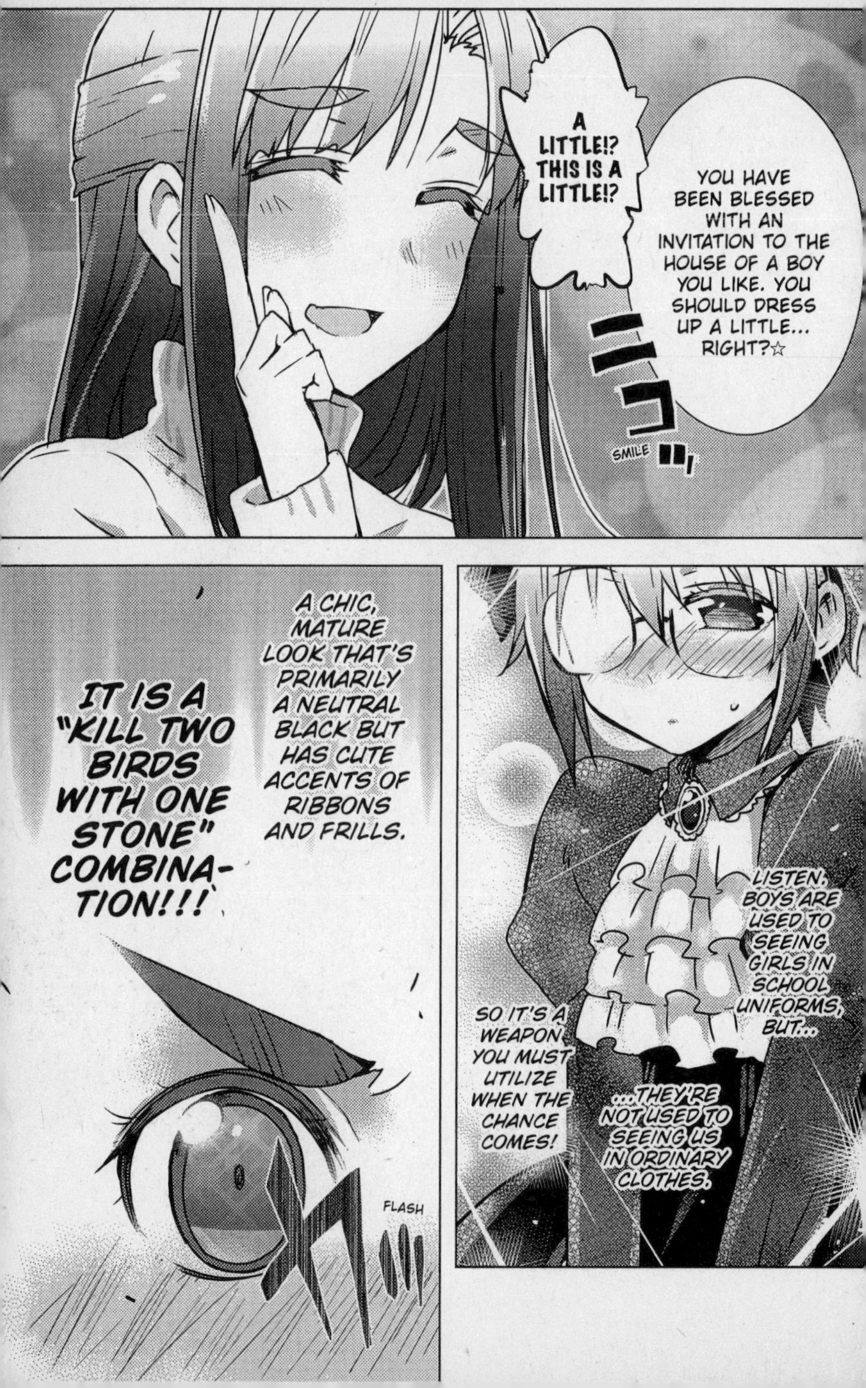
YOU HAVE BEEN BLESSED WITH AN INVITATION TO THE HOUSE OF A BOY YOU LIKE. YOU SHOULD DRESS UP A LITTLE... RIGHT?☆
A LITTLE!? THIS IS A LITTLE!?
SMILE
LISTEN. BOYS ARE USED TO SEEING GIRLS IN SCHOOL UNIFORMS, BUT...
...THEY'RE NOT USED TO SEEING US IN ORDINARY CLOTHES.
SO IT'S A WEAPON YOU MUST UTILIZE WHEN THE CHANCE COMES!
A CHIC, MATURE LOOK THAT'S PRIMARILY A NEUTRAL BLACK BUT HAS CUTE ACCENTS OF RIBBONS AND FRILLS.
IT IS A "KILL TWO BIRDS WITH ONE STONE" COMBINA-TION!!!
FLASH

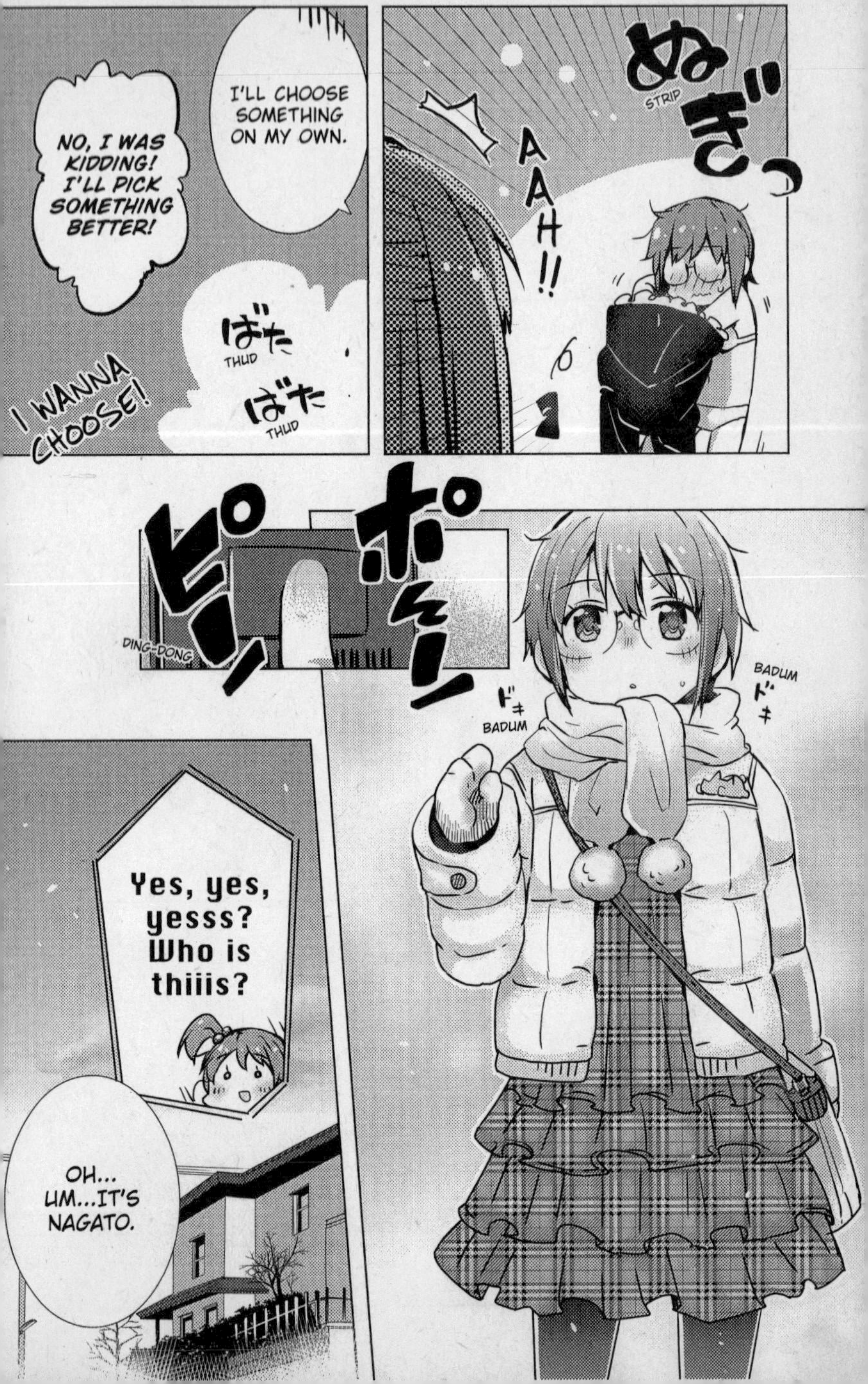

ぬぎっ
STRIP
AAH!!
I'LL CHOOSE SOMETHING ON MY OWN.
NO, I WAS KIDDING! I'LL PICK SOMETHING BETTER!
ばた
THUD
ばた
THUD
I WANNA CHOOSE!
ドキ
BADUM
ドキ
BADUM
ピンポーン
DING-DONG
Yes, yes, yesss? Who is thiiis?
OH... UM...IT'S NAGATO.

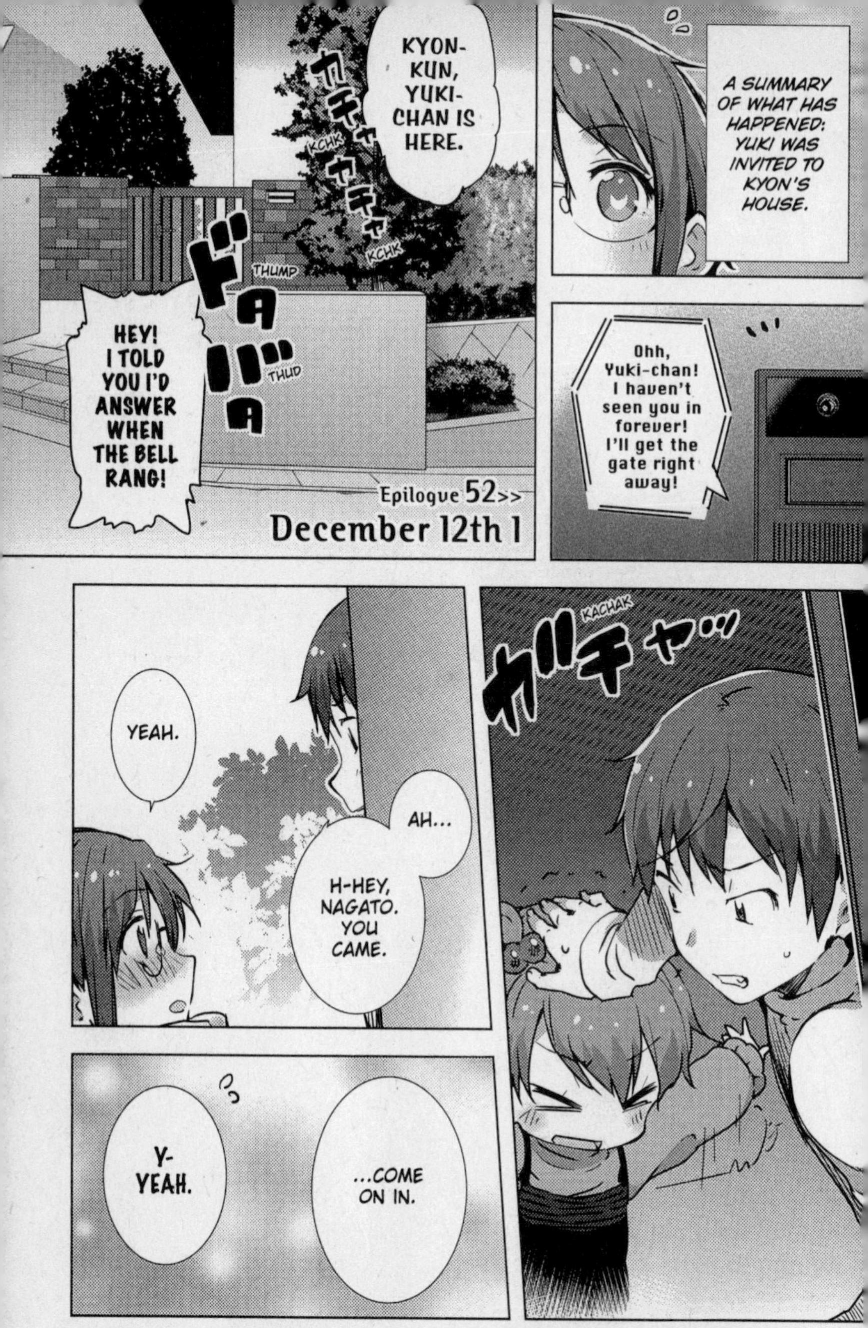
A SUMMARY OF WHAT HAS HAPPENED: YUKI WAS INVITED TO KYON'S HOUSE.
Ohh, Yuki-chan! I haven't seen you in forever! I'll get the gate right away!
KYON-KUN, YUKI-CHAN IS HERE.
KCHK
KCHK
THUMP
THUD
HEY! I TOLD YOU I'D ANSWER WHEN THE BELL RANG!
Epilogue 52>>
December 12th 1
KACHAK
AH...
H-HEY, NAGATO. YOU CAME.
YEAH.
...COME ON IN.
Y-YEAH.

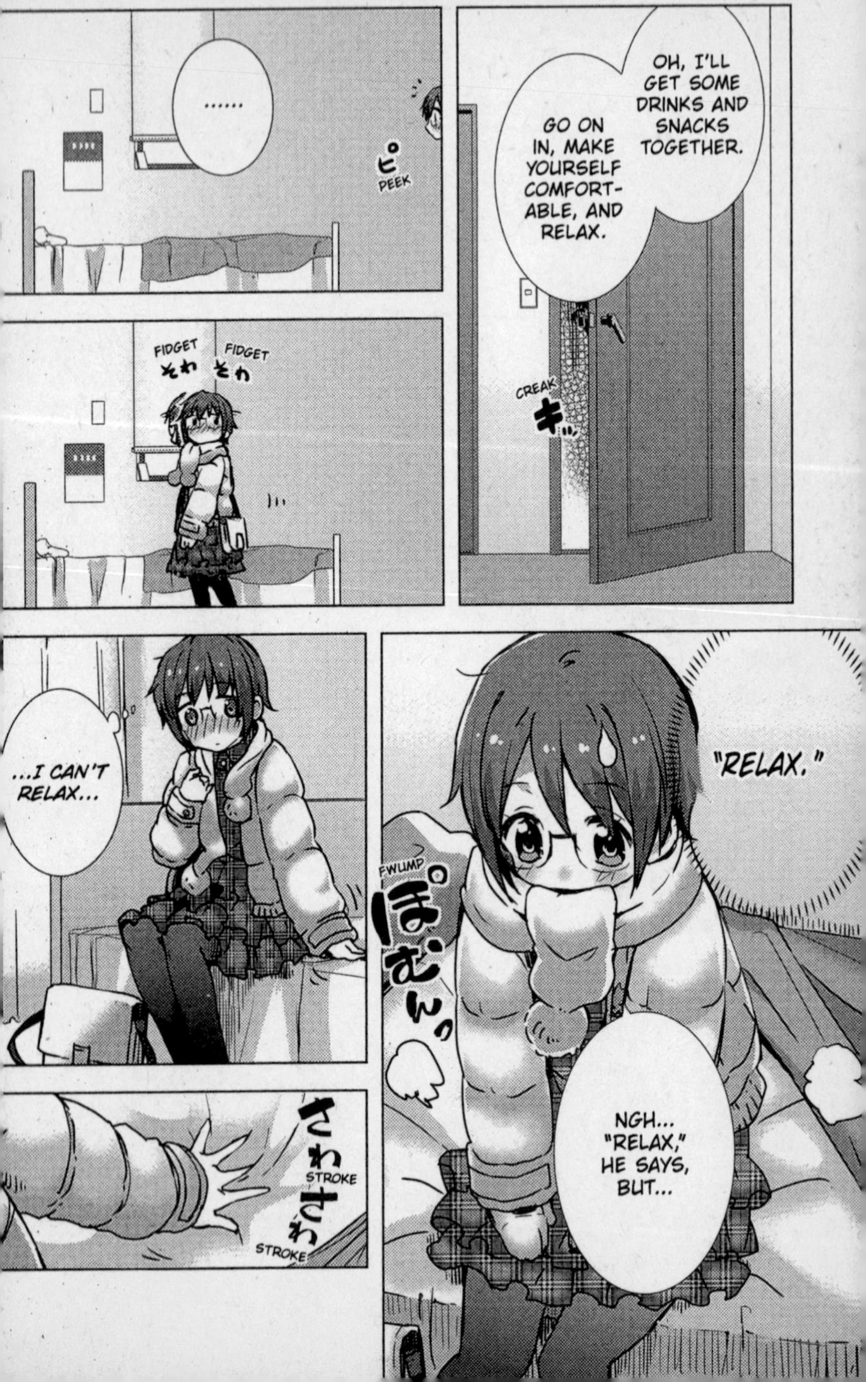
OH, I'LL GET SOME DRINKS AND SNACKS TOGETHER.
GO ON IN, MAKE YOURSELF COMFORT-ABLE, AND RELAX.
キ
CREAK
......
ピ
PEEK
そわ そわ
FIDGET FIDGET
"RELAX."
ぽむんっ
FWUMP
NGH... "RELAX," HE SAYS, BUT...
...I CAN'T RELAX...
さわさわ
STROKE STROKE

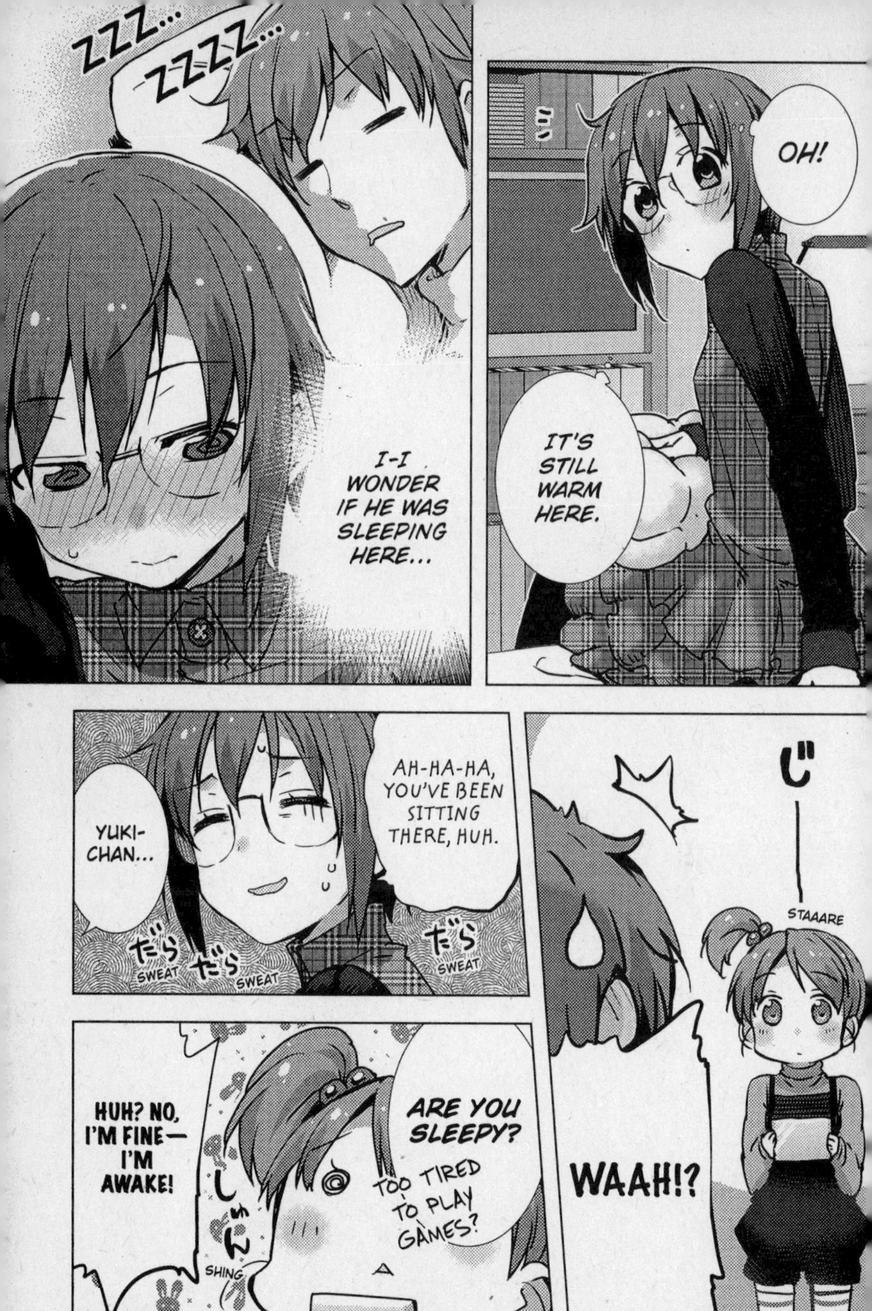
OH!
IT'S STILL WARM HERE.
ZZZ...
ZZZZ...
I-I WONDER IF HE WAS SLEEPING HERE...
じー
STAAARE
WAAH!?
AH-HA-HA, YOU'VE BEEN SITTING THERE, HUH.
YUKI-CHAN...
だら SWEAT だら SWEAT だら SWEAT
ARE YOU SLEEPY?
TOO TIRED TO PLAY GAMES?
しゅん SHING
HUH? NO, I'M FINE— I'M AWAKE!

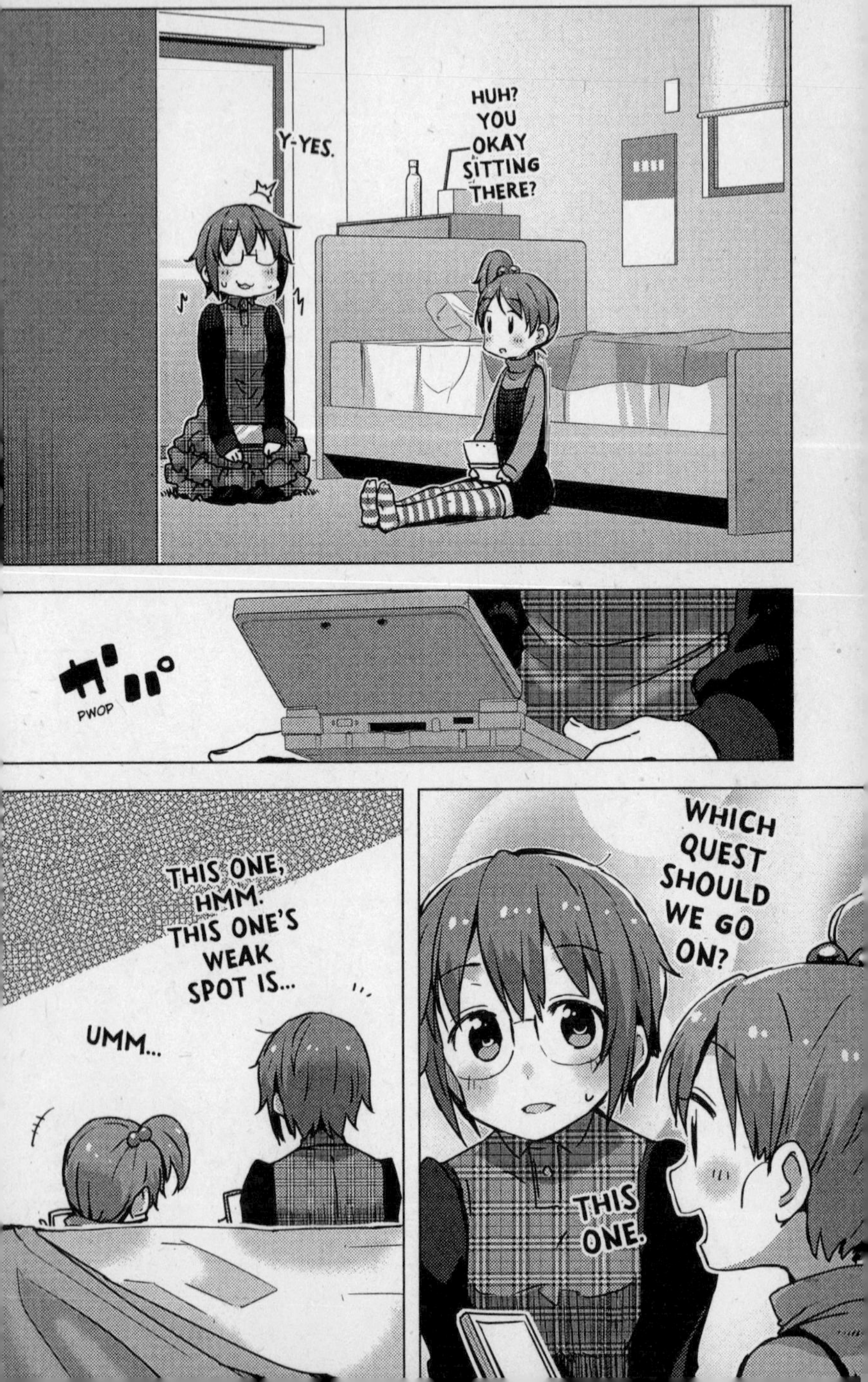
HUH? YOU OKAY SITTING THERE?
Y-YES.
ガパ
PWOP
WHICH QUEST SHOULD WE GO ON?
THIS ONE.
THIS ONE, HMM. THIS ONE'S WEAK SPOT IS...
UMM...

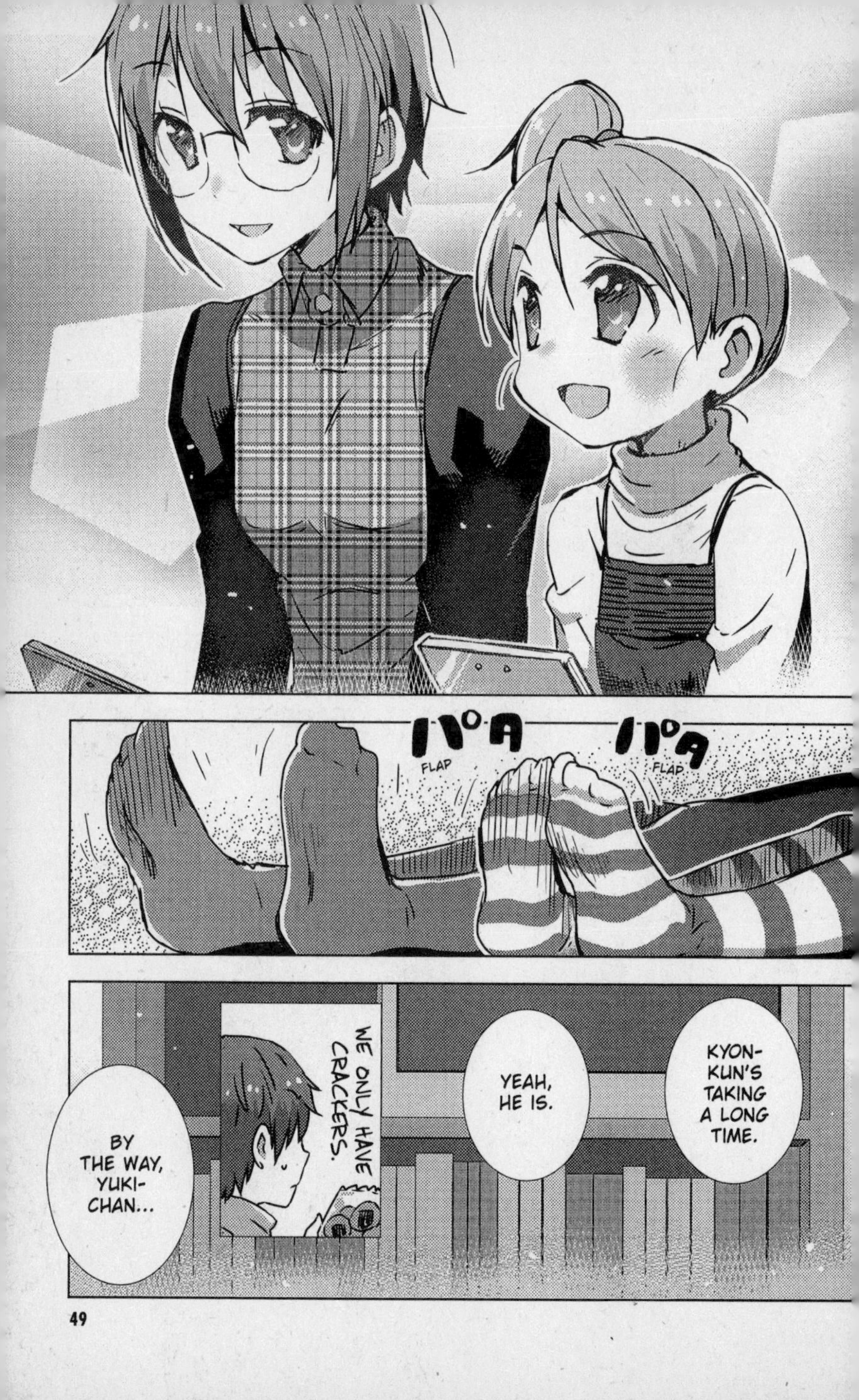
パタ
FLAP
パタ
FLAP
KYON-KUN'S TAKING A LONG TIME.
YEAH, HE IS.
WE ONLY HAVE CRACKERS.
BY THE WAY, YUKI-CHAN...

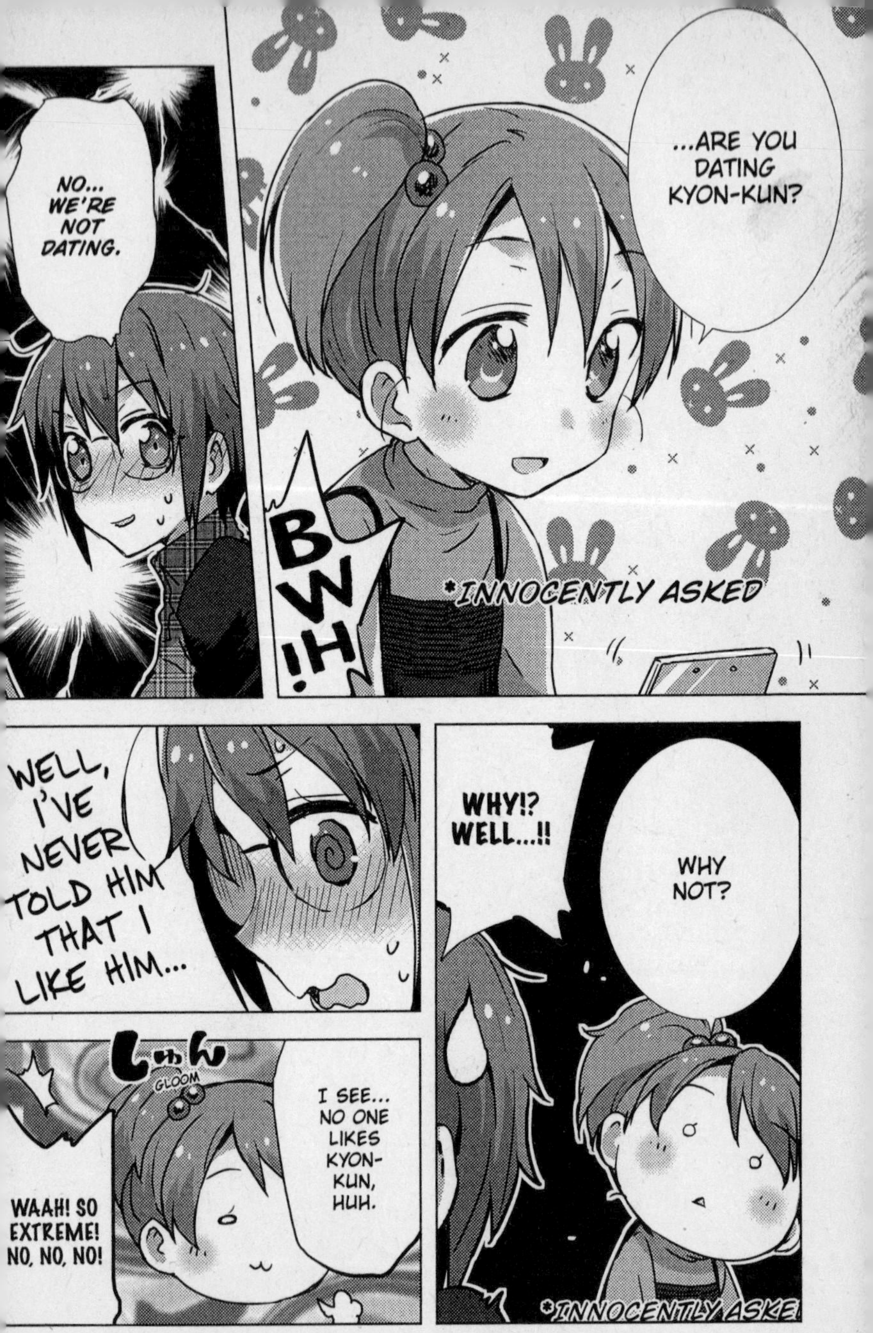
...ARE YOU DATING KYON-KUN?
*INNOCENTLY ASKED
BWH!!
NO... WE'RE NOT DATING.
WHY NOT?
WHY!? WELL...!!
*INNOCENTLY ASKE
WELL, I'VE NEVER TOLD HIM THAT I LIKE HIM...
I SEE... NO ONE LIKES KYON-KUN, HUH.
しゅん
GLOOM
WAAH! SO EXTREME! NO, NO, NO!

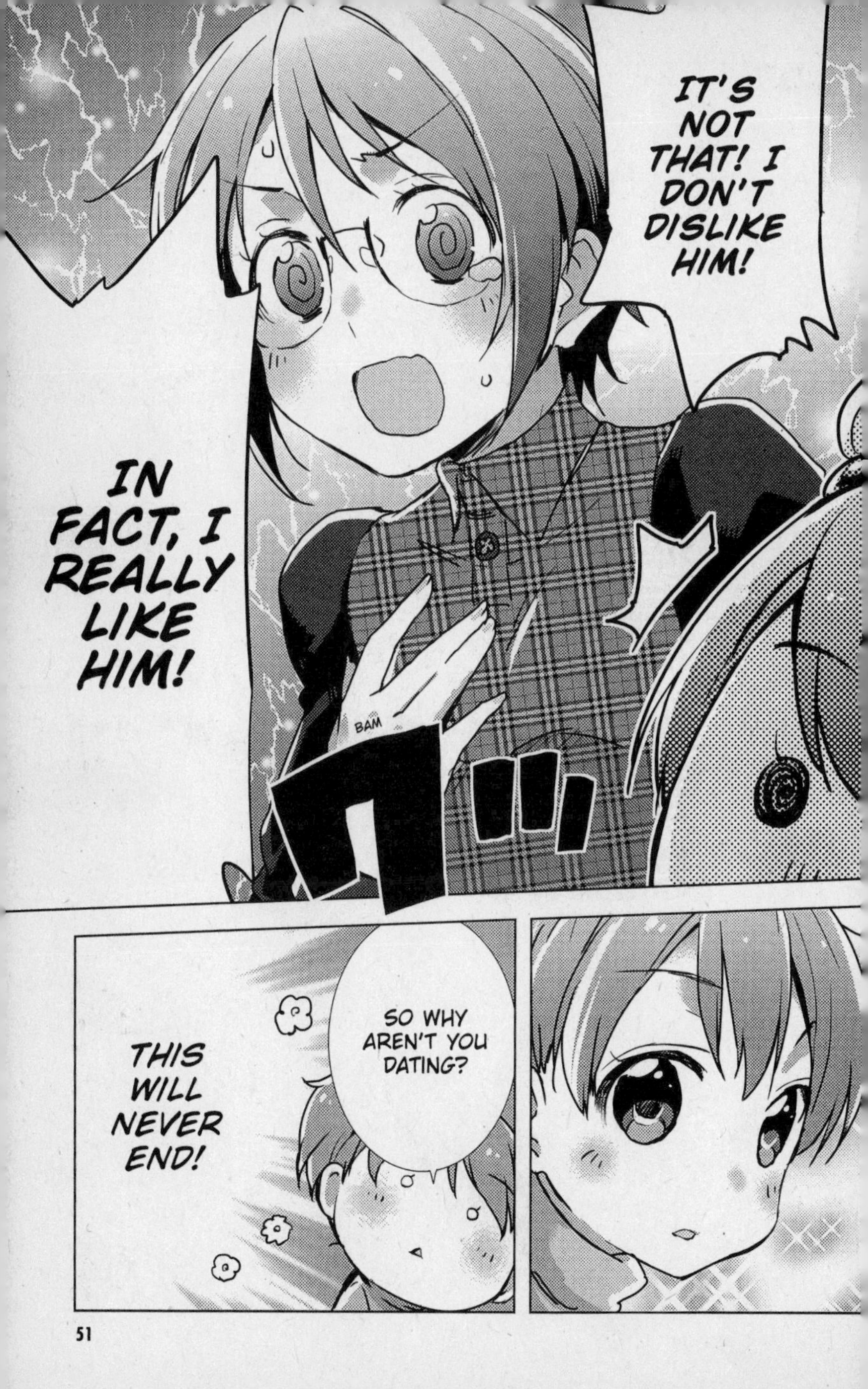
IT'S NOT THAT! I DON'T DISLIKE HIM!
BAM
IN FACT, I REALLY LIKE HIM!
SO WHY AREN'T YOU DATING?
THIS WILL NEVER END!

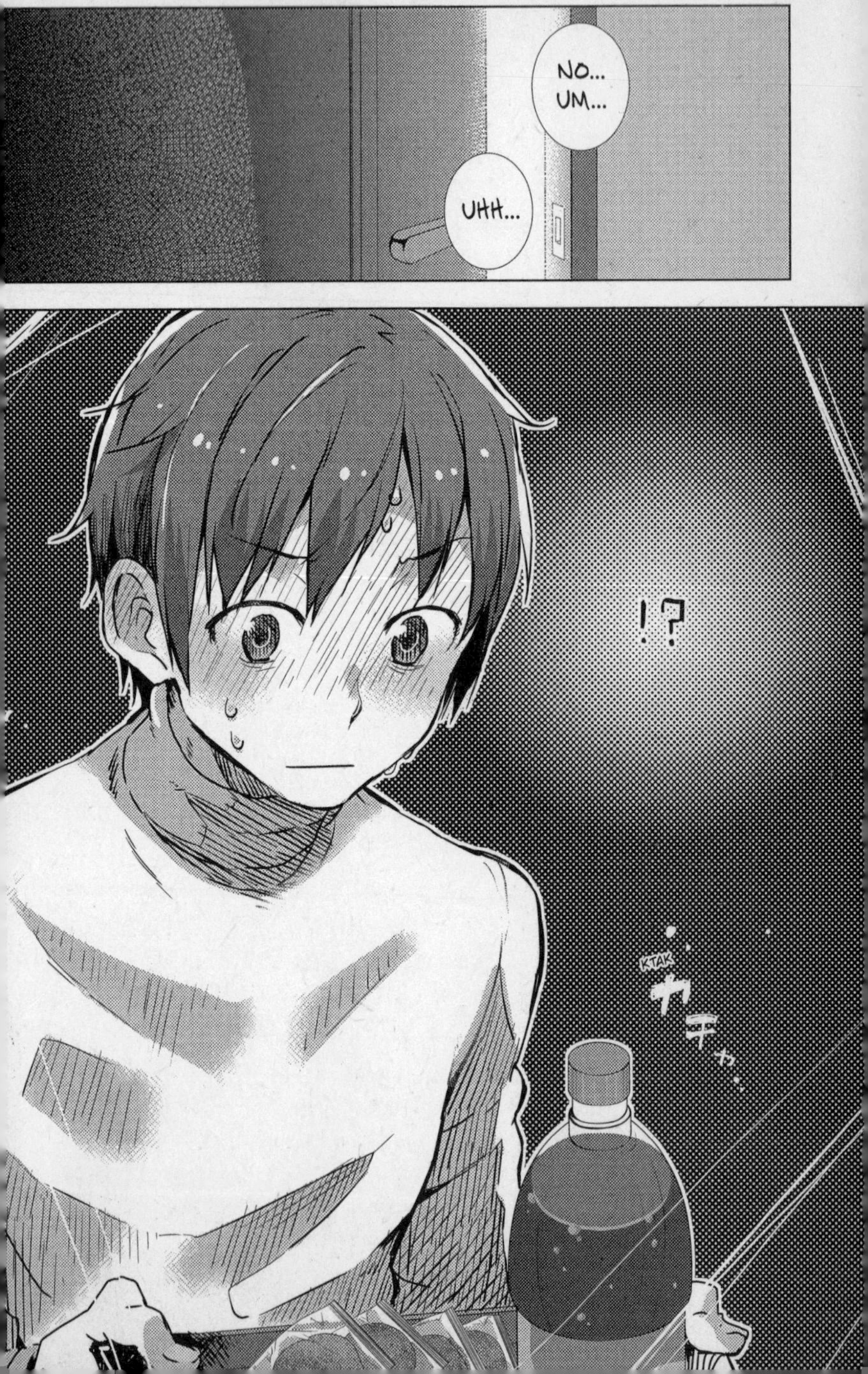
NO...
UM...
UHH...
!?
KTAK

Epilogue 53>> December 12th 2

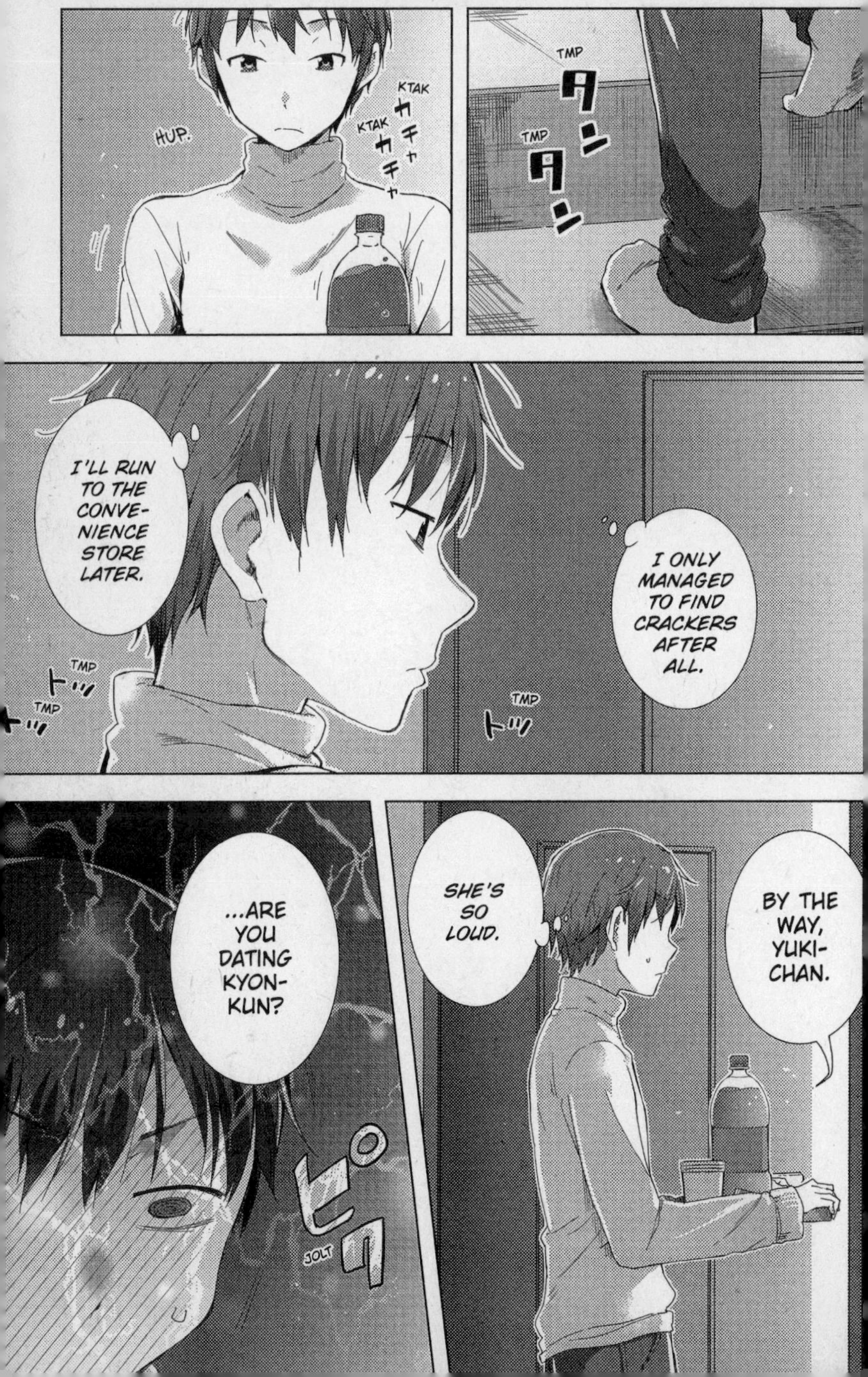
TMP
TMP
HUP.
KTAK
KTAK
I ONLY MANAGED TO FIND CRACKERS AFTER ALL.
TMP
I'LL RUN TO THE CONVE-NIENCE STORE LATER.
TMP
TMP
BY THE WAY, YUKI-CHAN.
SHE'S SO LOUD.
...ARE YOU DATING KYON-KUN?
JOLT

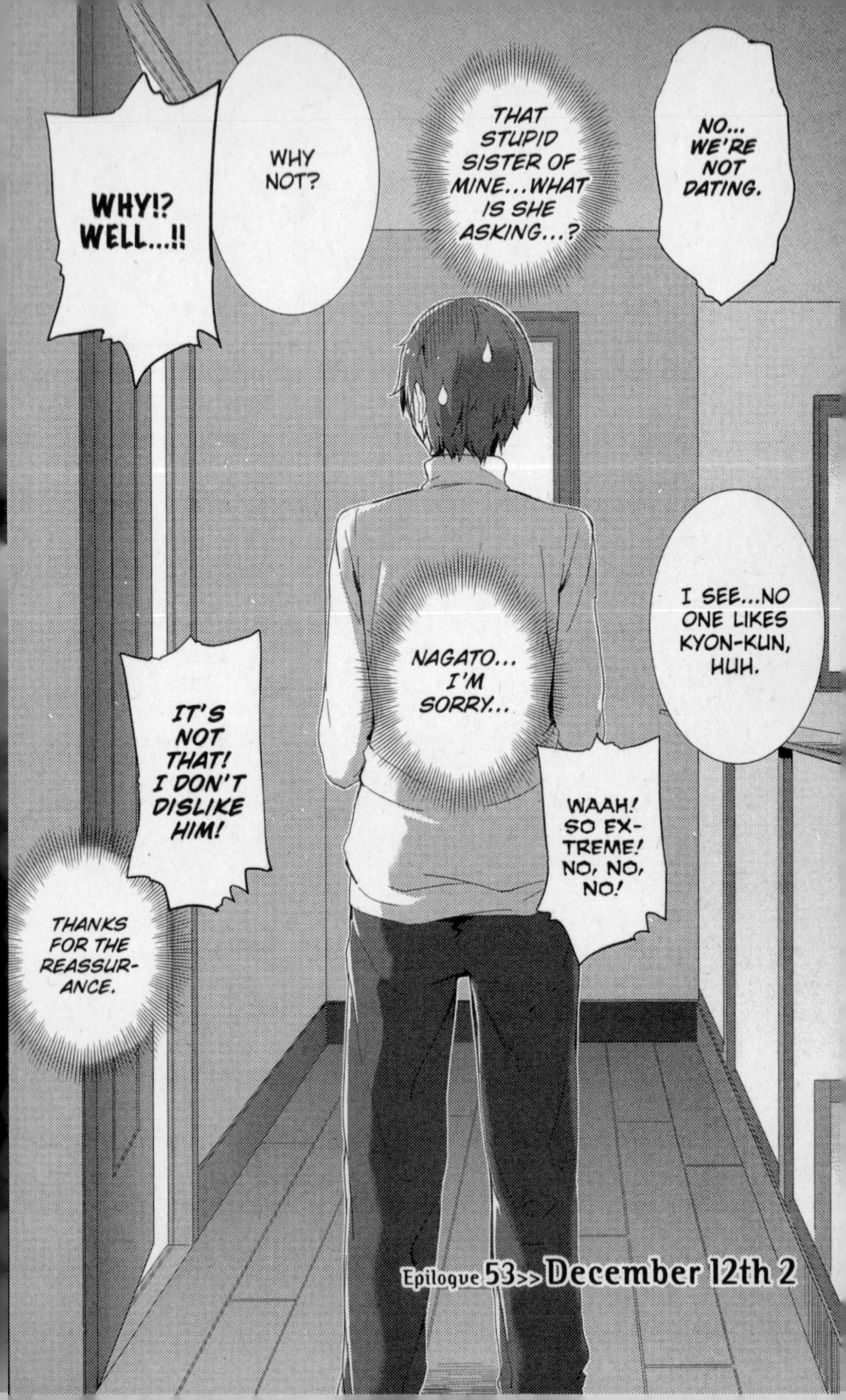
NO... WE'RE NOT DATING.
THAT STUPID SISTER OF MINE...WHAT IS SHE ASKING...?
WHY NOT?
WHY!? WELL...!!
I SEE...NO ONE LIKES KYON-KUN, HUH.
WAAH! SO EX-TREME! NO, NO, NO!
NAGATO... I'M SORRY...
IT'S NOT THAT! I DON'T DISLIKE HIM!
THANKS FOR THE REASSUR-ANCE.

## Epilogue 53>> December 12th 2

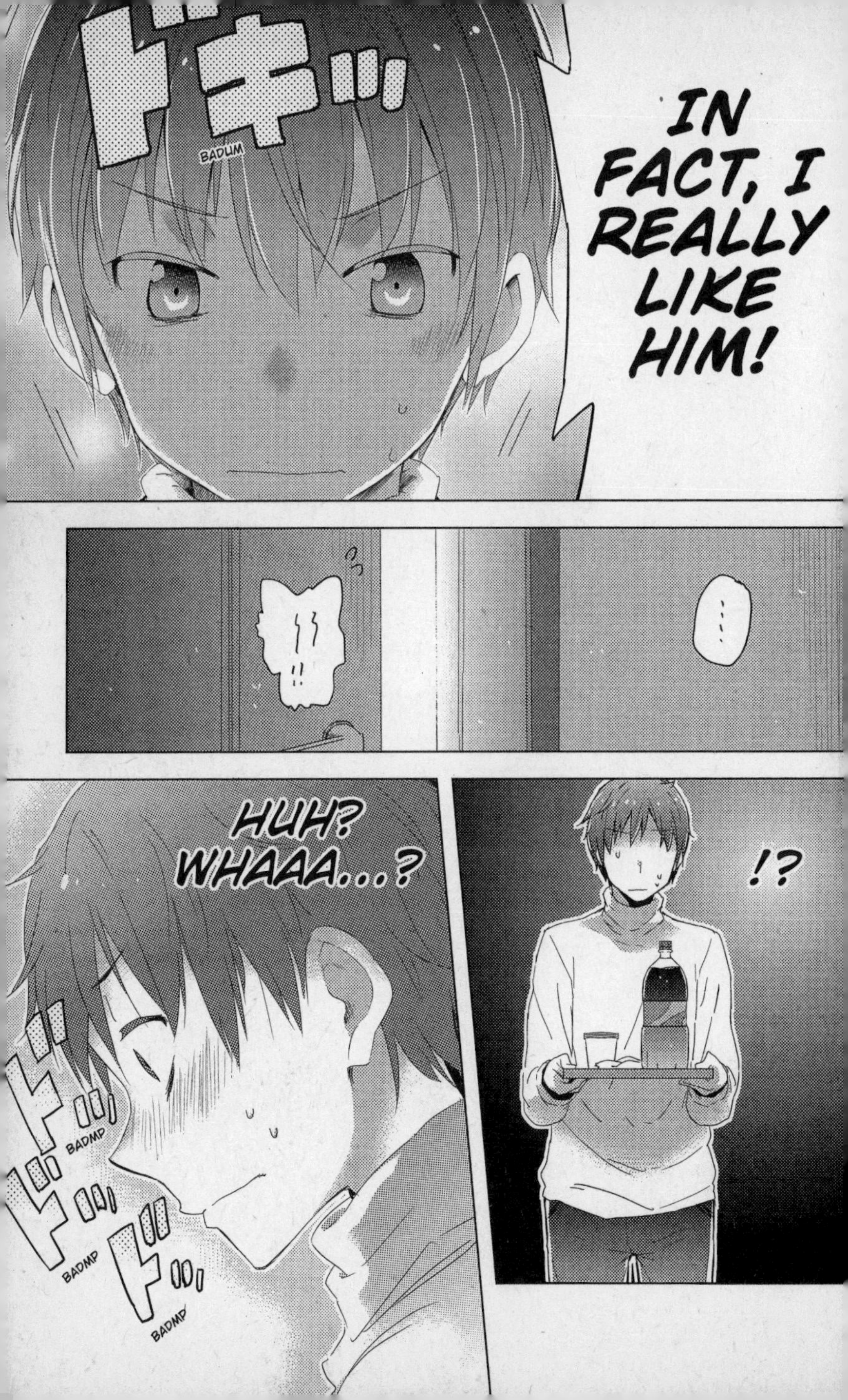
IN FACT, I REALLY LIKE HIM!
ドキッ
BADUM
…
!!
!?
HUH? WHAAA...?
BADMP
BADMP
BADMP

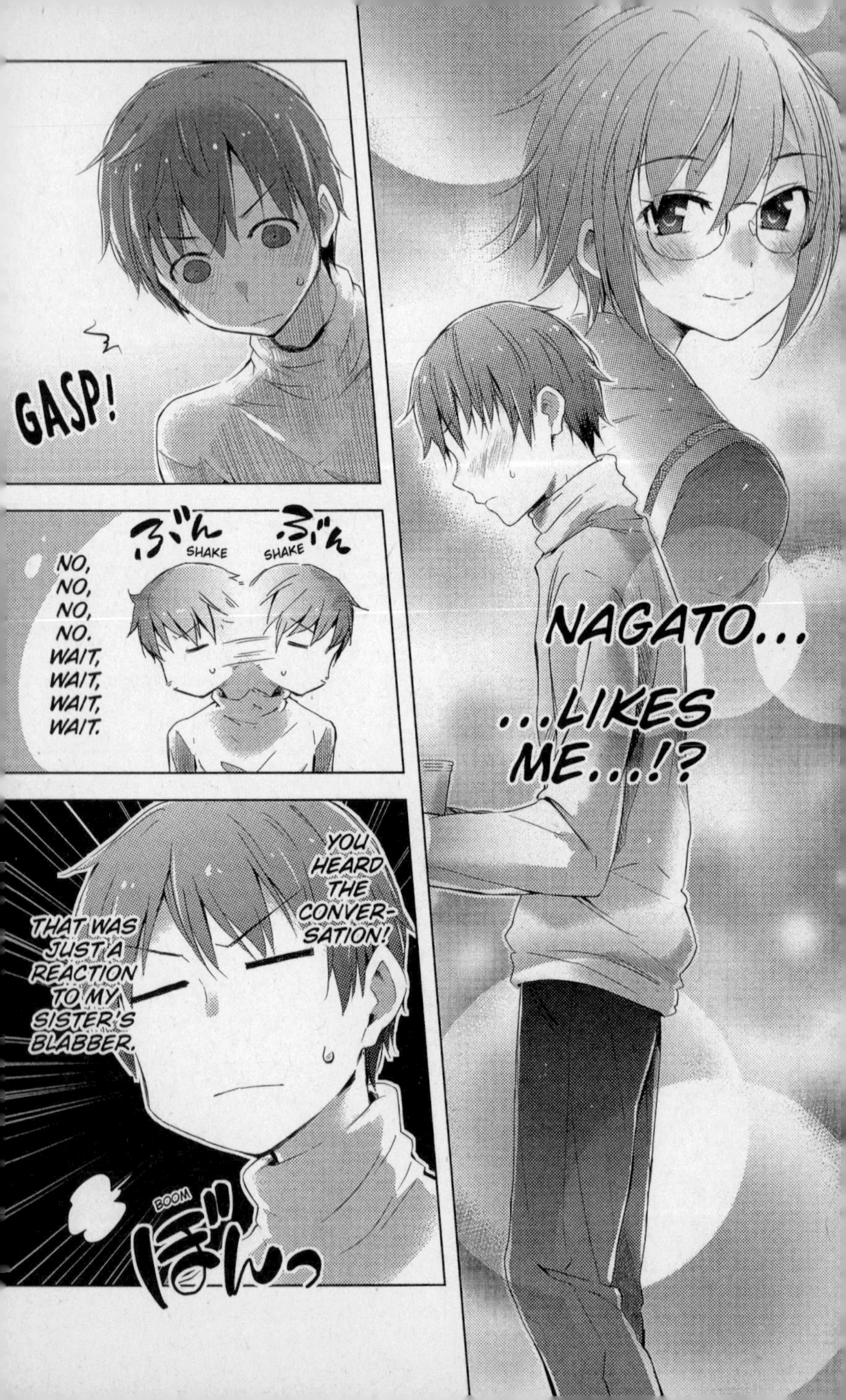
NAGATO...
...LIKES ME...!?
GASP!
ぶん SHAKE ぶん SHAKE
NO, NO, NO, NO. WAIT, WAIT, WAIT, WAIT.
YOU HEARD THE CONVER-SATION!
THAT WAS JUST A REACTION TO MY SISTER'S BLABBER.
ぼんっ BOOM

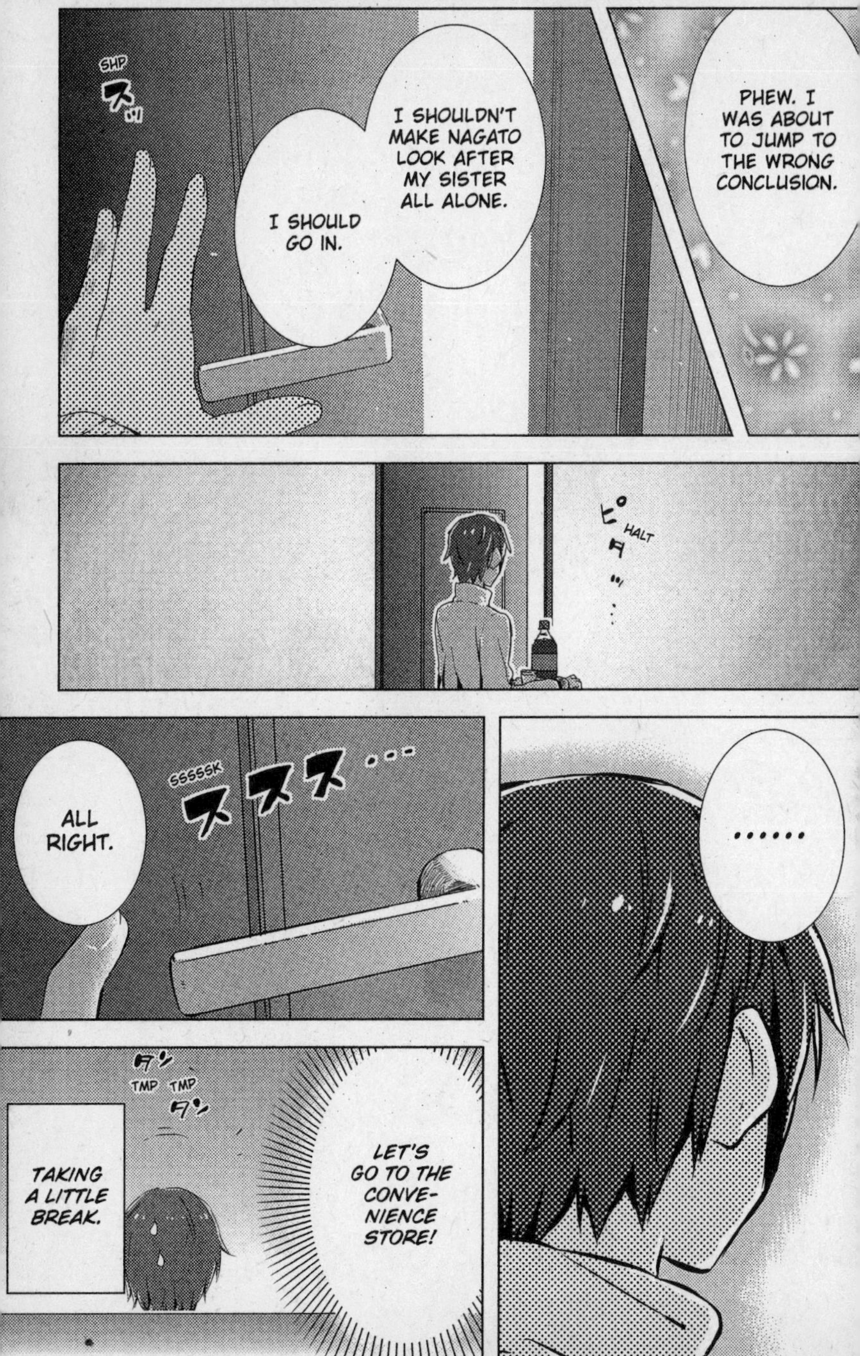
PHEW. I WAS ABOUT TO JUMP TO THE WRONG CONCLUSION.
I SHOULDN'T MAKE NAGATO LOOK AFTER MY SISTER ALL ALONE.
I SHOULD GO IN.
SHP
HALT
......
SSSSSK
ALL RIGHT.
TMP TMP
LET'S GO TO THE CONVE-NIENCE STORE!
TAKING A LITTLE BREAK.

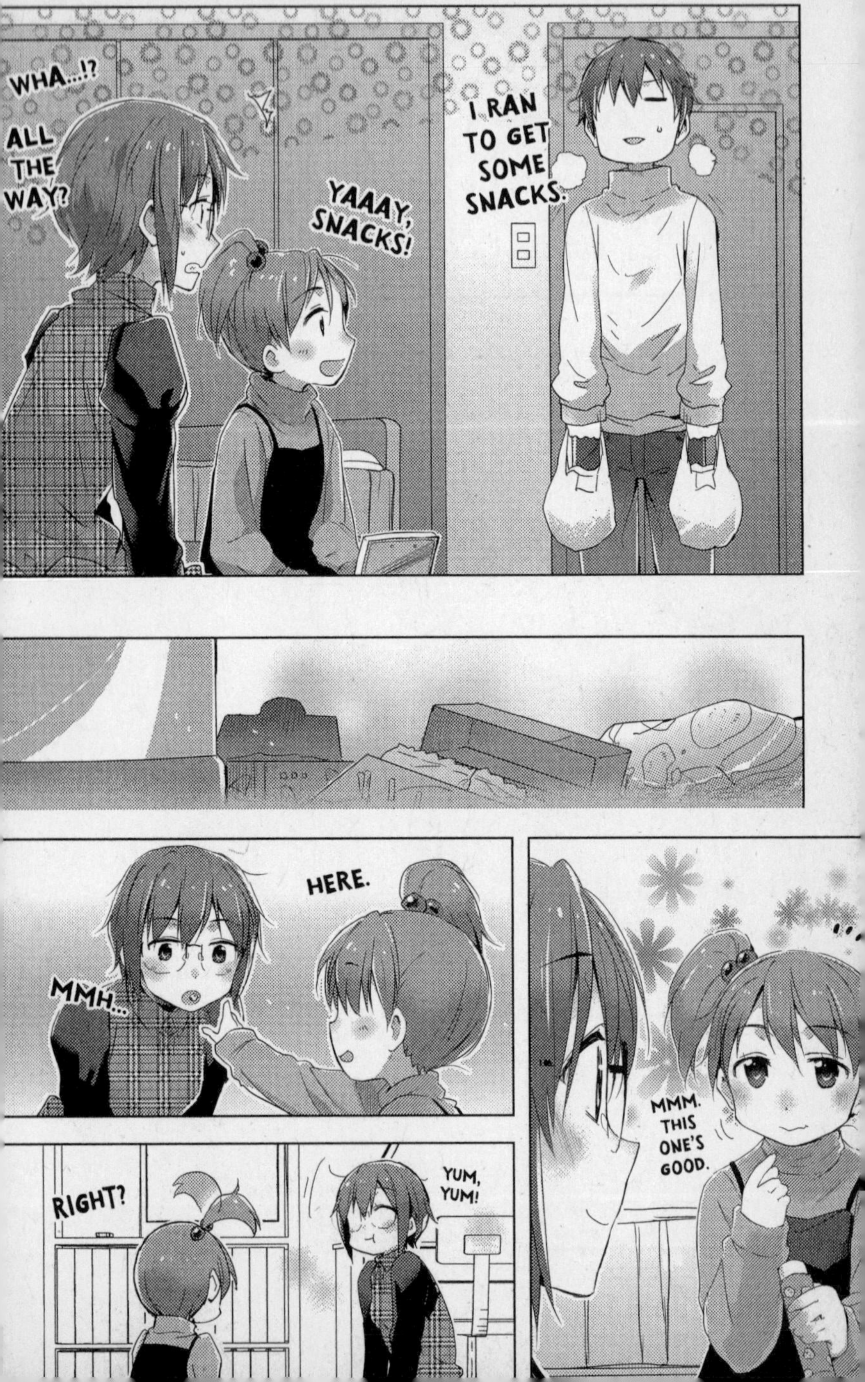
I RAN TO GET SOME SNACKS.
YAAAY, SNACKS!
WHA...!?
ALL THE WAY?
...
MMM. THIS ONE'S GOOD.
HERE.
MMH...
YUM, YUM!
RIGHT?

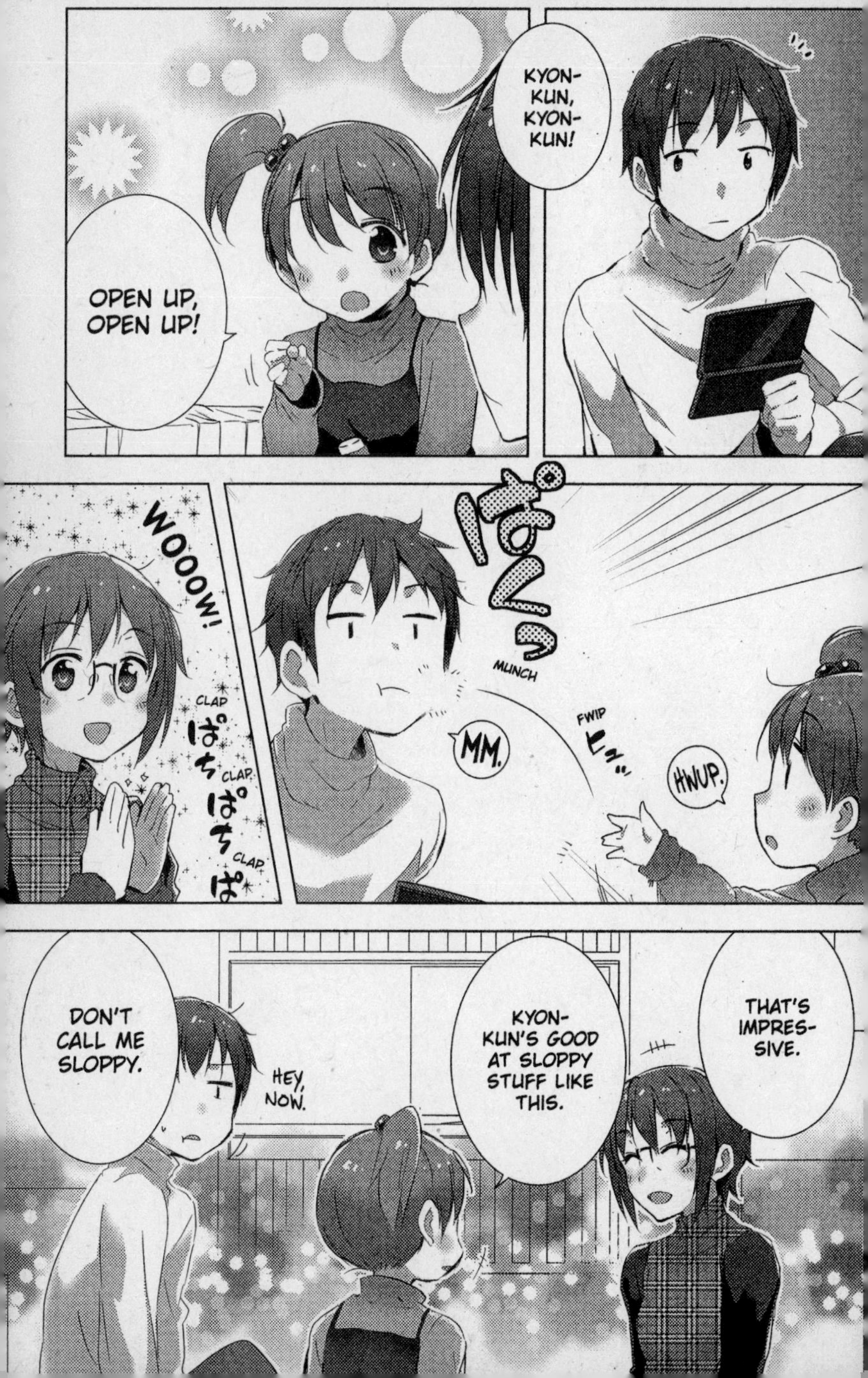
KYON-KUN, KYON-KUN!
OPEN UP, OPEN UP!
ぱくっ
MUNCH
FWIP
ヒュッ
HWUP.
MM.
WOOOOW!
CLAP
ぱち
CLAP
ぱち
CLAP
ぱ
THAT'S IMPRES-SIVE.
KYON-KUN'S GOOD AT SLOPPY STUFF LIKE THIS.
HEY, NOW.
DON'T CALL ME SLOPPY.

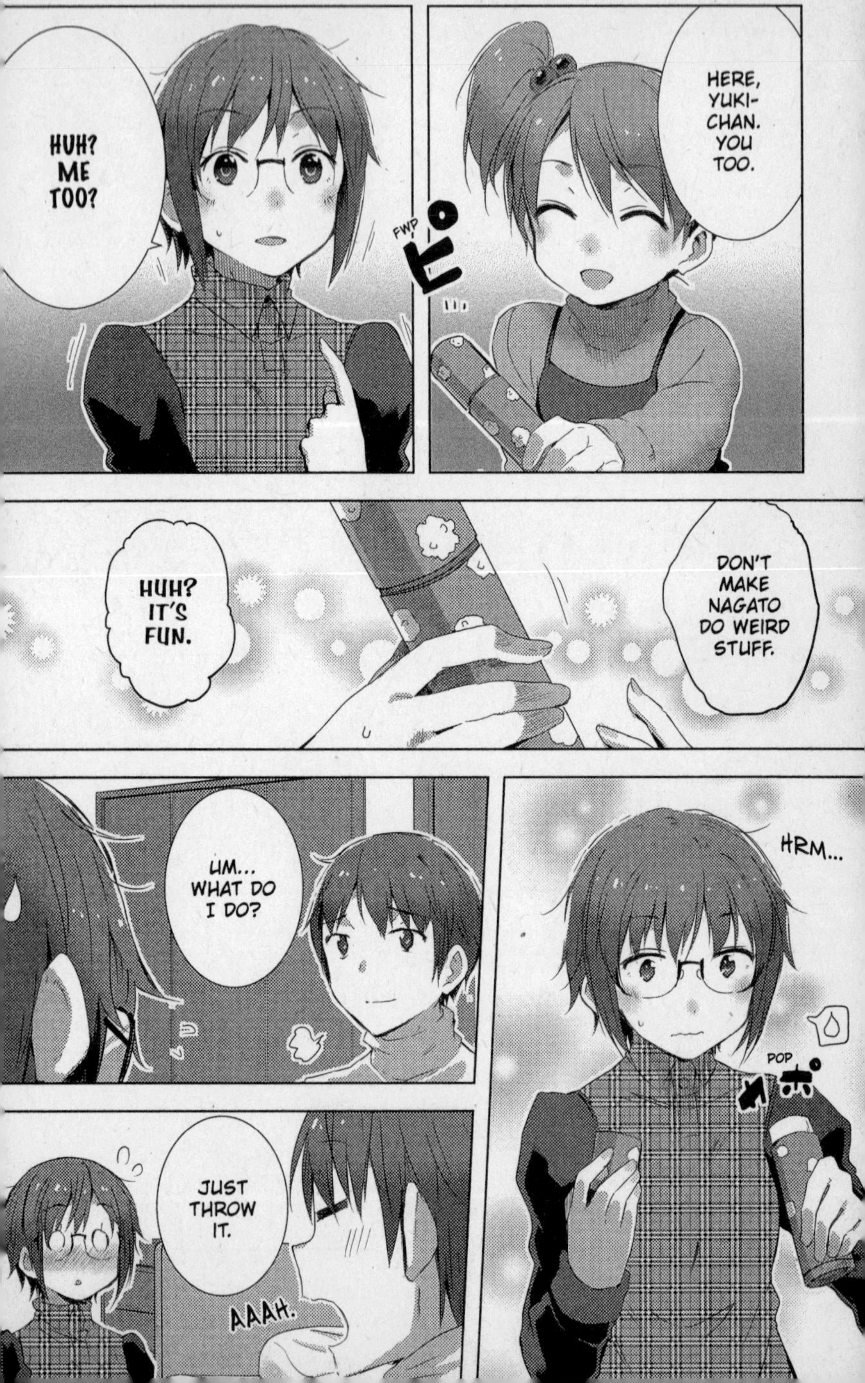
HERE, YUKI-CHAN. YOU TOO.
FWP
ピ
HUH? ME TOO?
DON'T MAKE NAGATO DO WEIRD STUFF.
HUH? IT'S FUN.
HRM...
POP
ポ
UM... WHAT DO I DO?
JUST THROW IT.
AAAH.

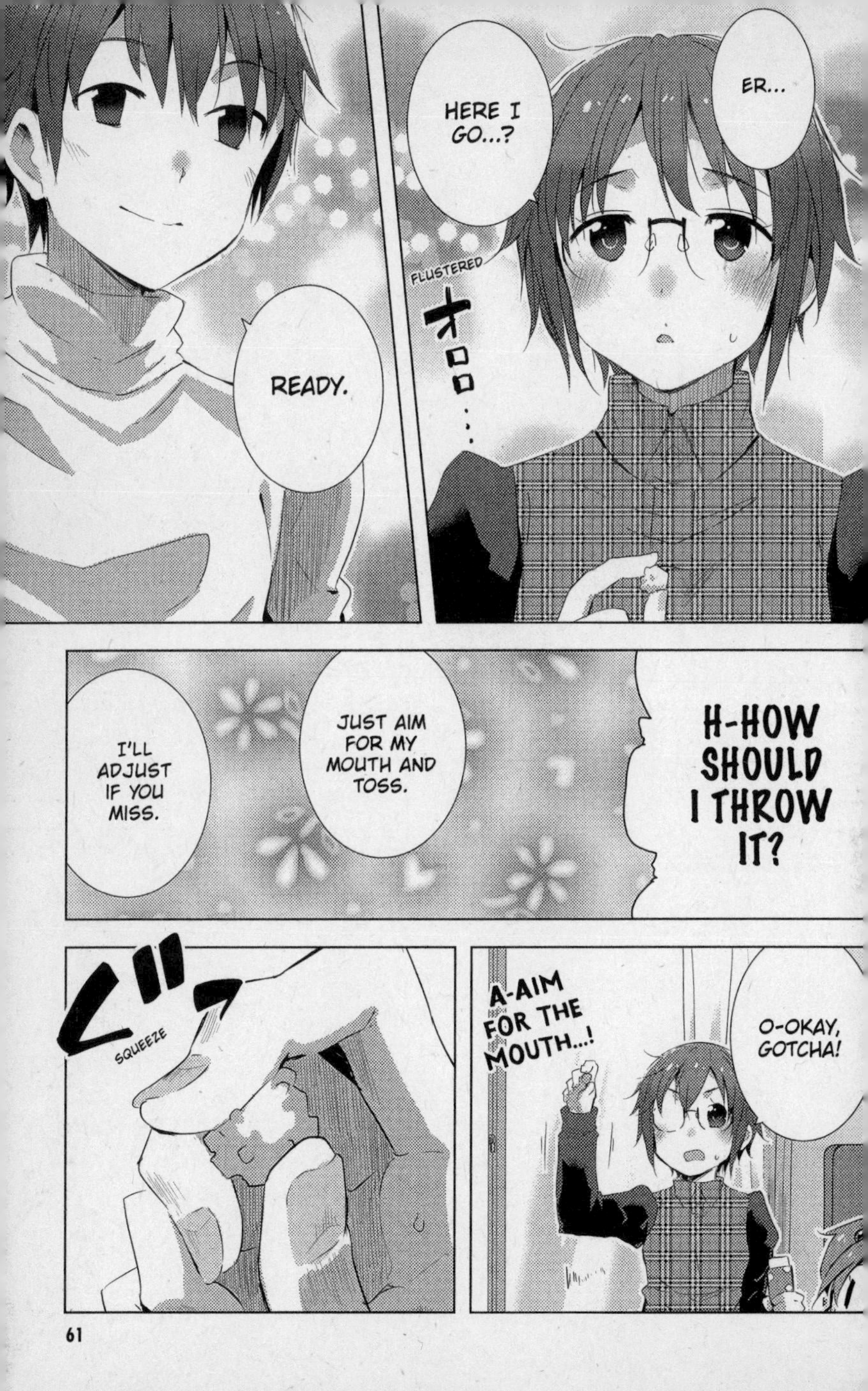
ER...
HERE I GO...?
FLUSTERED
オロロ...
READY.
H-HOW SHOULD I THROW IT?
JUST AIM FOR MY MOUTH AND TOSS.
I'LL ADJUST IF YOU MISS.
O-OKAY, GOTCHA!
A-AIM FOR THE MOUTH...!
SQUEEZE

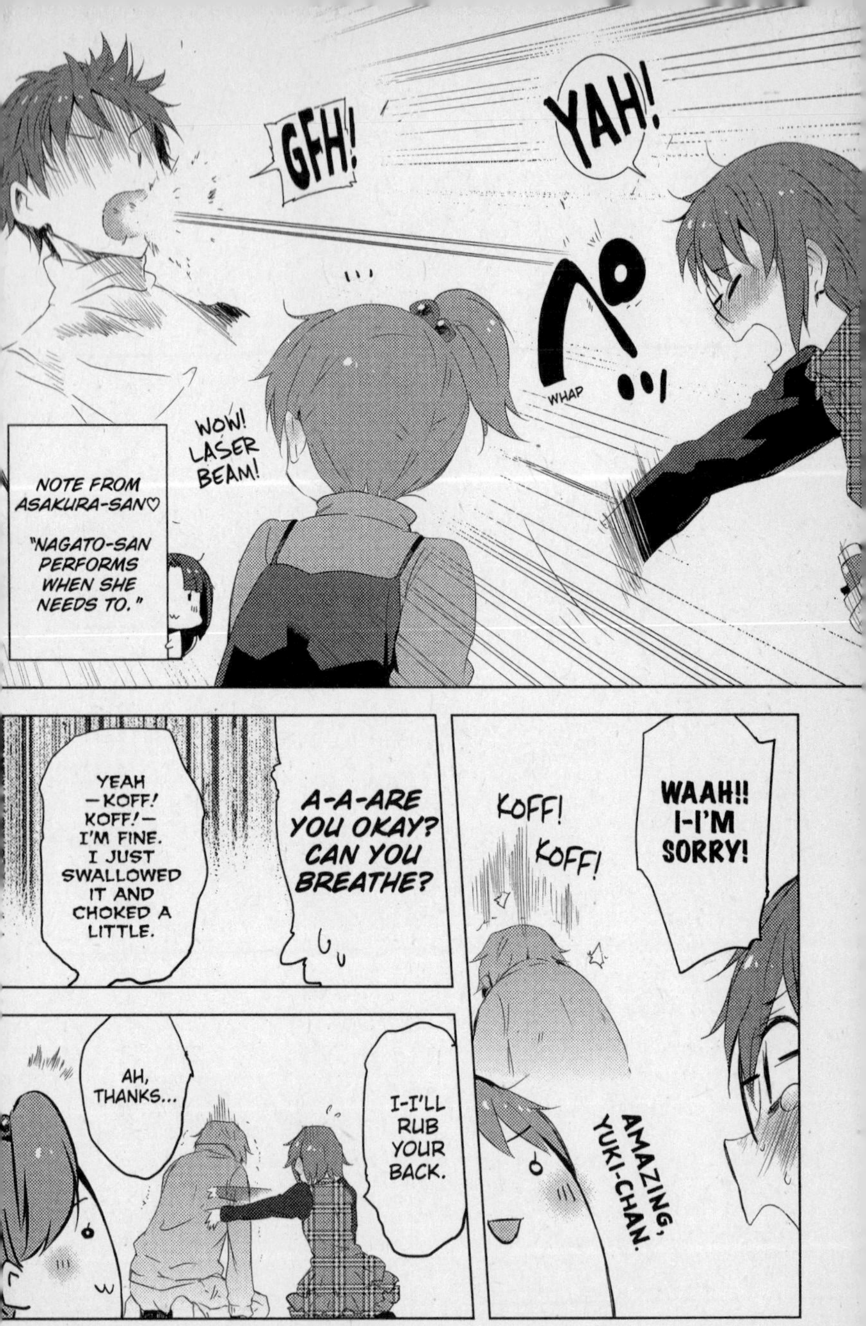
YAH!
GFH!
WHAP
WOW! LASER BEAM!
NOTE FROM ASAKURA-SAN♡
"NAGATO-SAN PERFORMS WHEN SHE NEEDS TO."
WAAH!! I-I'M SORRY!
KOFF! KOFF!
AMAZING, YUKI-CHAN.
A-A-ARE YOU OKAY? CAN YOU BREATHE?
YEAH —KOFF! KOFF!— I'M FINE. I JUST SWALLOWED IT AND CHOKED A LITTLE.
I-I'LL RUB YOUR BACK.
AH, THANKS...

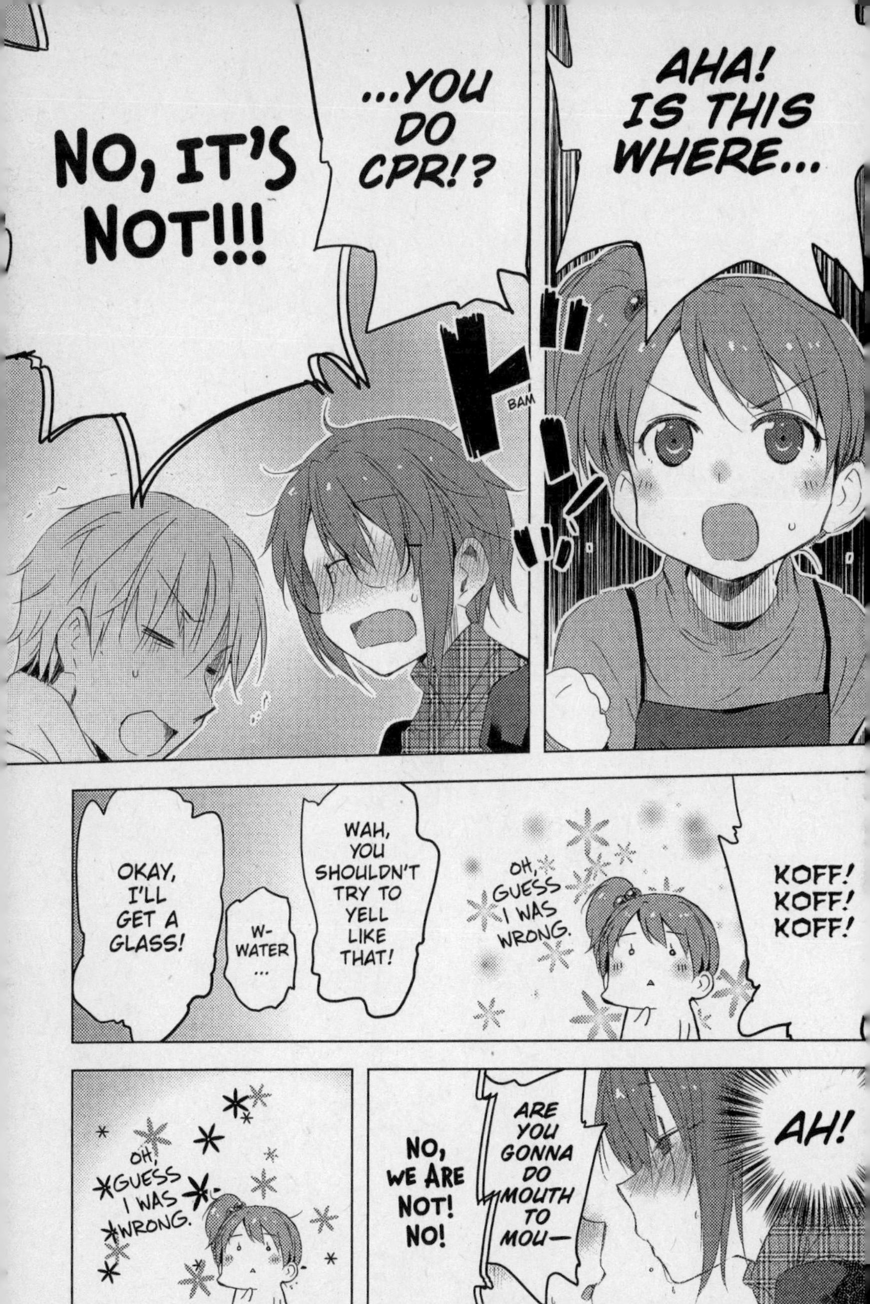
AHA! IS THIS WHERE...
...YOU DO CPR!?
BAM
NO, IT'S NOT!!!
KOFF! KOFF! KOFF!
OH, GUESS I WAS WRONG.
WAH, YOU SHOULDN'T TRY TO YELL LIKE THAT!
W-WATER...
OKAY, I'LL GET A GLASS!
AH!
ARE YOU GONNA DO MOUTH TO MOU—
NO, WE ARE NOT! NO!
OH, GUESS I WAS WRONG.

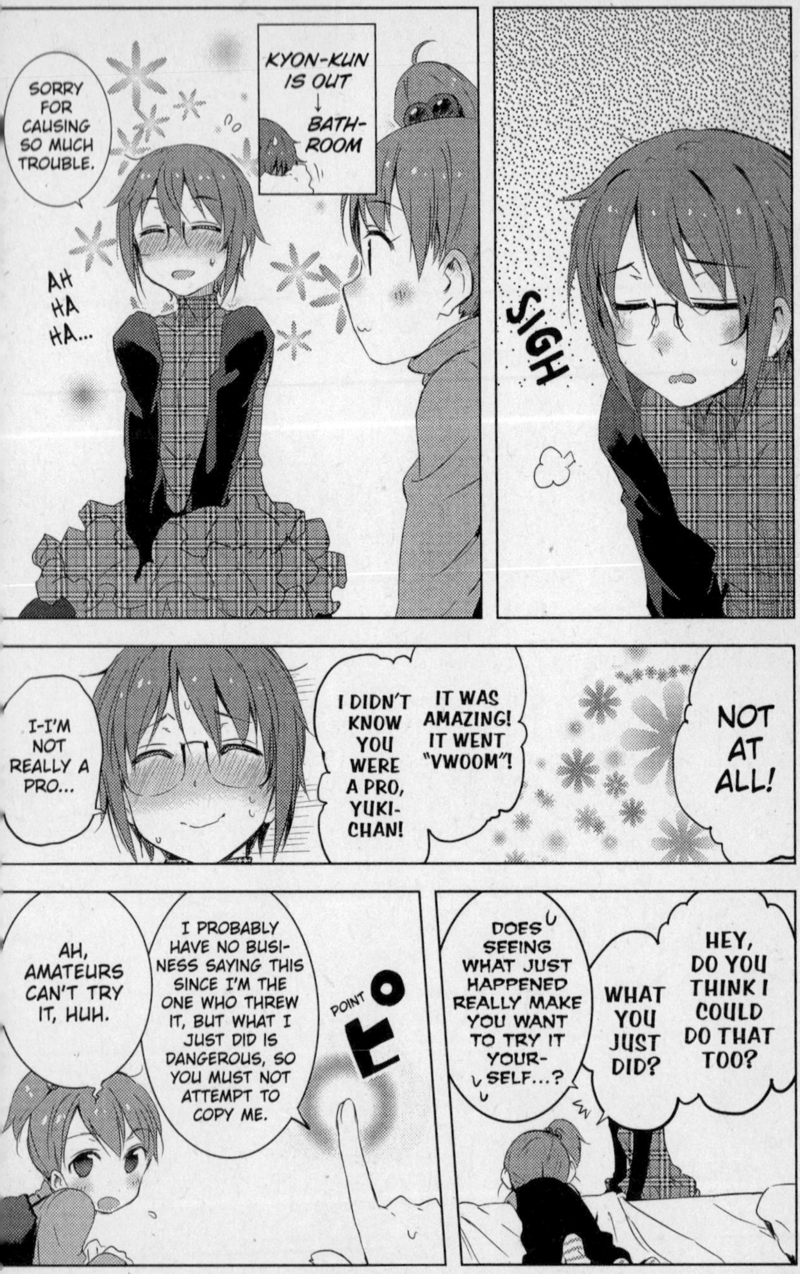
SIGH
KYON-KUN IS OUT → BATHROOM
SORRY FOR CAUSING SO MUCH TROUBLE.
AH HA HA...
NOT AT ALL!
IT WAS AMAZING! IT WENT "VWOOM"!
I DIDN'T KNOW YOU WERE A PRO, YUKI-CHAN!
I-I'M NOT REALLY A PRO...
HEY, DO YOU THINK I COULD DO THAT TOO?
WHAT YOU JUST DID?
DOES SEEING WHAT JUST HAPPENED REALLY MAKE YOU WANT TO TRY IT YOURSELF...?
I PROBABLY HAVE NO BUSINESS SAYING THIS SINCE I'M THE ONE WHO THREW IT, BUT WHAT I JUST DID IS DANGEROUS, SO YOU MUST NOT ATTEMPT TO COPY ME.
POINT
AH, AMATEURS CAN'T TRY IT, HUH.

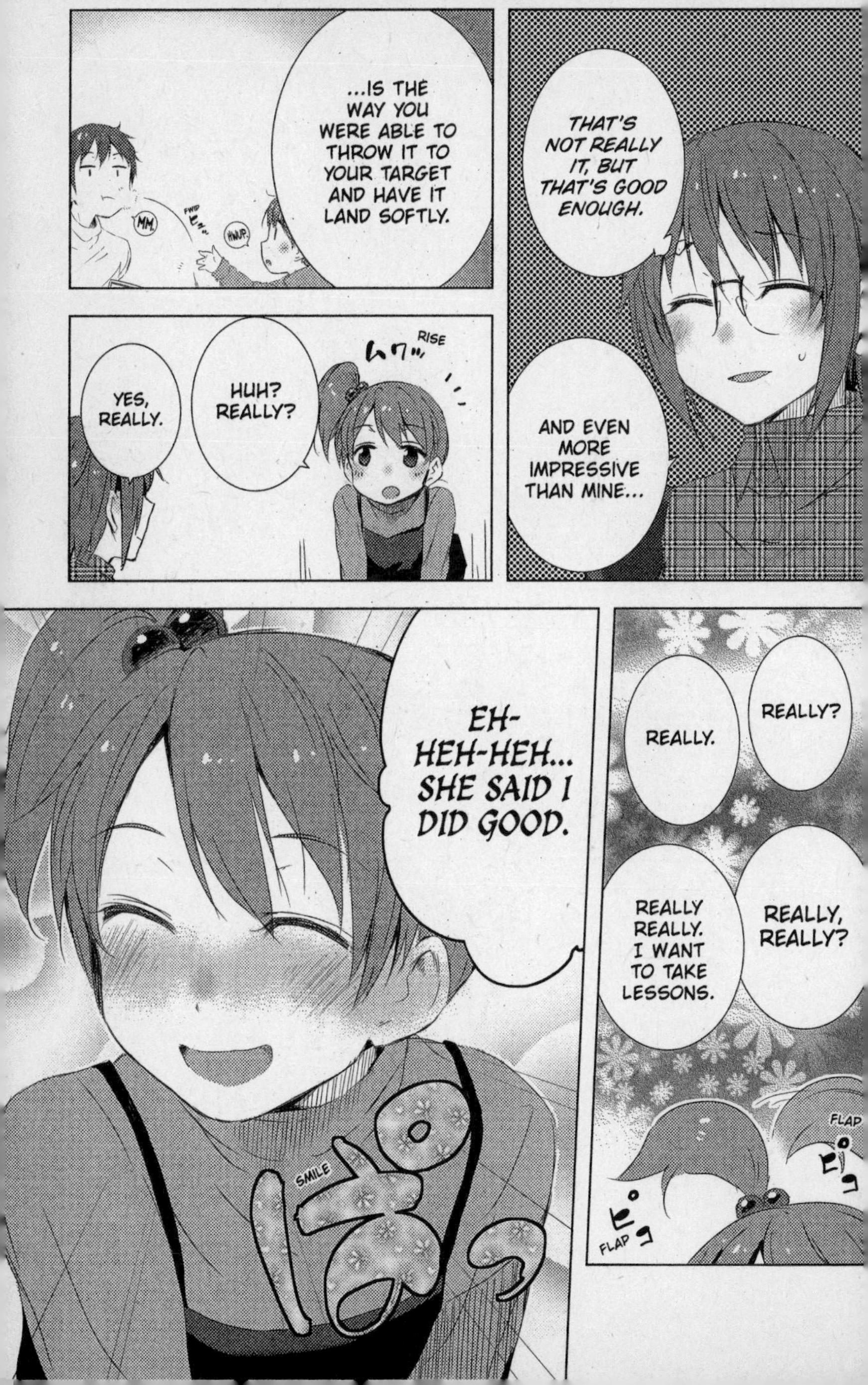
THAT'S NOT REALLY IT, BUT THAT'S GOOD ENOUGH.
AND EVEN MORE IMPRESSIVE THAN MINE...
...IS THE WAY YOU WERE ABLE TO THROW IT TO YOUR TARGET AND HAVE IT LAND SOFTLY.
FWIP
MM.
HWUP.
RISE
HUH? REALLY?
YES, REALLY.
REALLY?
REALLY.
REALLY, REALLY?
REALLY REALLY. I WANT TO TAKE LESSONS.
FLAP
FLAP
EH-HEH-HEH... SHE SAID I DID GOOD.
SMILE

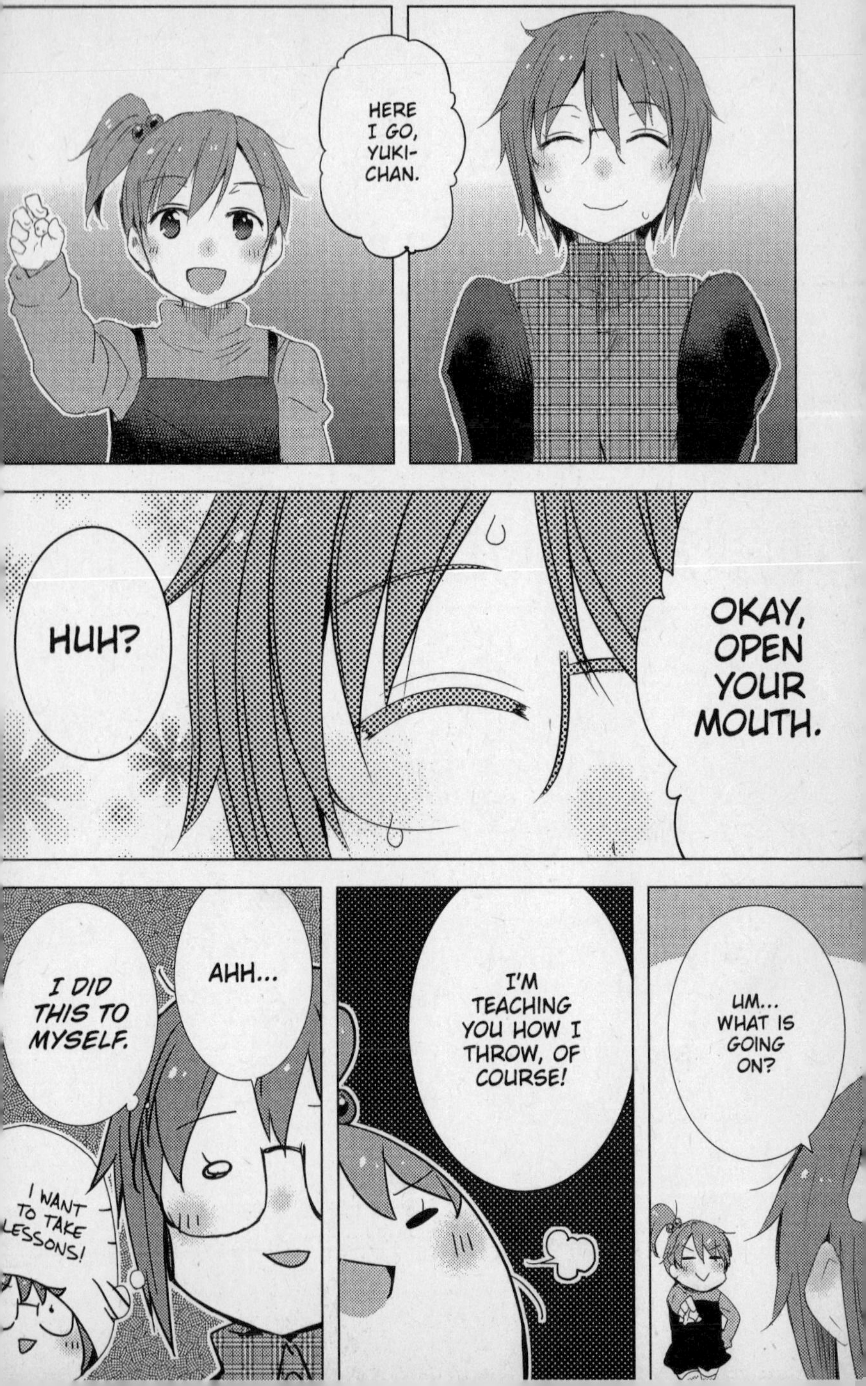
HERE I GO, YUKI-CHAN.
OKAY, OPEN YOUR MOUTH.
HUH?
UM... WHAT IS GOING ON?
I'M TEACHING YOU HOW I THROW, OF COURSE!
AHH...
I DID THIS TO MYSELF.
I WANT TO TAKE LESSONS!

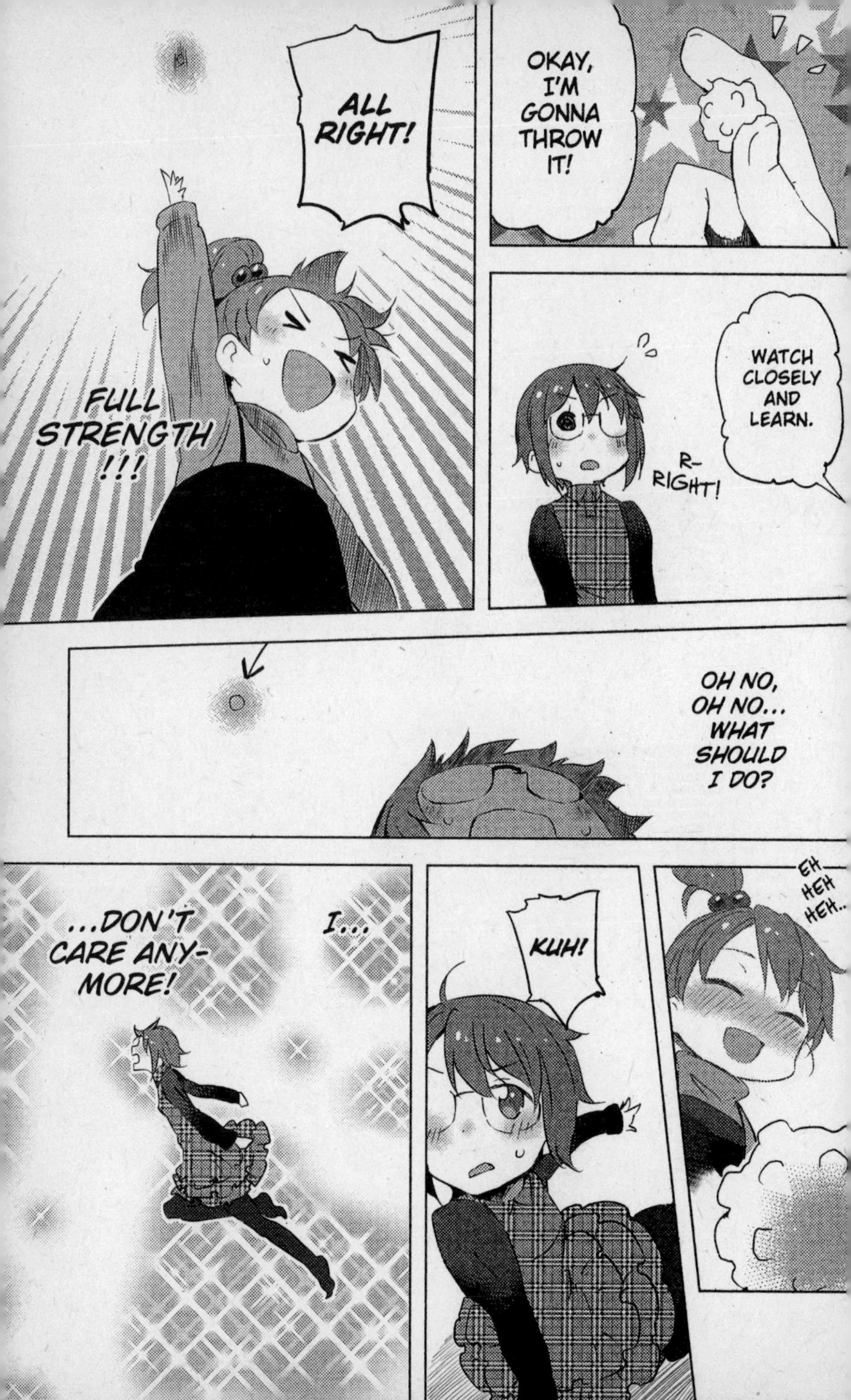
OKAY, I'M GONNA THROW IT!
WATCH CLOSELY AND LEARN.
R-RIGHT!
ALL RIGHT!
FULL STRENGTH!!!
OH NO, OH NO... WHAT SHOULD I DO?
EH HEH HEH..
KUH!
I...
...DON'T CARE ANY-MORE!

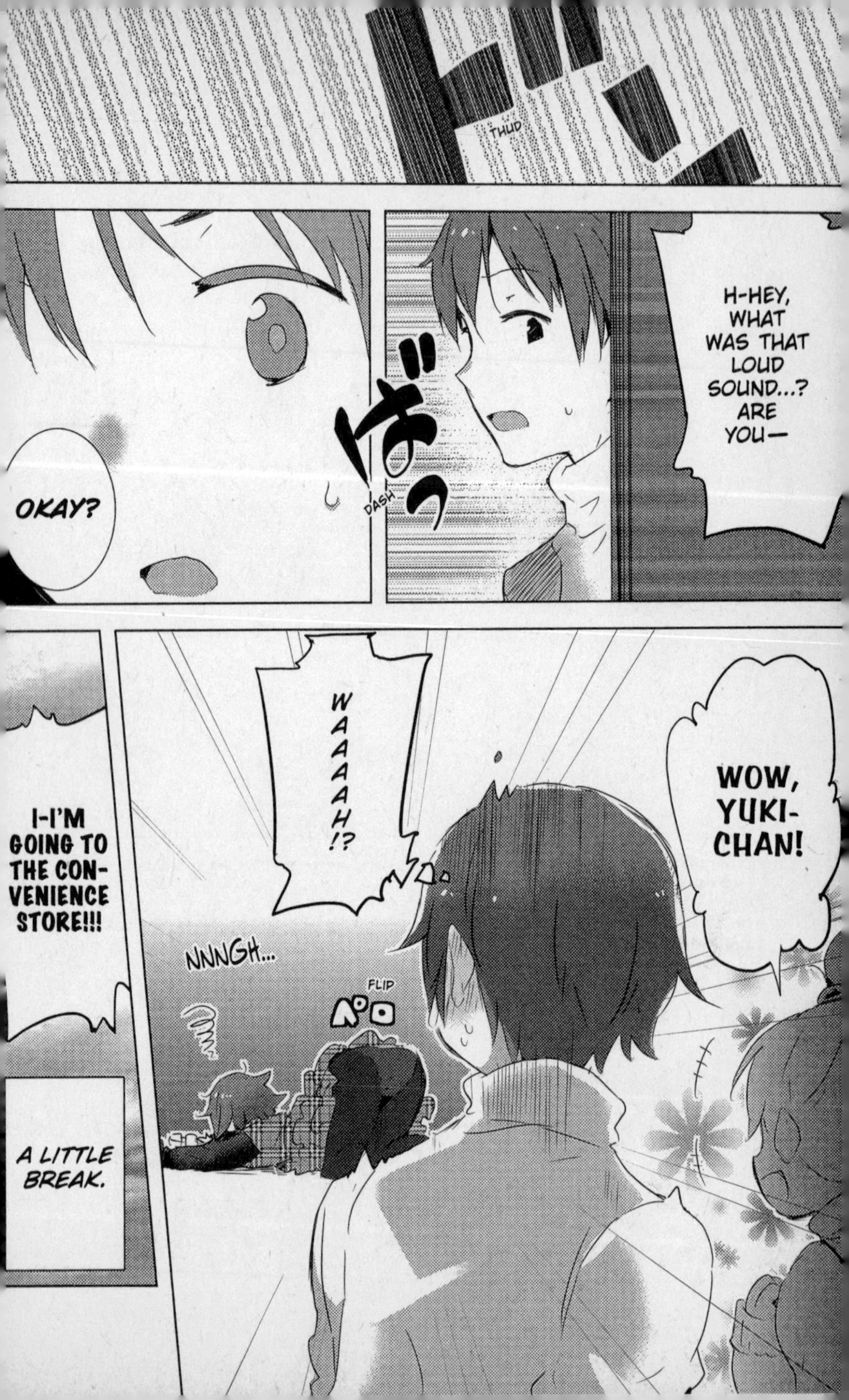
THUD
H-HEY, WHAT WAS THAT LOUD SOUND...? ARE YOU—
DASH
OKAY?
WOW, YUKI-CHAN!
WAAAAAH!?
FLIP
NNNGH...
I-I'M GOING TO THE CON-VENIENCE STORE!!!
A LITTLE BREAK.

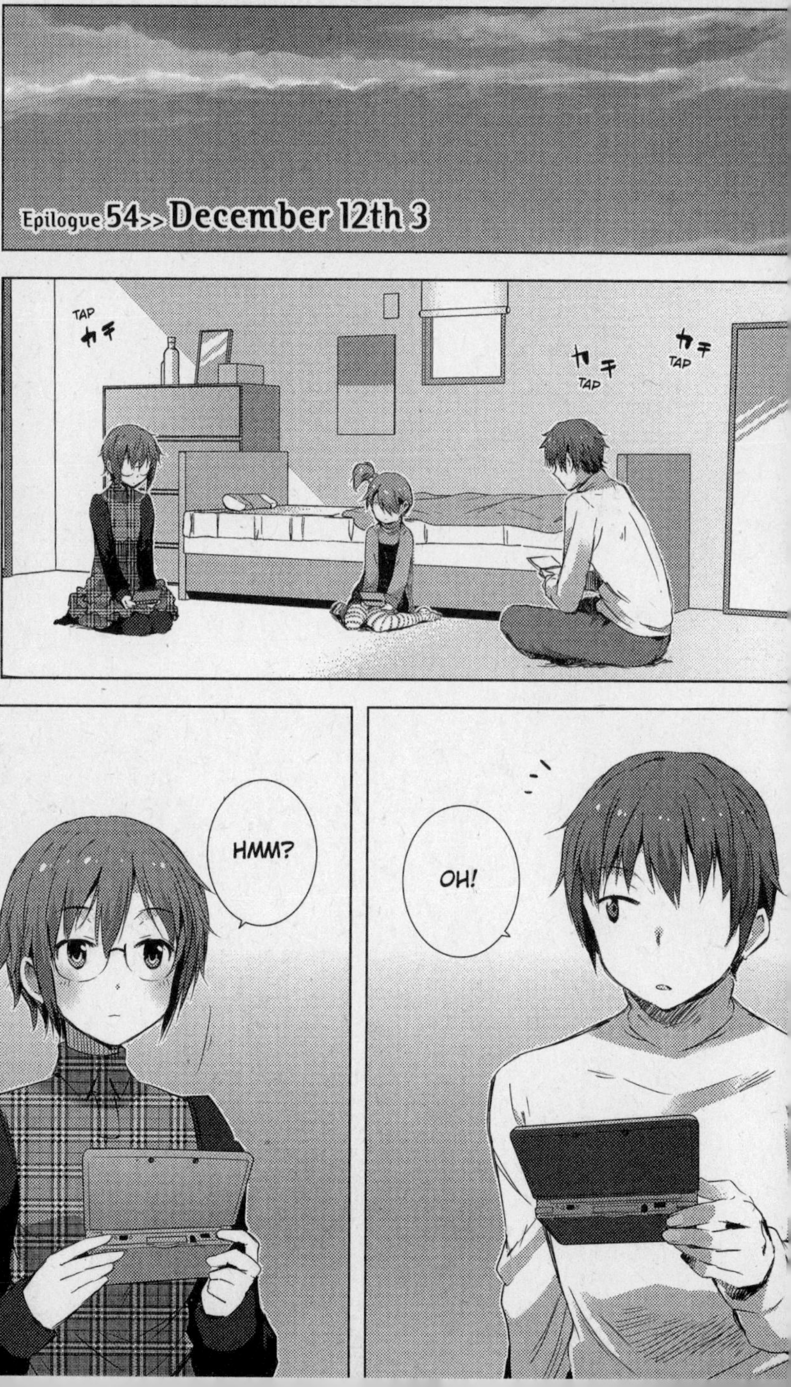
Epilogue 54>> December 12th 3
カチ
TAP
カチ
TAP
TAP
カチ
OH!
HMM?

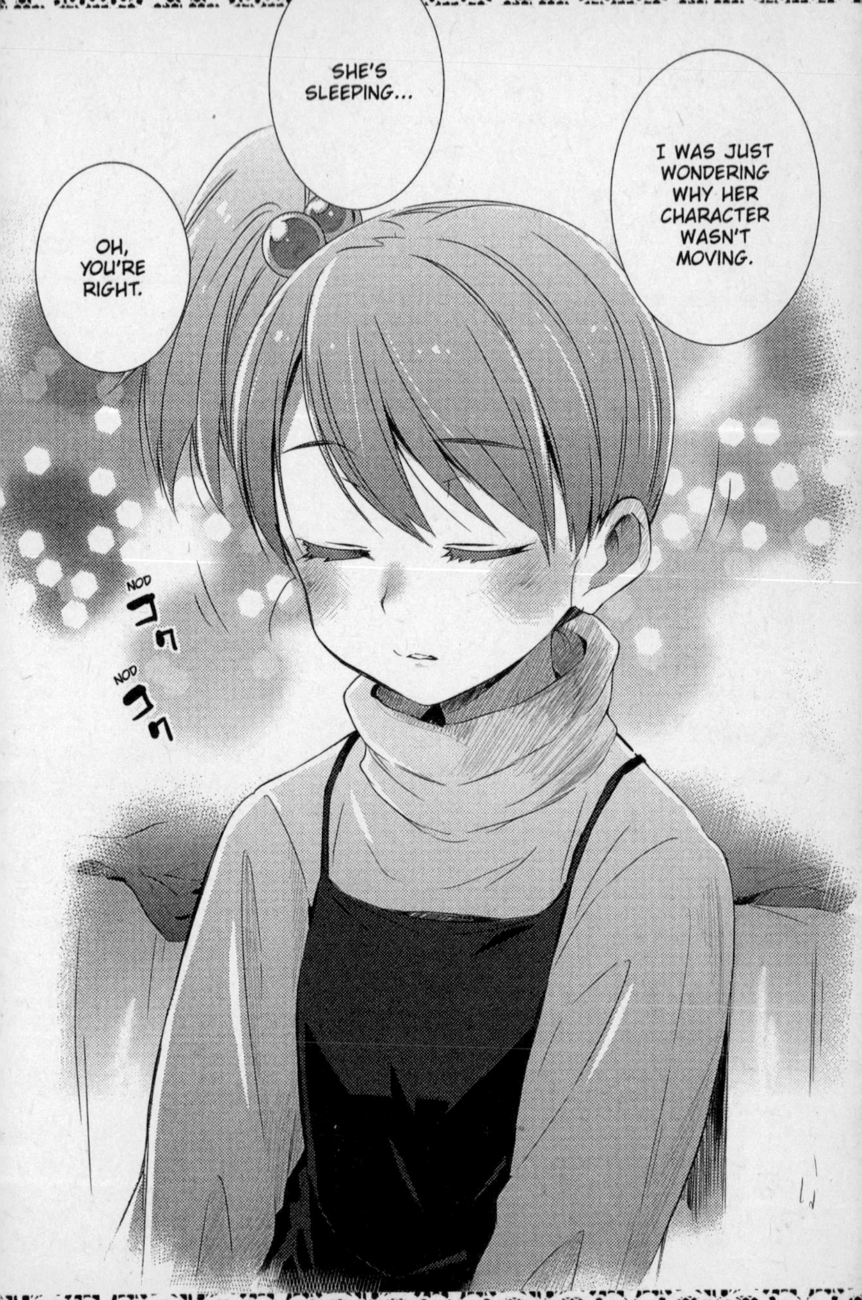
I WAS JUST WONDERING WHY HER CHARACTER WASN'T MOVING.
SHE'S SLEEPING...
OH, YOU'RE RIGHT.
NOD コク
NOD コク

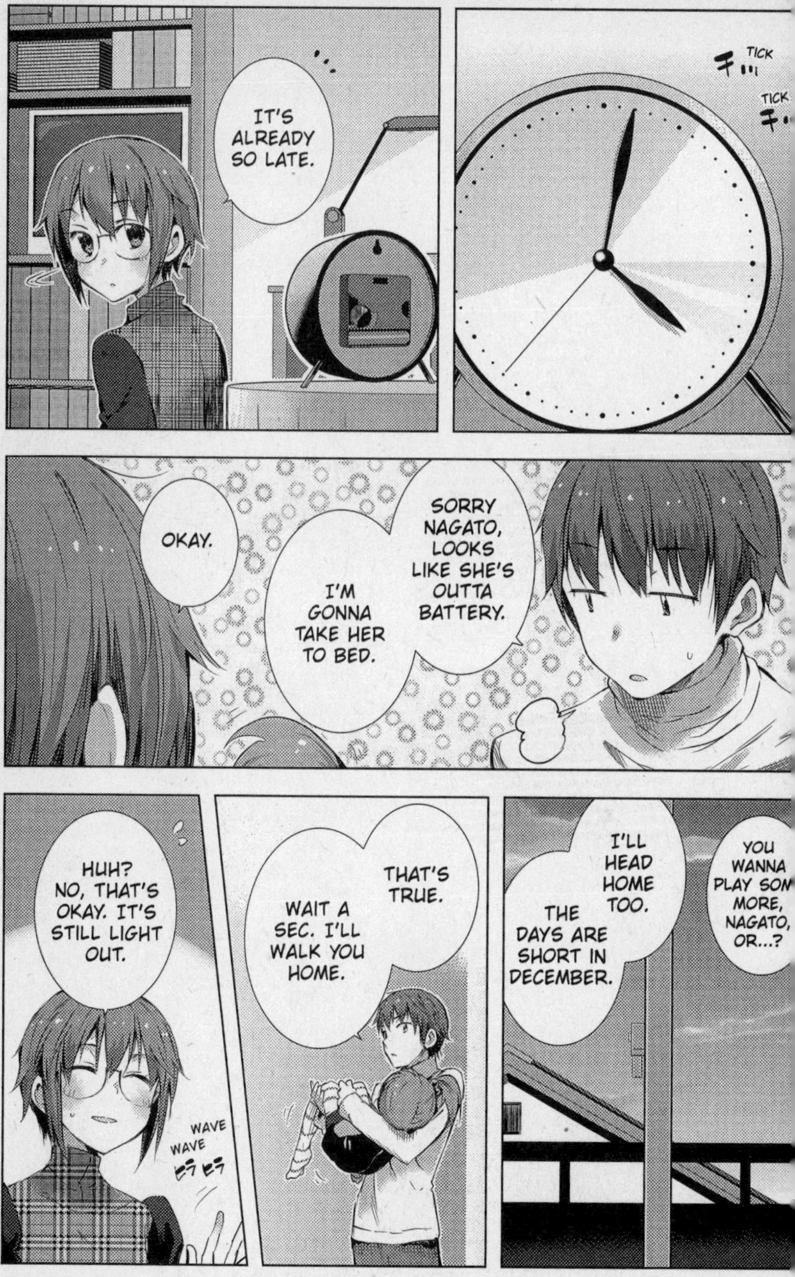
TICK
チッ
TICK
チッ
...
IT'S ALREADY SO LATE.
SORRY NAGATO, LOOKS LIKE SHE'S OUTTA BATTERY.
I'M GONNA TAKE HER TO BED.
OKAY.
YOU WANNA PLAY SOM MORE, NAGATO, OR...?
I'LL HEAD HOME TOO.
THE DAYS ARE SHORT IN DECEMBER.
THAT'S TRUE.
WAIT A SEC. I'LL WALK YOU HOME.
HUH? NO, THAT'S OKAY. IT'S STILL LIGHT OUT.
WAVE WAVE
ヒラヒラ

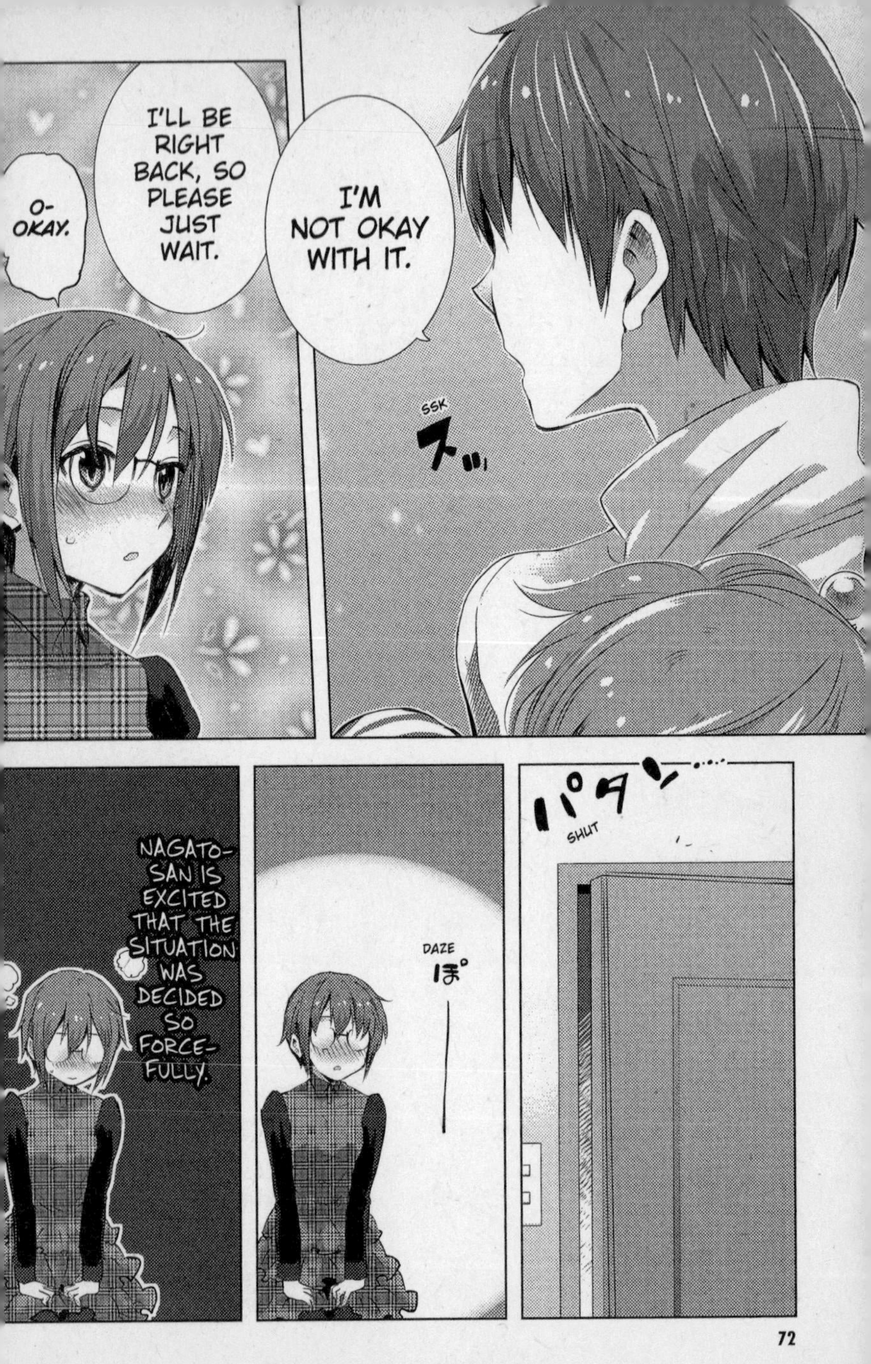
I'M NOT OKAY WITH IT.
SSK
スッ
I'LL BE RIGHT BACK, SO PLEASE JUST WAIT.
O-OKAY.
パタン
SHUT
DAZE
ぽ
NAGATO-SAN IS EXCITED THAT THE SITUATION WAS DECIDED SO FORCE-FULLY.

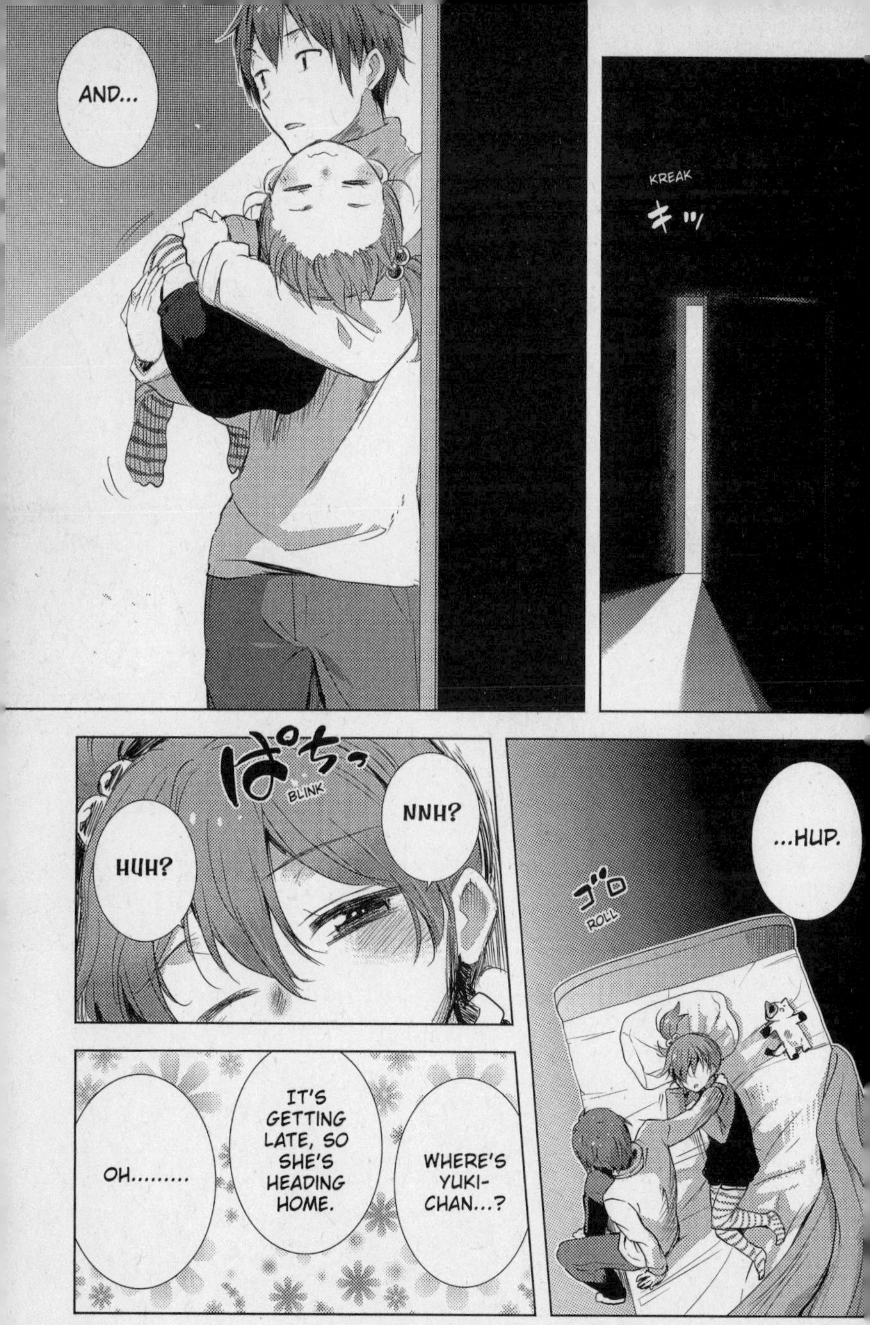
KREAK
キッ
AND...
...HUP.
ゴロ
ROLL
ぱちっ
BLINK
NNH?
HUH?
WHERE'S YUKI-CHAN...?
IT'S GETTING LATE, SO SHE'S HEADING HOME.
OH.........

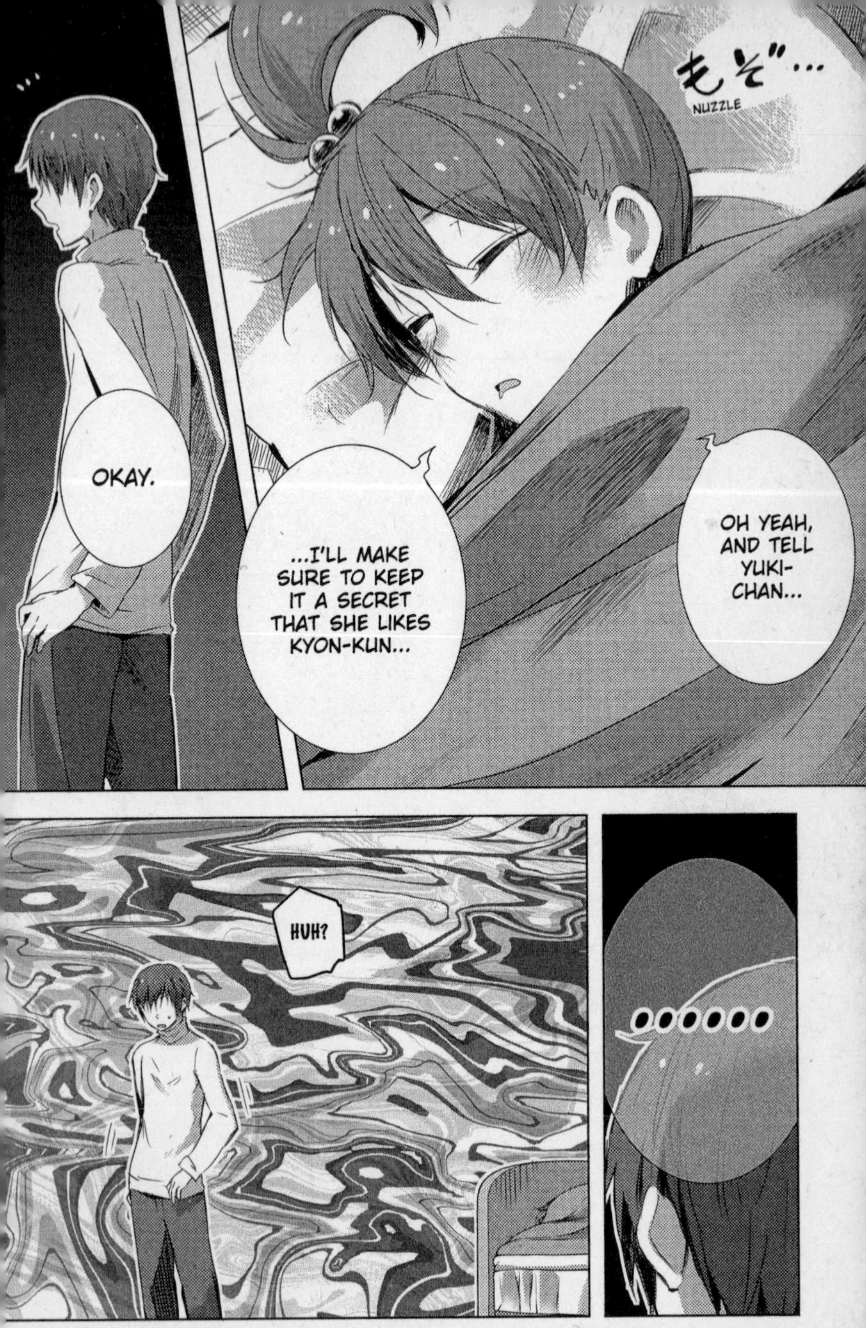
もぞ…
NUZZLE
OH YEAH, AND TELL YUKI-CHAN...
...I'LL MAKE SURE TO KEEP IT A SECRET THAT SHE LIKES KYON-KUN...
...
OKAY.
......
HUH?

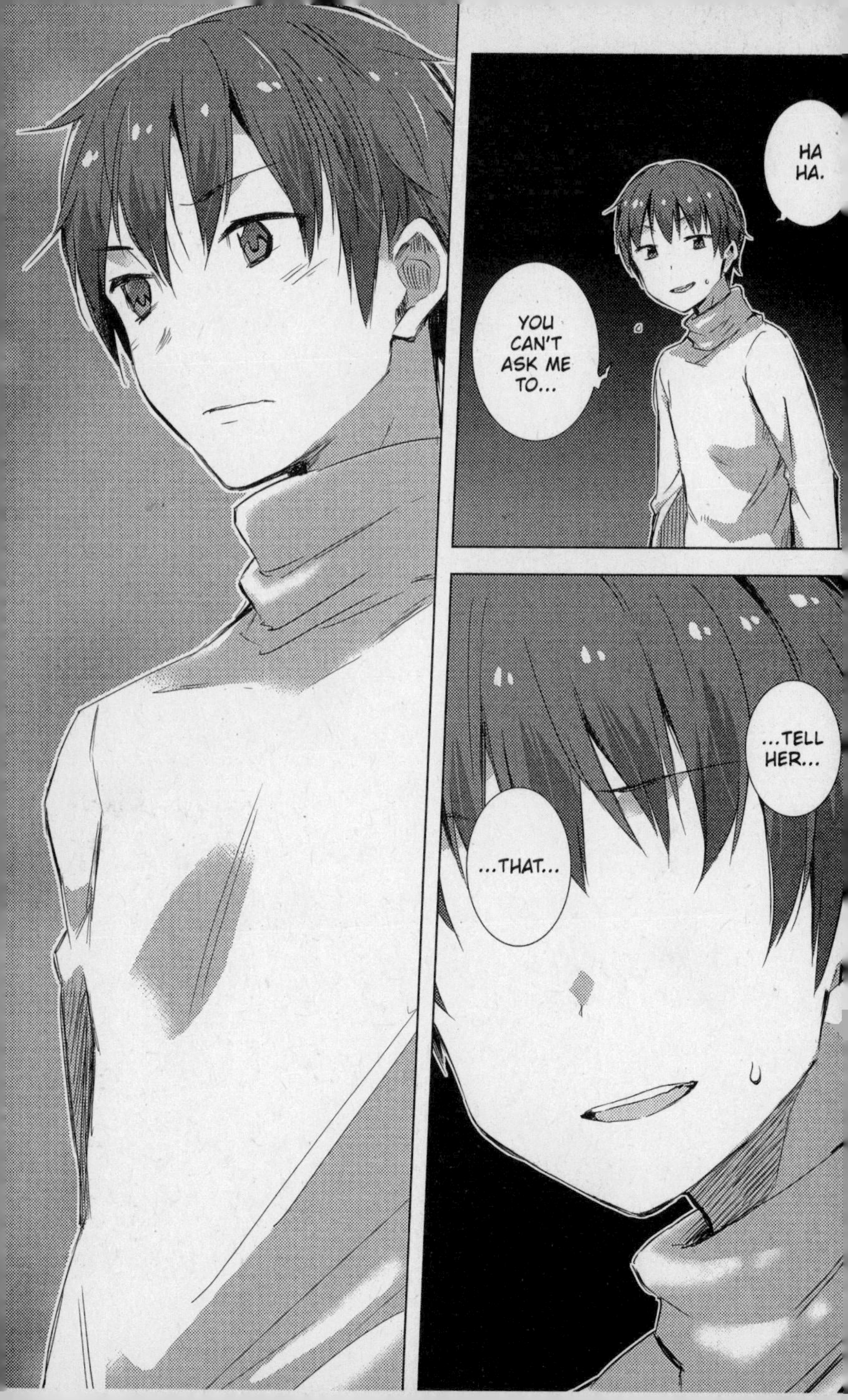
HA HA.
YOU CAN'T ASK ME TO...
...TELL HER...
...THAT...

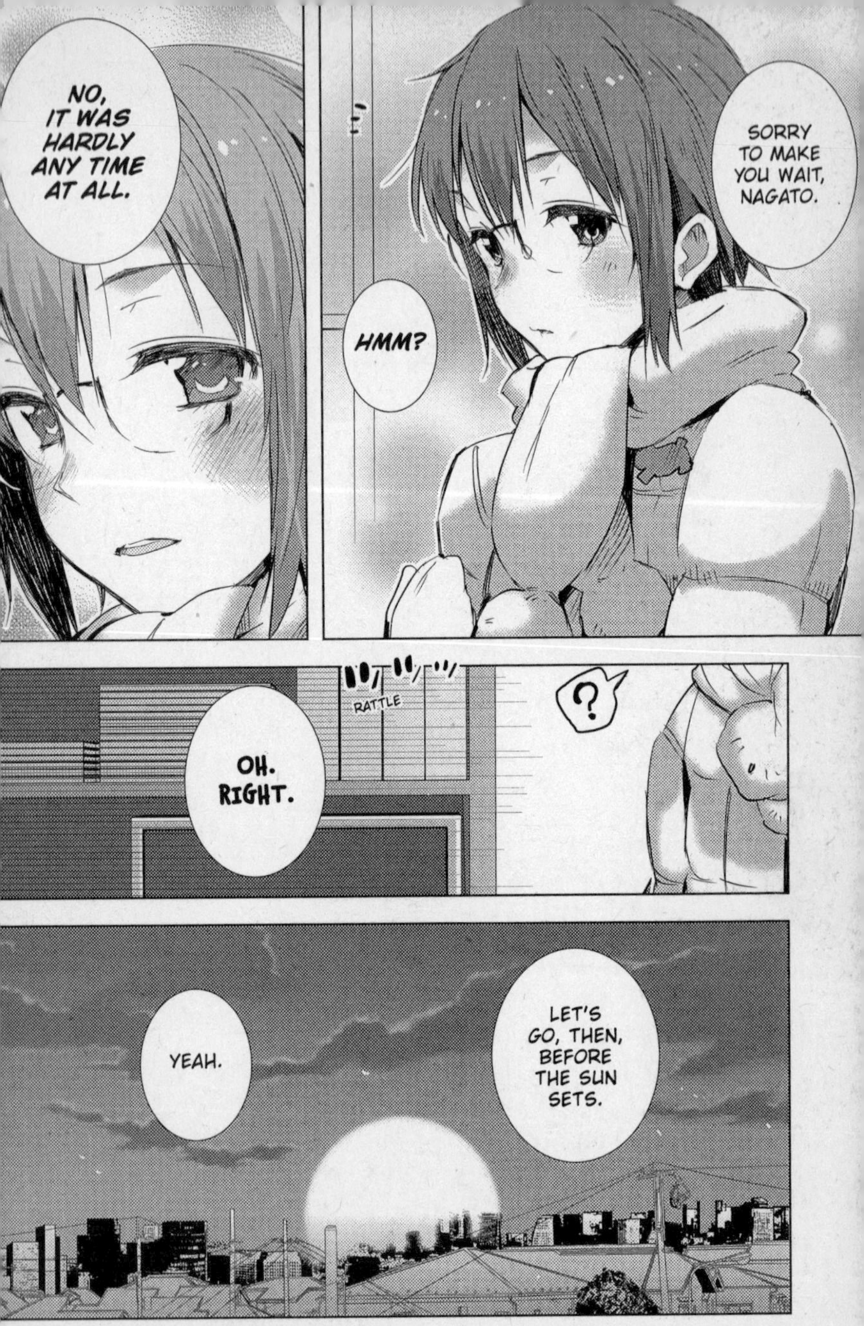
SORRY TO MAKE YOU WAIT, NAGATO.
HMM?
NO, IT WAS HARDLY ANY TIME AT ALL.
?
RATTLE
OH. RIGHT.
LET'S GO, THEN, BEFORE THE SUN SETS.
YEAH.

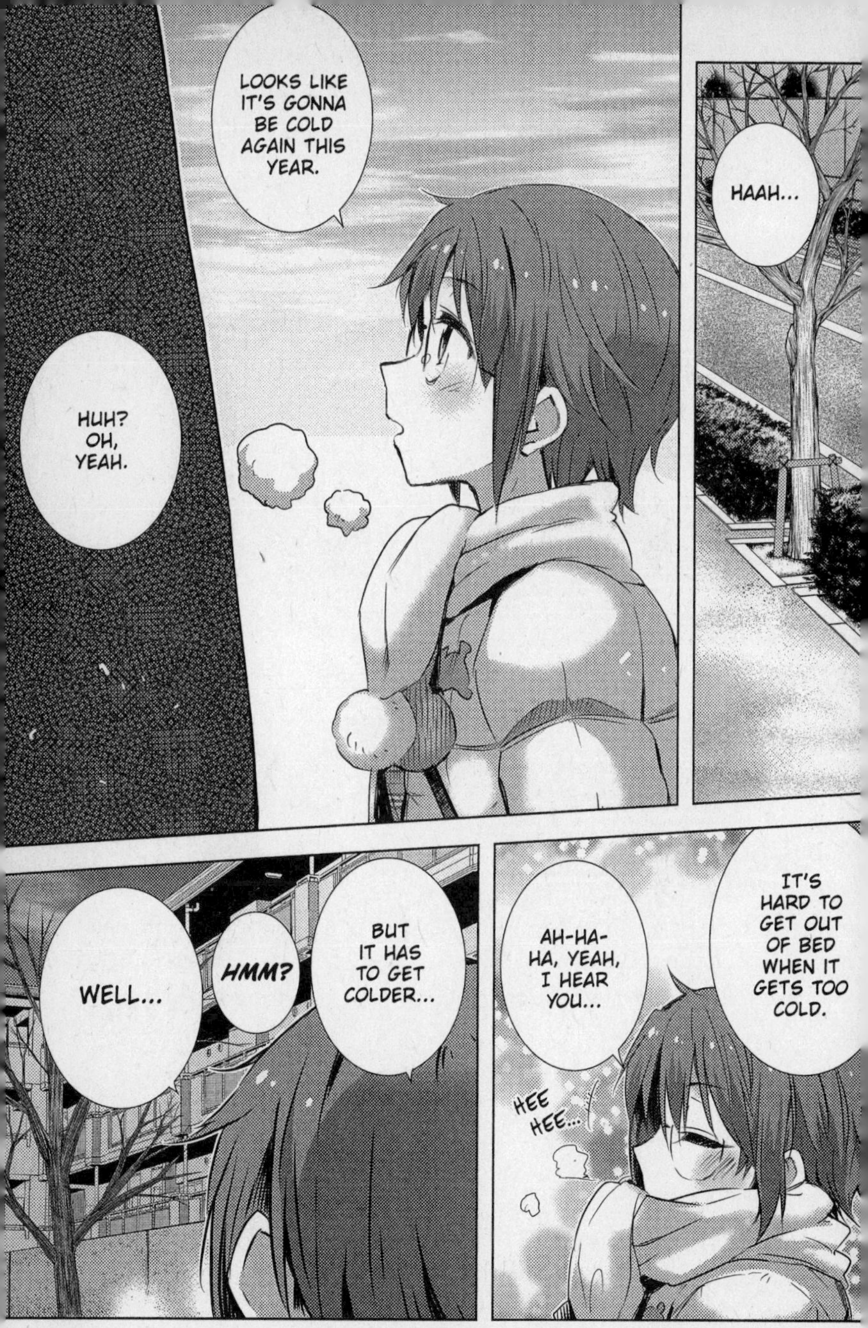
HAAH...
LOOKS LIKE IT'S GONNA BE COLD AGAIN THIS YEAR.
HUH? OH, YEAH.
IT'S HARD TO GET OUT OF BED WHEN IT GETS TOO COLD.
AH-HA-HA, YEAH, I HEAR YOU...
HEE HEE...
BUT IT HAS TO GET COLDER...
HMM?
WELL...

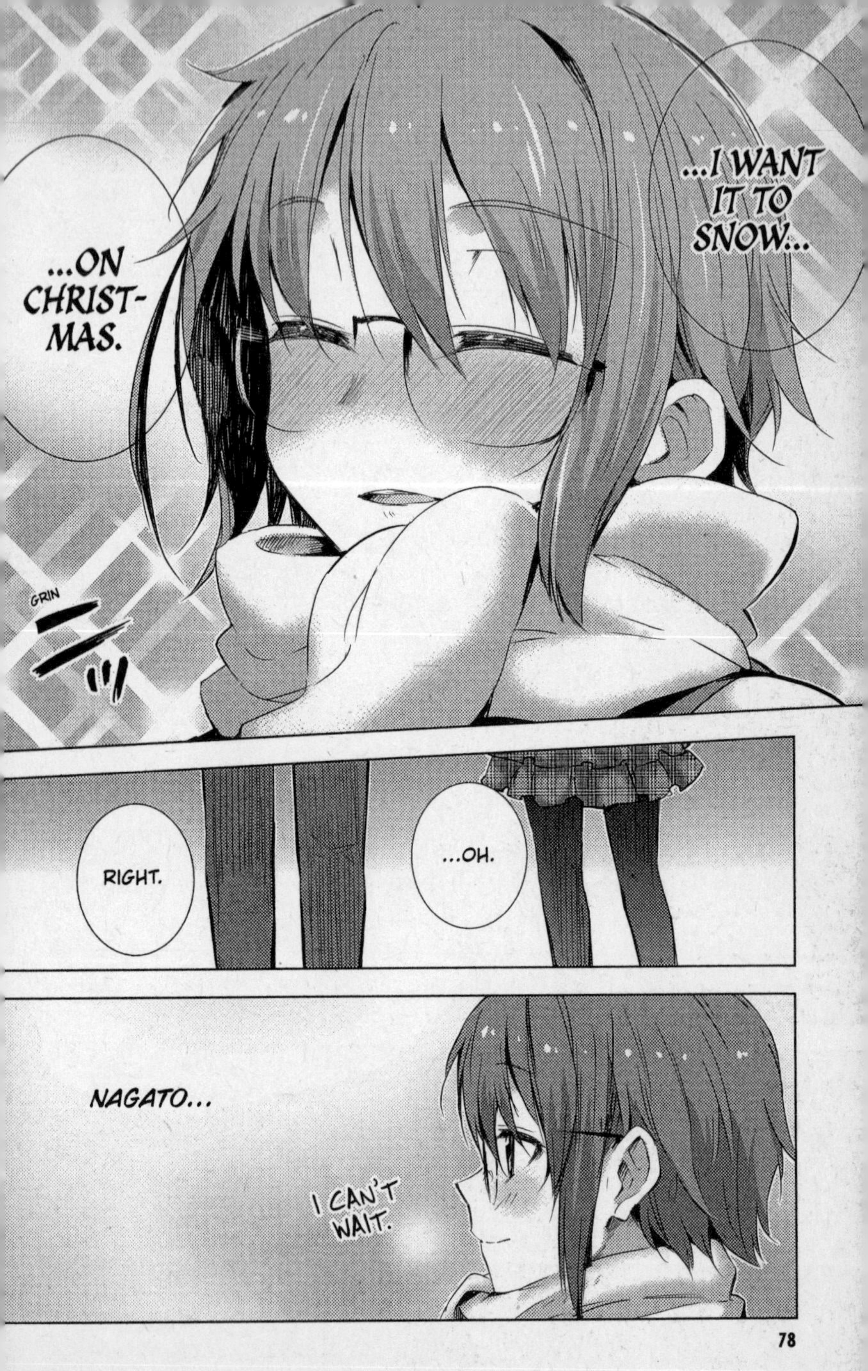
...I WANT IT TO SNOW...
...ON CHRISTMAS.
GRIN
...OH.
RIGHT.
NAGATO...
I CAN'T WAIT.

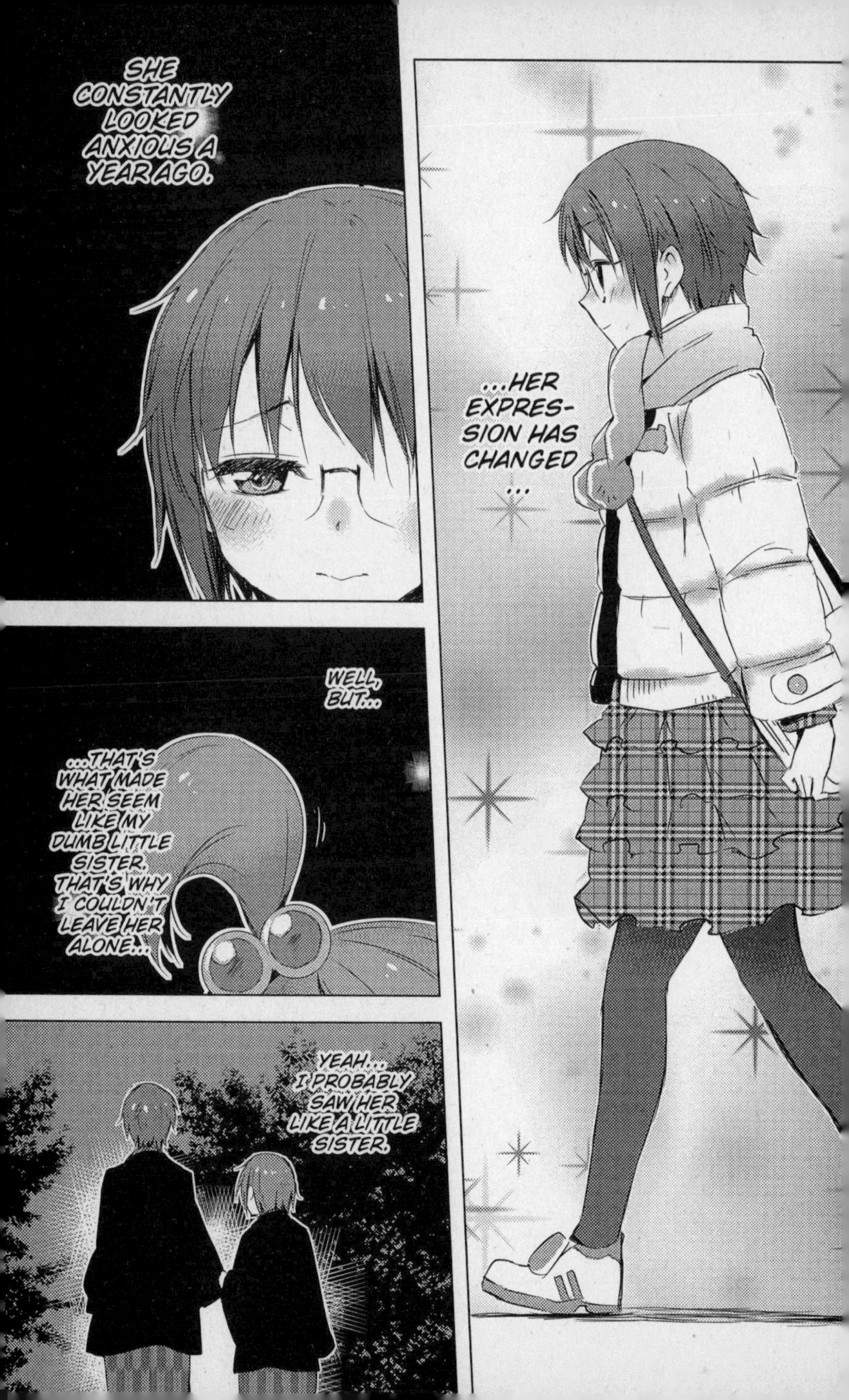
...HER EXPRES-SION HAS CHANGED ...
SHE CONSTANTLY LOOKED ANXIOUS A YEAR AGO.
WELL, BUT...
...THAT'S WHAT MADE HER SEEM LIKE MY DUMB LITTLE SISTER. THAT'S WHY I COULDN'T LEAVE HER ALONE...
YEAH... I PROBABLY SAW HER LIKE A LITTLE SISTER.

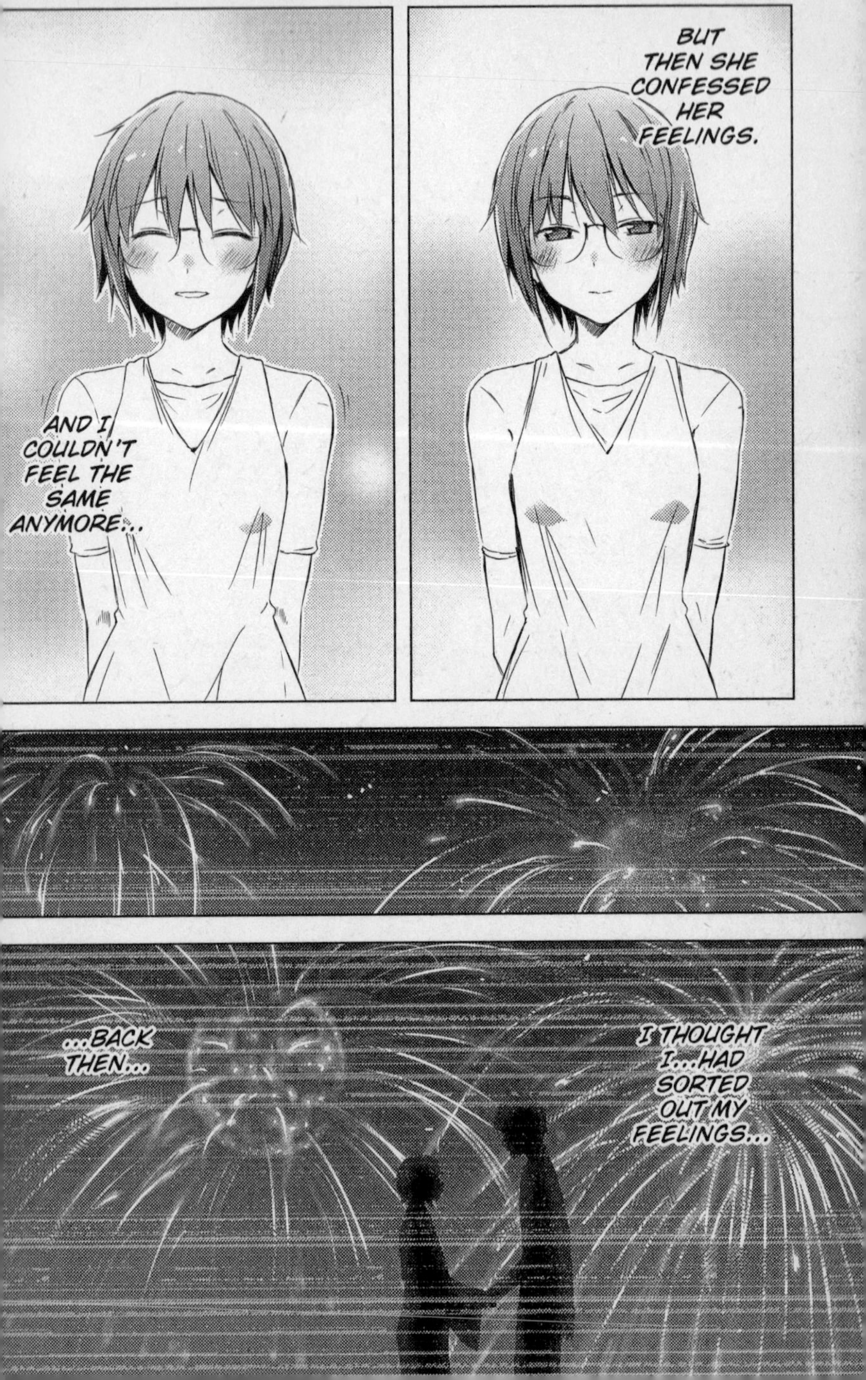
BUT THEN SHE CONFESSED HER FEELINGS.
AND I COULDN'T FEEL THE SAME ANYMORE...
I THOUGHT I...HAD SORTED OUT MY FEELINGS...
...BACK THEN...

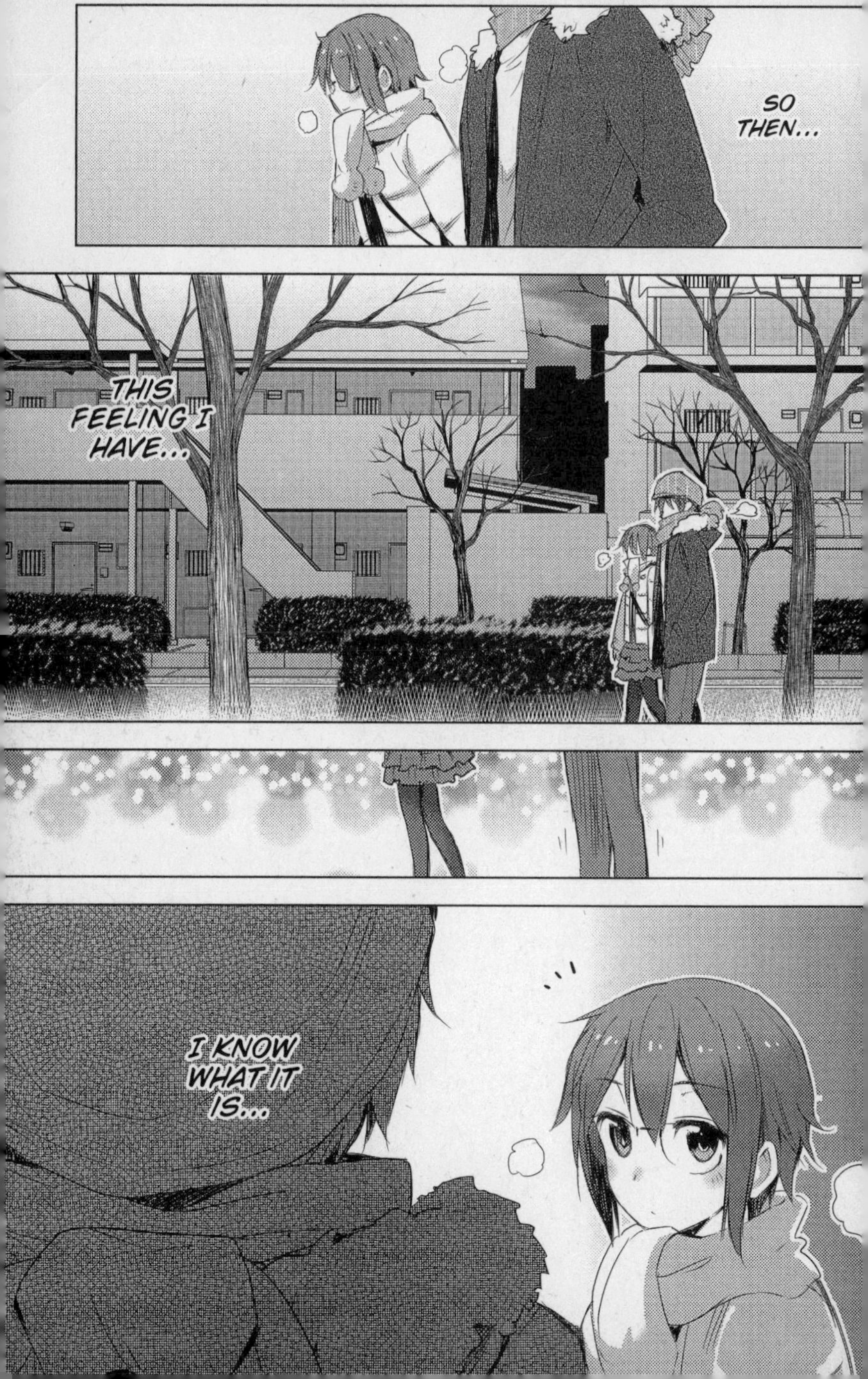
SO THEN...
THIS FEELING I HAVE...
I KNOW WHAT IT IS...

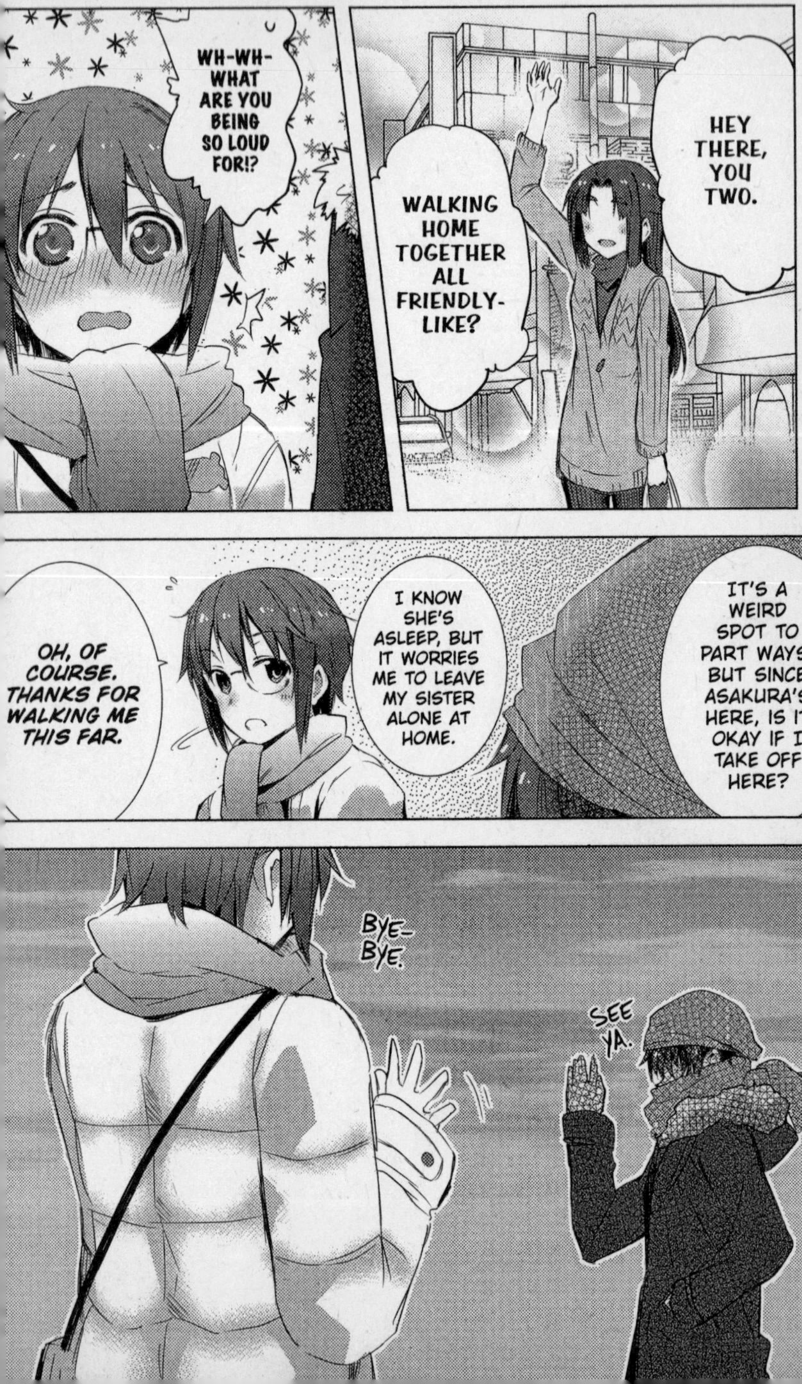
HEY THERE, YOU TWO.
WALKING HOME TOGETHER ALL FRIENDLY-LIKE?
WH-WH-WHAT ARE YOU BEING SO LOUD FOR!?
IT'S A WEIRD SPOT TO PART WAYS, BUT SINCE ASAKURA'S HERE, IS IT OKAY IF I TAKE OFF HERE?
I KNOW SHE'S ASLEEP, BUT IT WORRIES ME TO LEAVE MY SISTER ALONE AT HOME.
OH, OF COURSE. THANKS FOR WALKING ME THIS FAR.
SEE YA.
BYE-BYE.

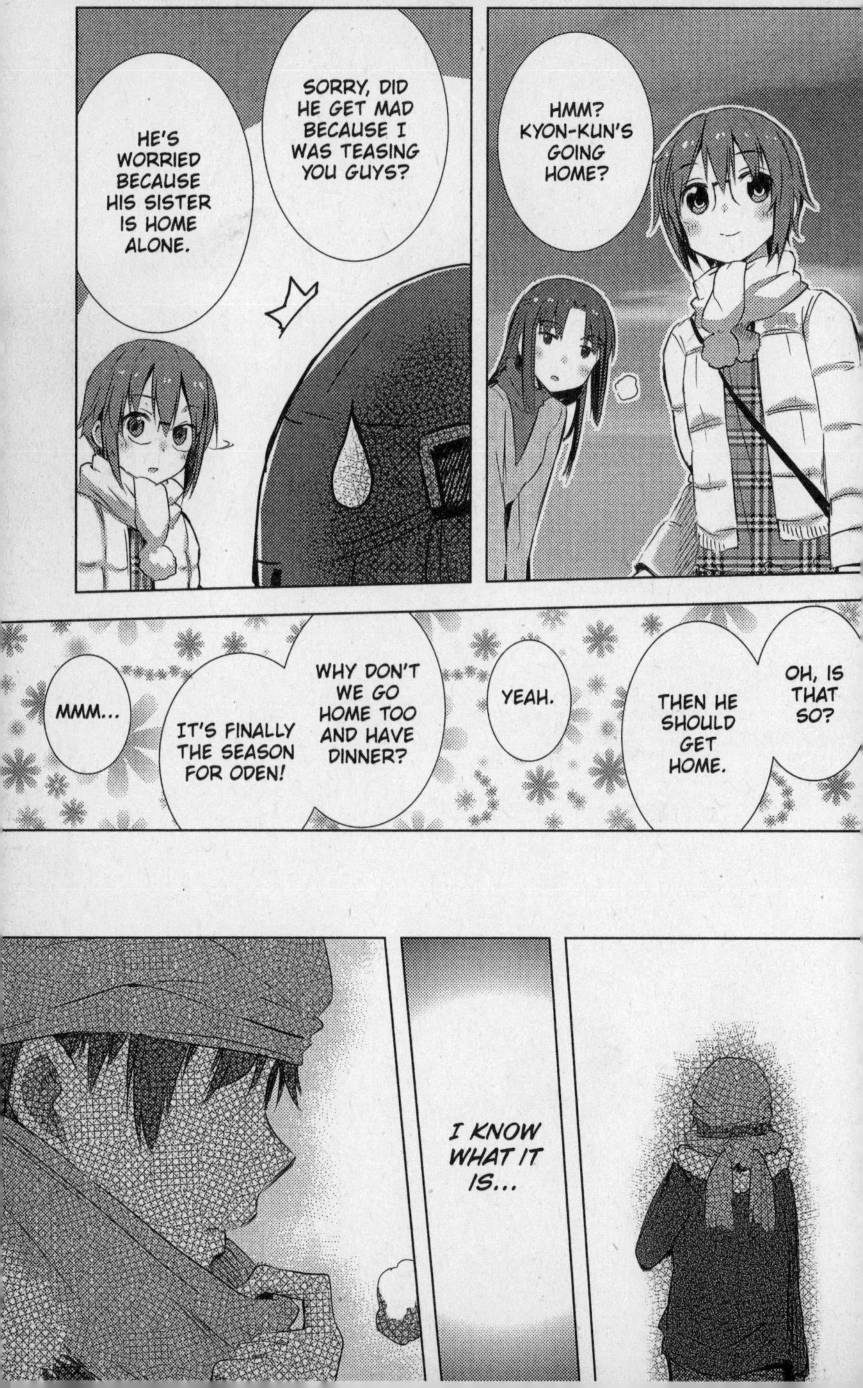
HMM? KYON-KUN'S GOING HOME?
SORRY, DID HE GET MAD BECAUSE I WAS TEASING YOU GUYS?
HE'S WORRIED BECAUSE HIS SISTER IS HOME ALONE.
OH, IS THAT SO?
THEN HE SHOULD GET HOME.
YEAH.
WHY DON'T WE GO HOME TOO AND HAVE DINNER?
IT'S FINALLY THE SEASON FOR ODEN!
MMM...
I KNOW WHAT IT IS...

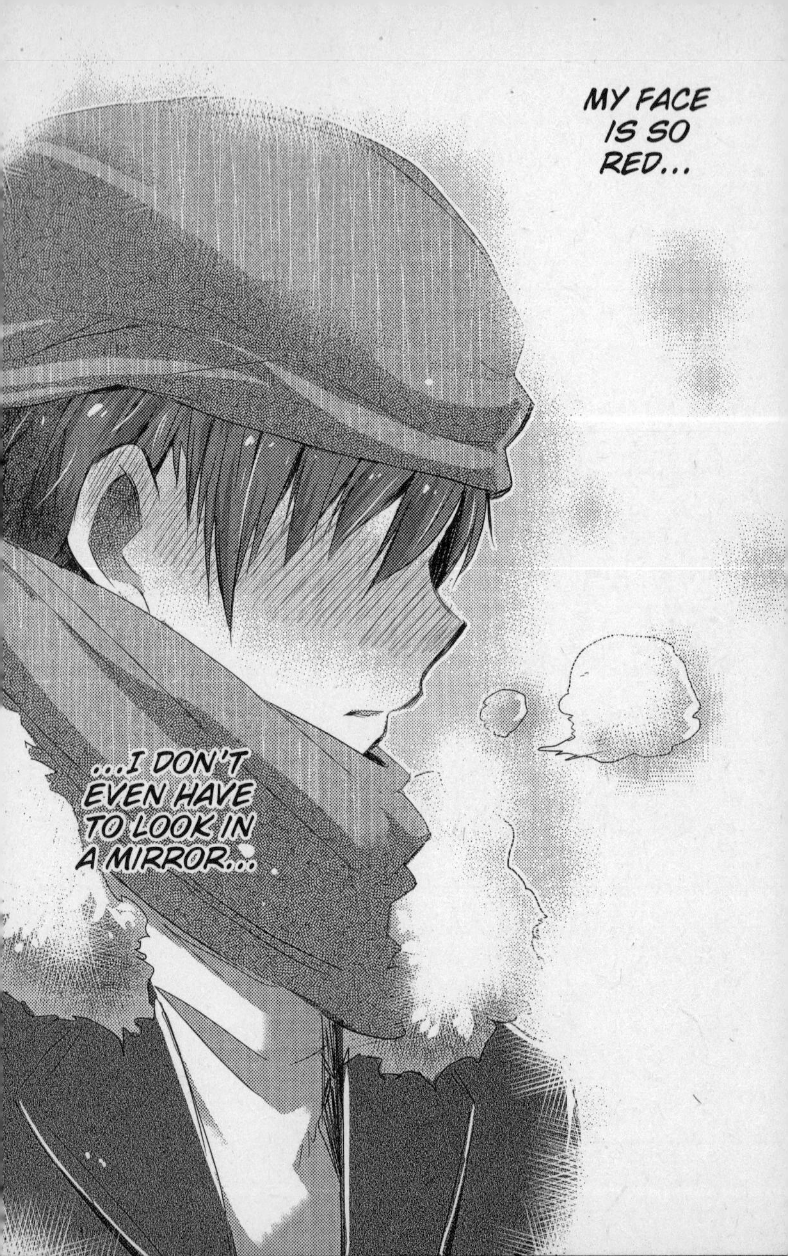
MY FACE IS SO RED...
...I DON'T EVEN HAVE TO LOOK IN A MIRROR...

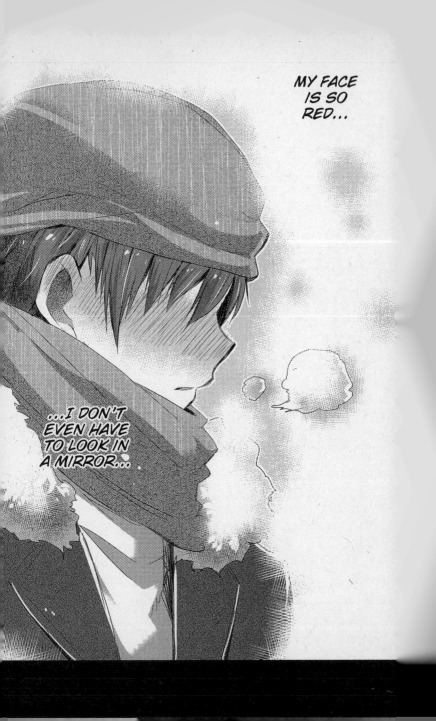

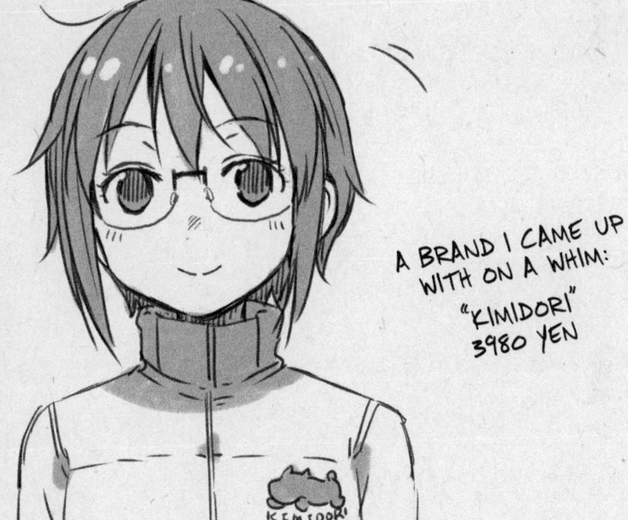
A BRAND I CAME UP WITH ON A WHIM:
"KIMIDORI"
3980 YEN
KIMIDORI

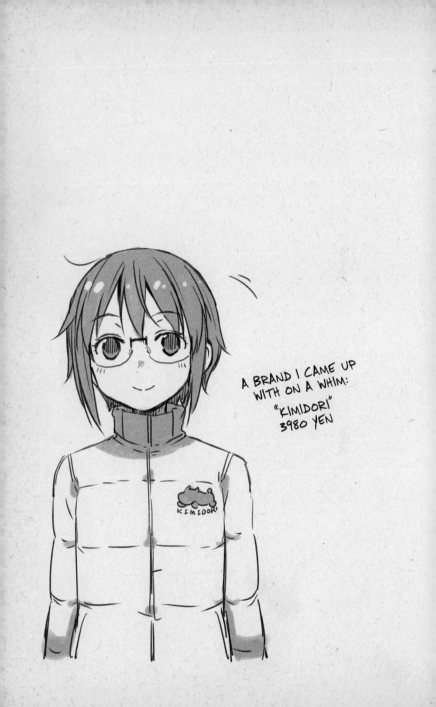

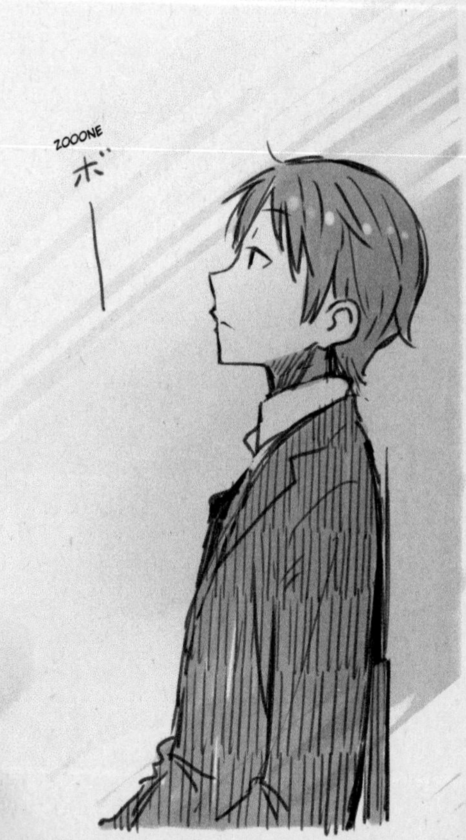
ZOOONE
ボー

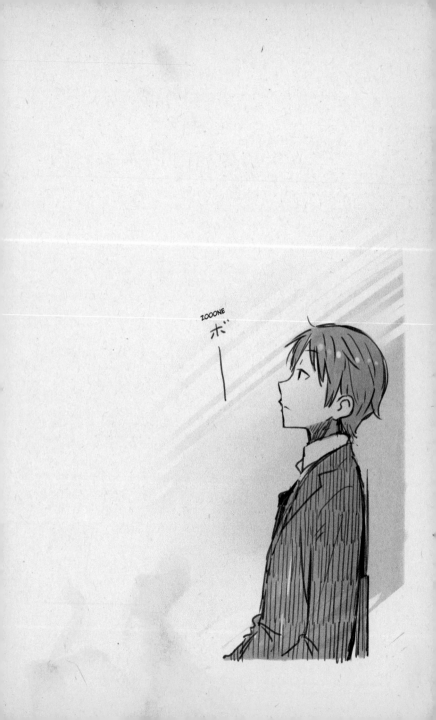

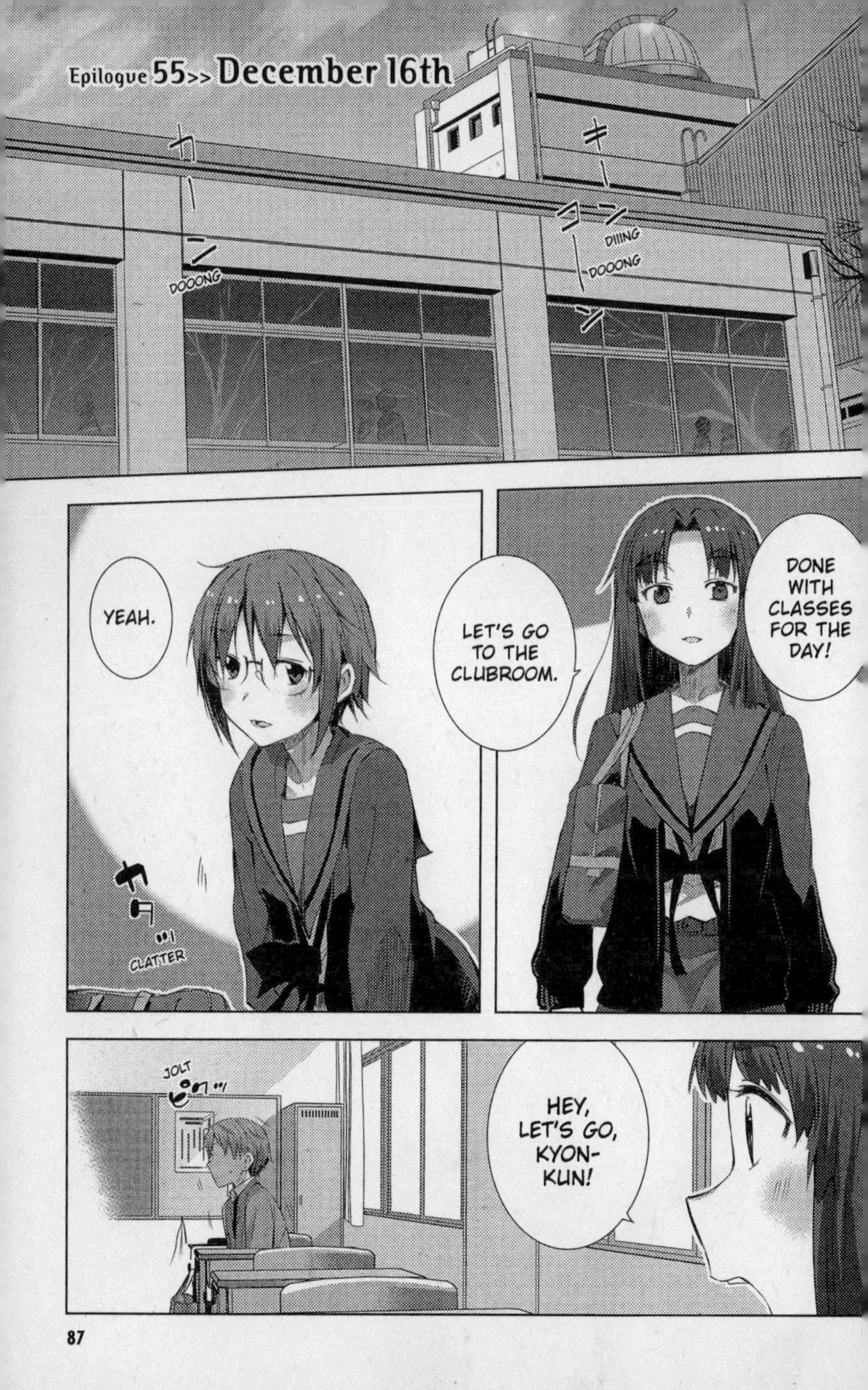
Epilogue 55>> December 16th
DIIING
DOOONG
DOOONG
DONE WITH CLASSES FOR THE DAY!
LET'S GO TO THE CLUBROOM.
YEAH.
CLATTER
HEY, LET'S GO, KYON-KUN!
JOLT

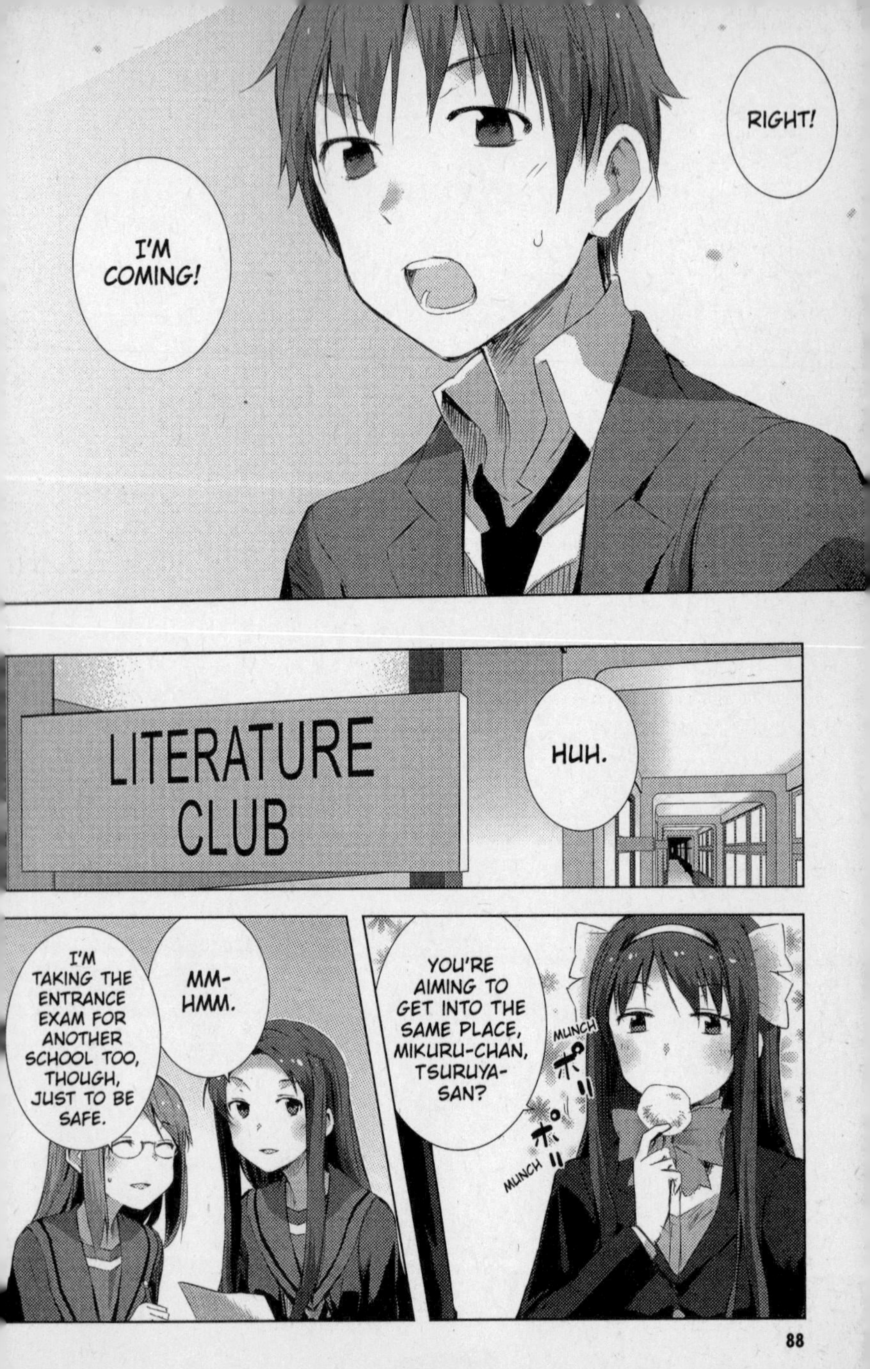
RIGHT!
I'M COMING!
HUH.
LITERATURE CLUB
YOU'RE AIMING TO GET INTO THE SAME PLACE, MIKURU-CHAN, TSURUYA-SAN?
MUNCH
MUNCH
MM-HMM.
I'M TAKING THE ENTRANCE EXAM FOR ANOTHER SCHOOL TOO, THOUGH, JUST TO BE SAFE.

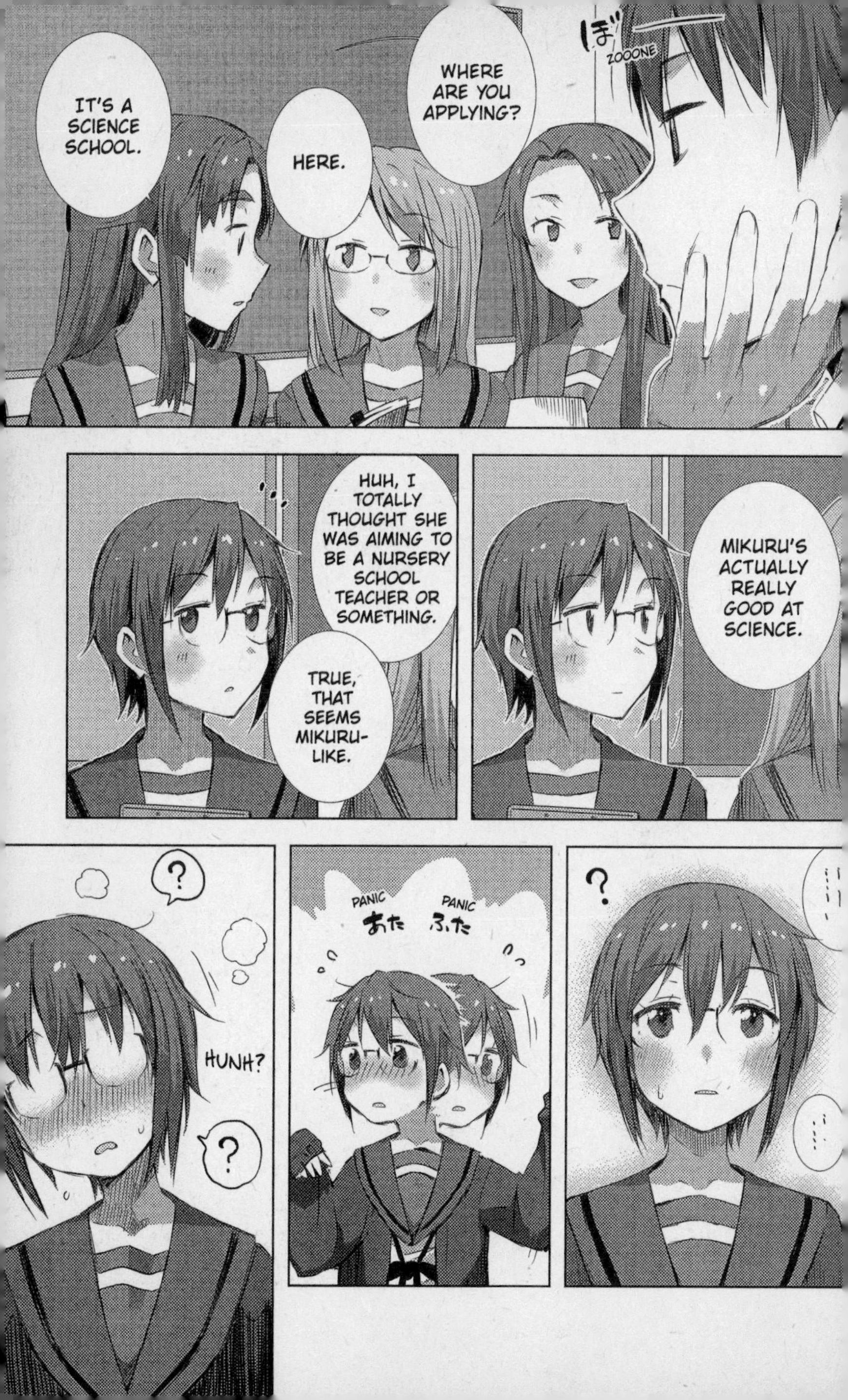
ぼ
ZOOONE
WHERE ARE YOU APPLYING?
HERE.
IT'S A SCIENCE SCHOOL.
MIKURU'S ACTUALLY REALLY GOOD AT SCIENCE.
HUH, I TOTALLY THOUGHT SHE WAS AIMING TO BE A NURSERY SCHOOL TEACHER OR SOMETHING.
TRUE, THAT SEEMS MIKURU-LIKE.
?
PANIC
あた
PANIC
ふた
?
HUNH?
?

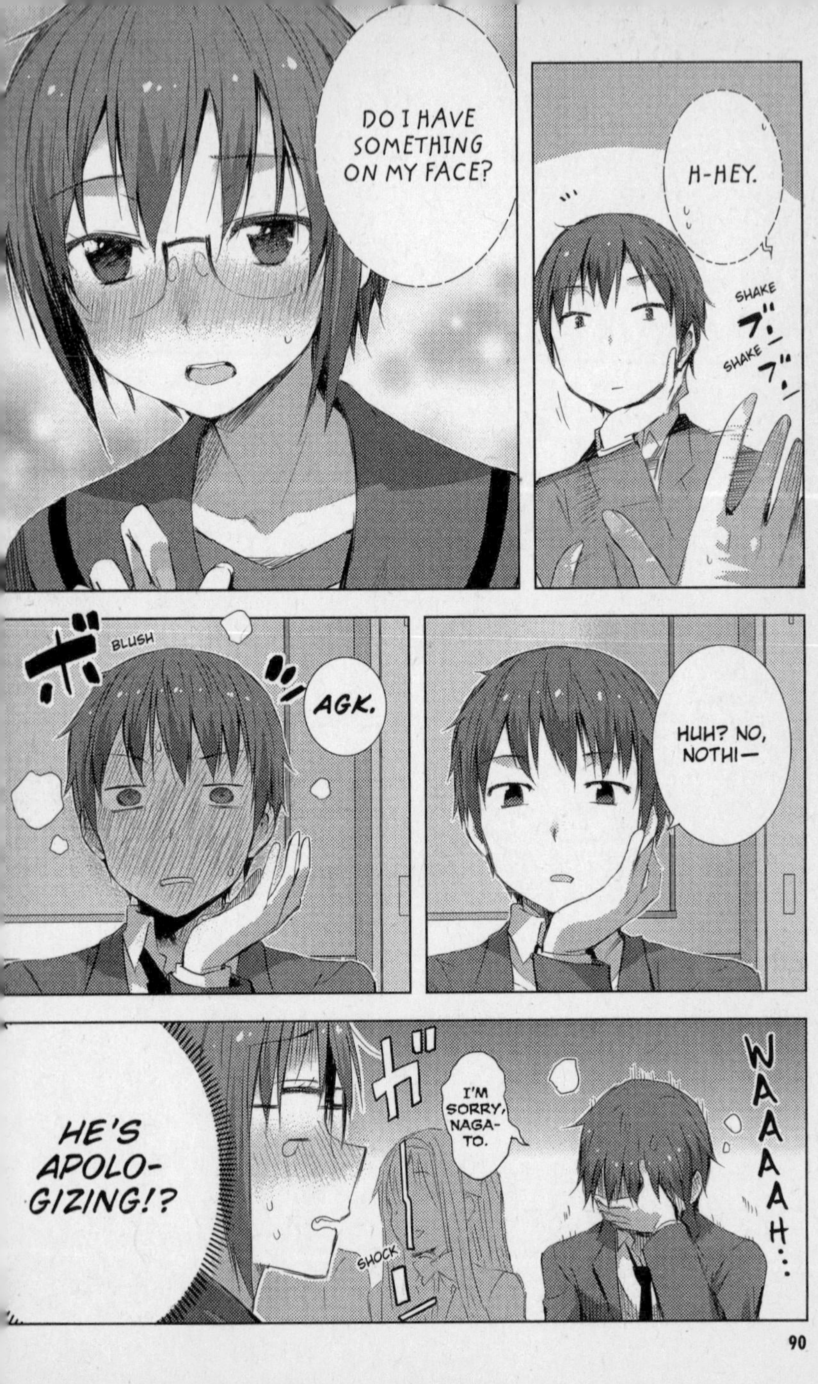
H-HEY.
SHAKE
SHAKE
DO I HAVE SOMETHING ON MY FACE?
HUH? NO, NOTHI—
BLUSH
AGK.
WAAAAH...
I'M SORRY, NAGA-TO.
SHOCK
HE'S APOLO-GIZING!?

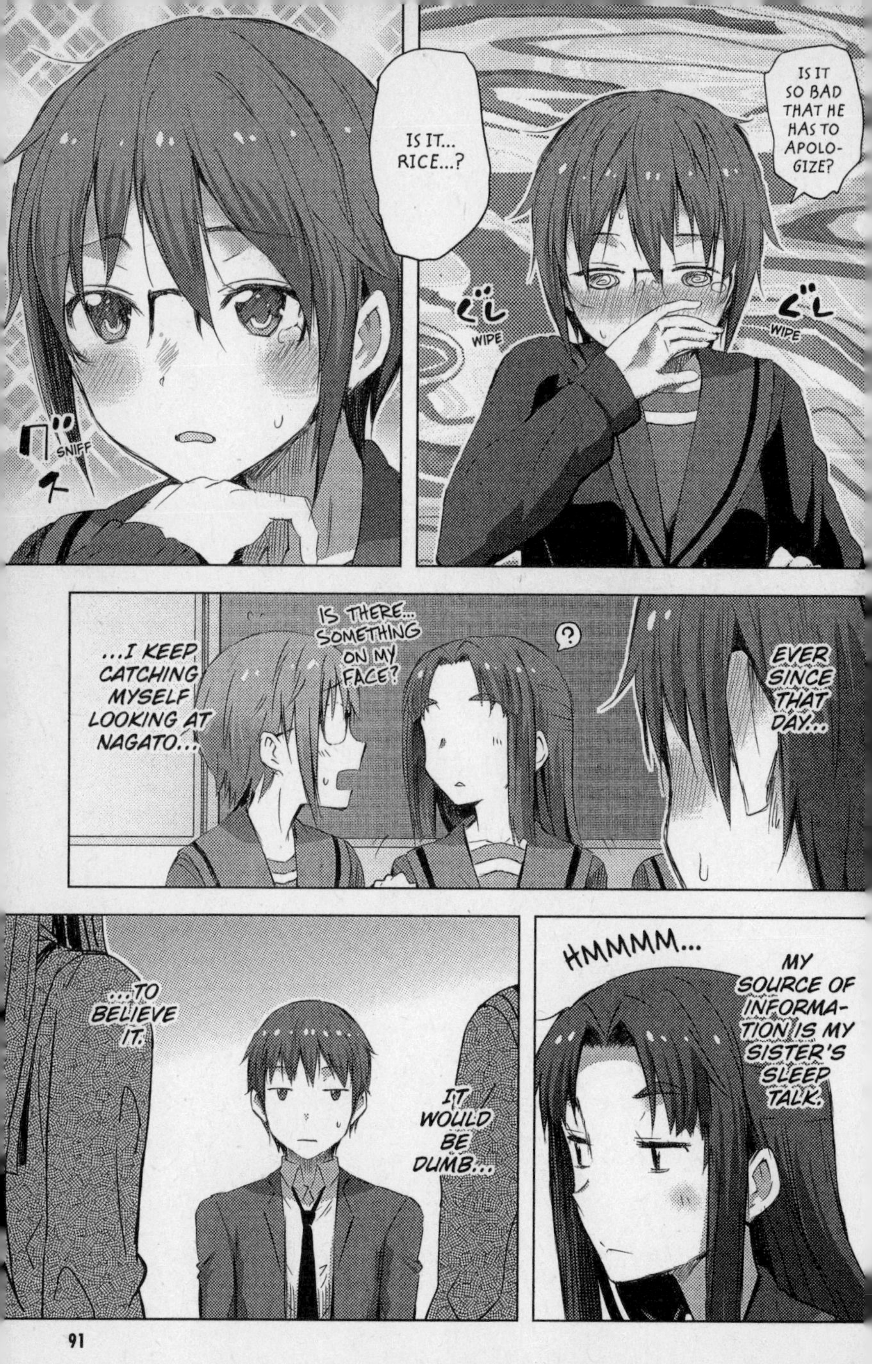
IS IT SO BAD THAT HE HAS TO APOLOGIZE?
WIPE
WIPE
IS IT... RICE...?
SNIFF
EVER SINCE THAT DAY...
?
IS THERE... SOMETHING ON MY FACE?
...I KEEP CATCHING MYSELF LOOKING AT NAGATO...
HMMMM...
MY SOURCE OF INFORMATION IS MY SISTER'S SLEEP TALK.
IT WOULD BE DUMB...
...TO BELIEVE IT.

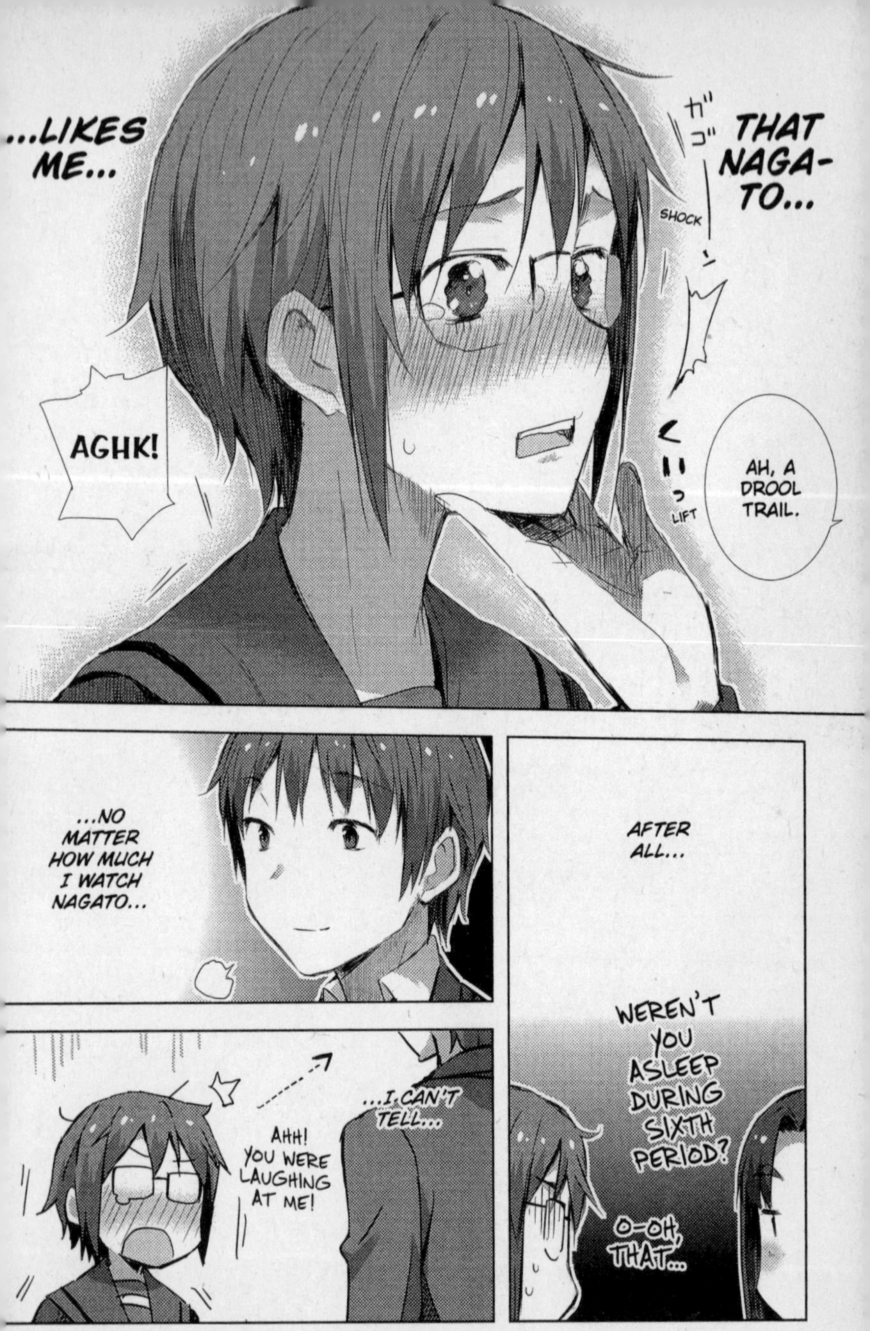

THAT NAGA-TO...
ガゴ
SHOCK
...LIKES ME...
AH, A DROOL TRAIL.
くいっ
LIFT
AGHK!
AFTER ALL...
WEREN'T YOU ASLEEP DURING SIXTH PERIOD?
O-OH, THAT...
...NO MATTER HOW MUCH I WATCH NAGATO...
...I CAN'T TELL...
AHH! YOU WERE LAUGHING AT ME!

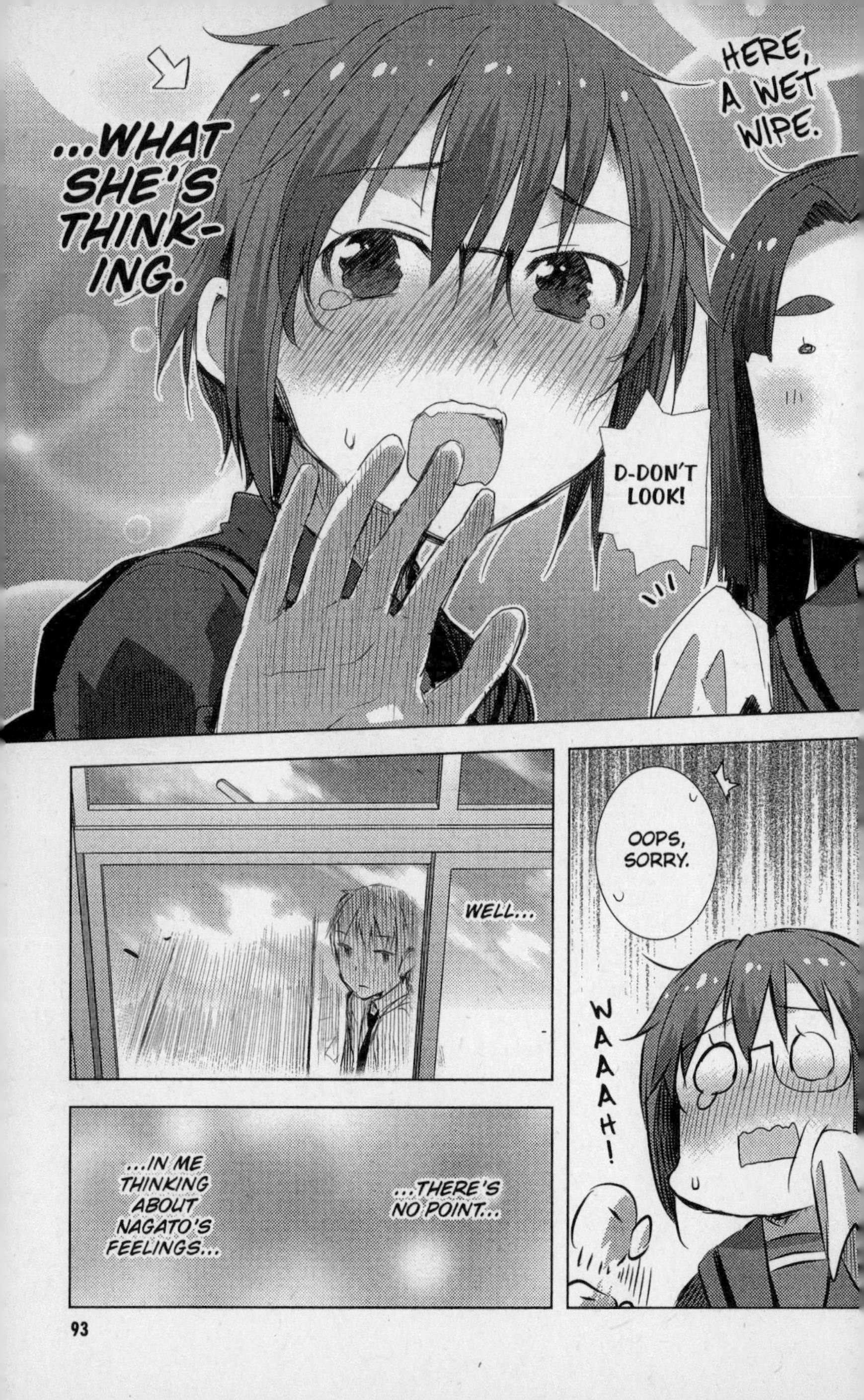
HERE, A WET WIPE.
...WHAT SHE'S THINK-ING.
D-DON'T LOOK!
OOPS, SORRY.
WAAAAH!
WELL...
...THERE'S NO POINT...
...IN ME THINKING ABOUT NAGATO'S FEELINGS...

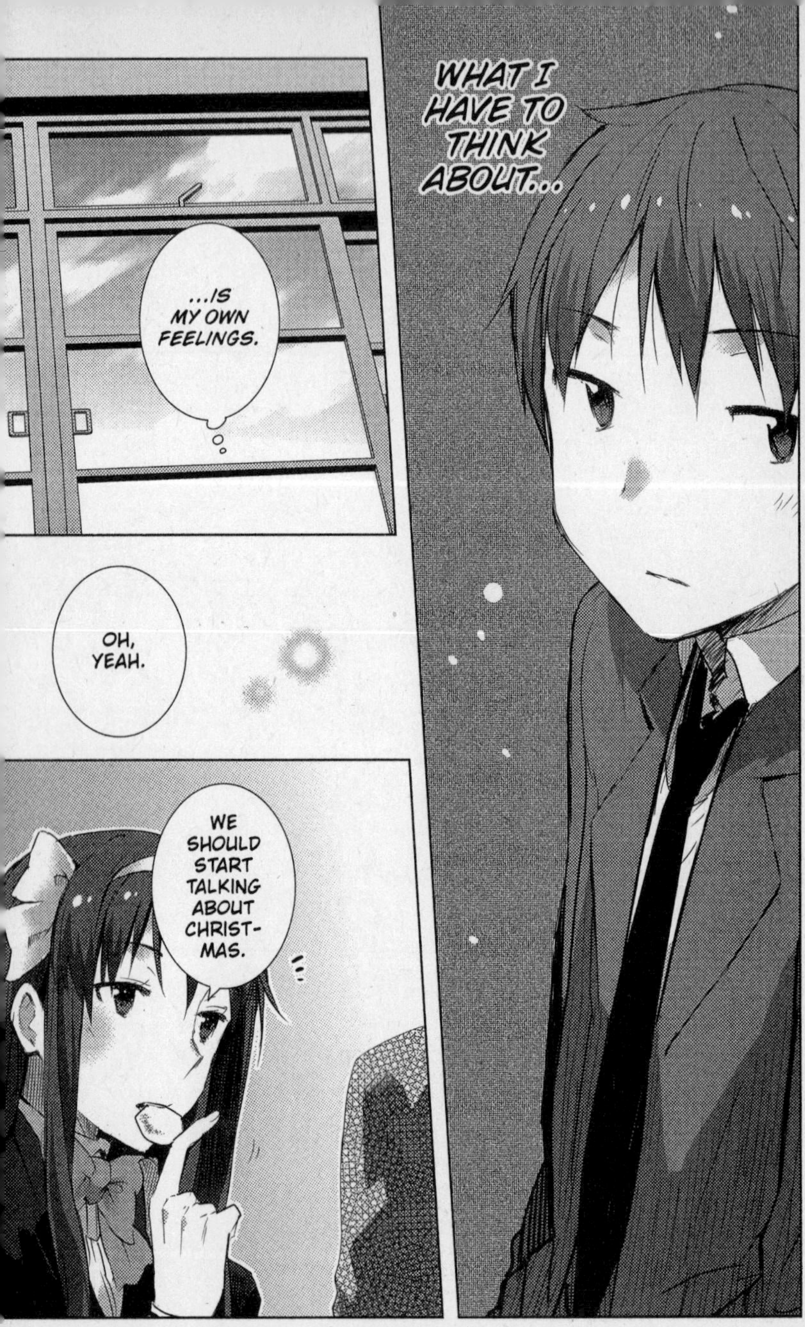
WHAT I HAVE TO THINK ABOUT...
...IS MY OWN FEELINGS.
OH, YEAH.
WE SHOULD START TALKING ABOUT CHRISTMAS.

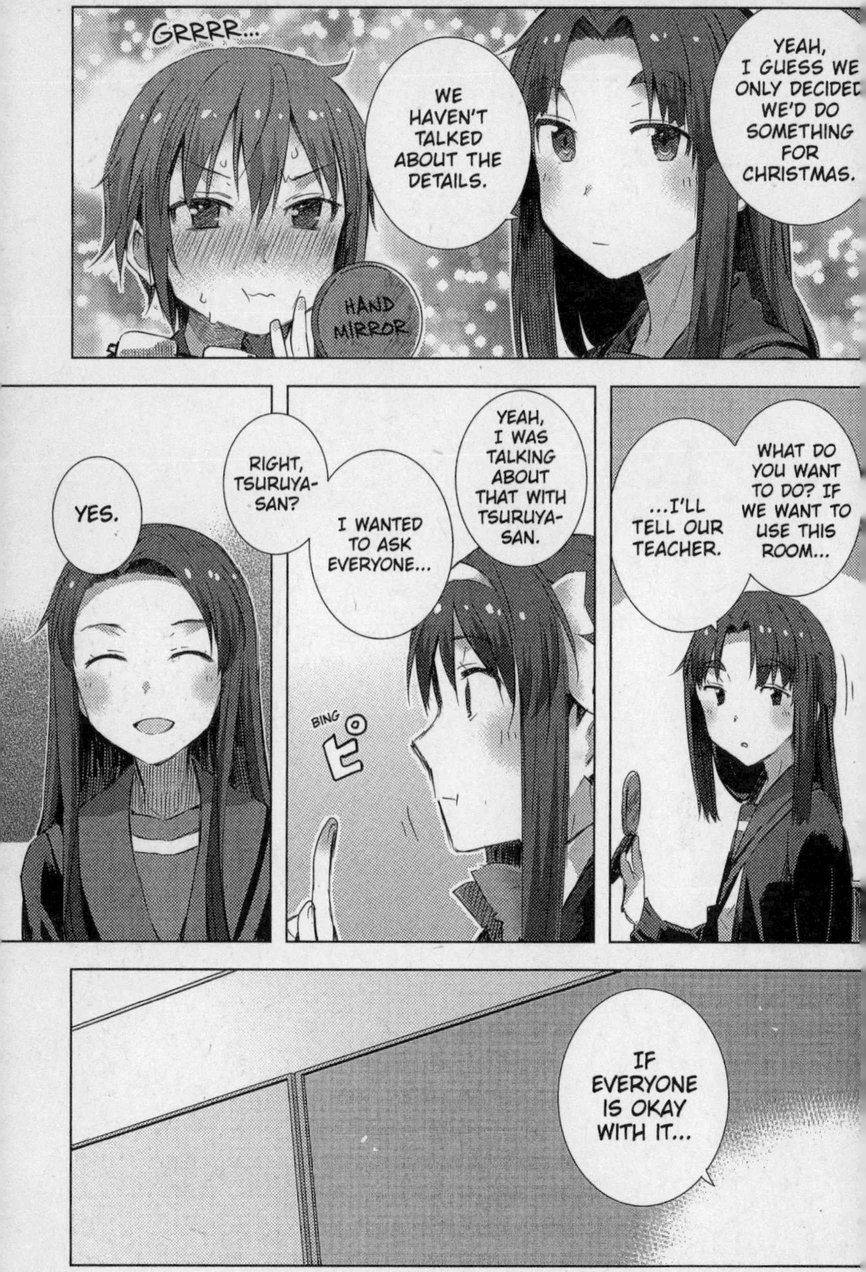
YEAH, I GUESS WE ONLY DECIDED WE'D DO SOMETHING FOR CHRISTMAS.
WE HAVEN'T TALKED ABOUT THE DETAILS.
GRRRR...
HAND MIRROR
WHAT DO YOU WANT TO DO? IF WE WANT TO USE THIS ROOM...
...I'LL TELL OUR TEACHER.
YEAH, I WAS TALKING ABOUT THAT WITH TSURUYA-SAN.
I WANTED TO ASK EVERYONE...
BING
ピ
RIGHT, TSURUYA-SAN?
YES.
IF EVERYONE IS OKAY WITH IT...

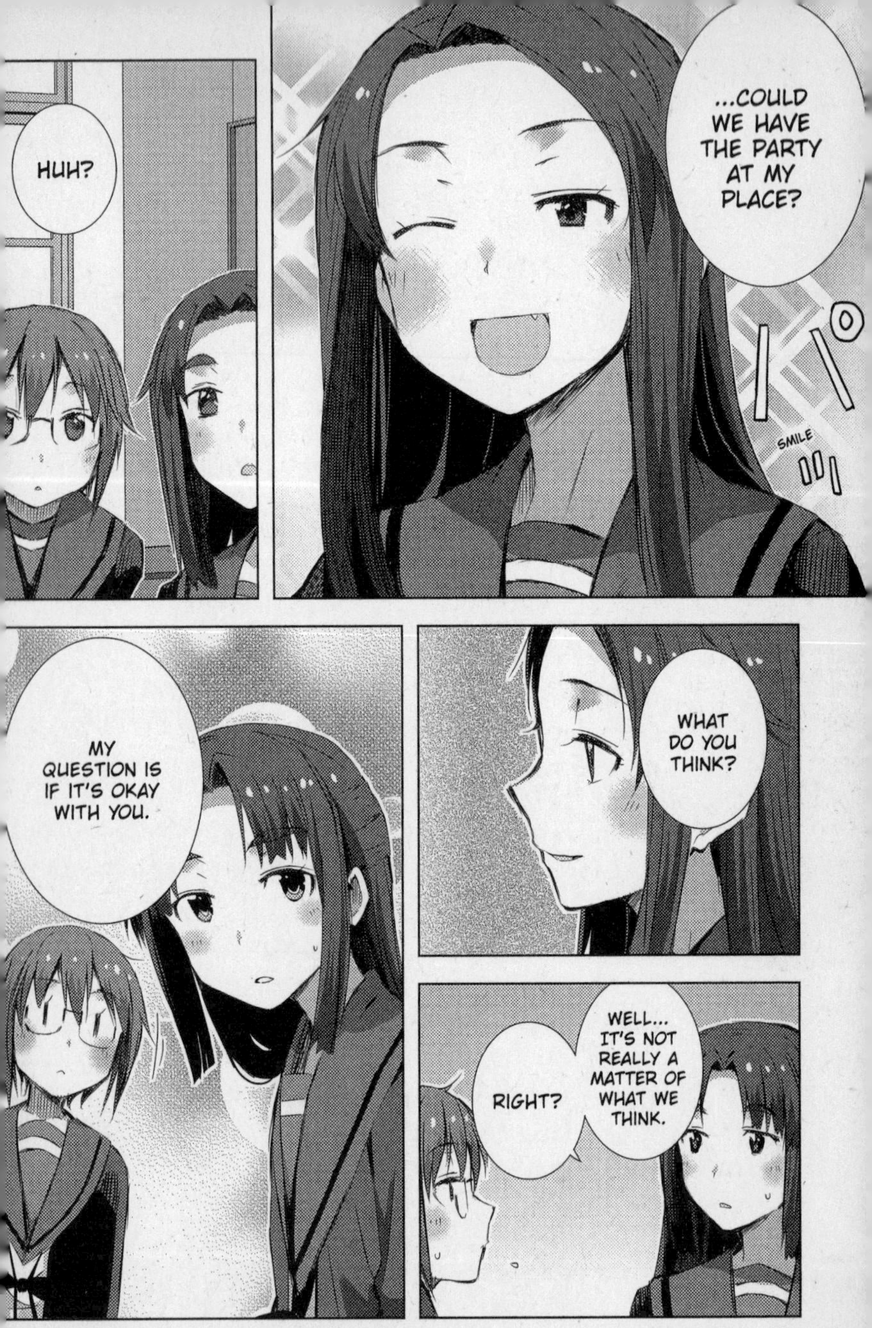
...COULD WE HAVE THE PARTY AT MY PLACE?
SMILE
HUH?
WHAT DO YOU THINK?
WELL... IT'S NOT REALLY A MATTER OF WHAT WE THINK.
RIGHT?
MY QUESTION IS IF IT'S OKAY WITH YOU.

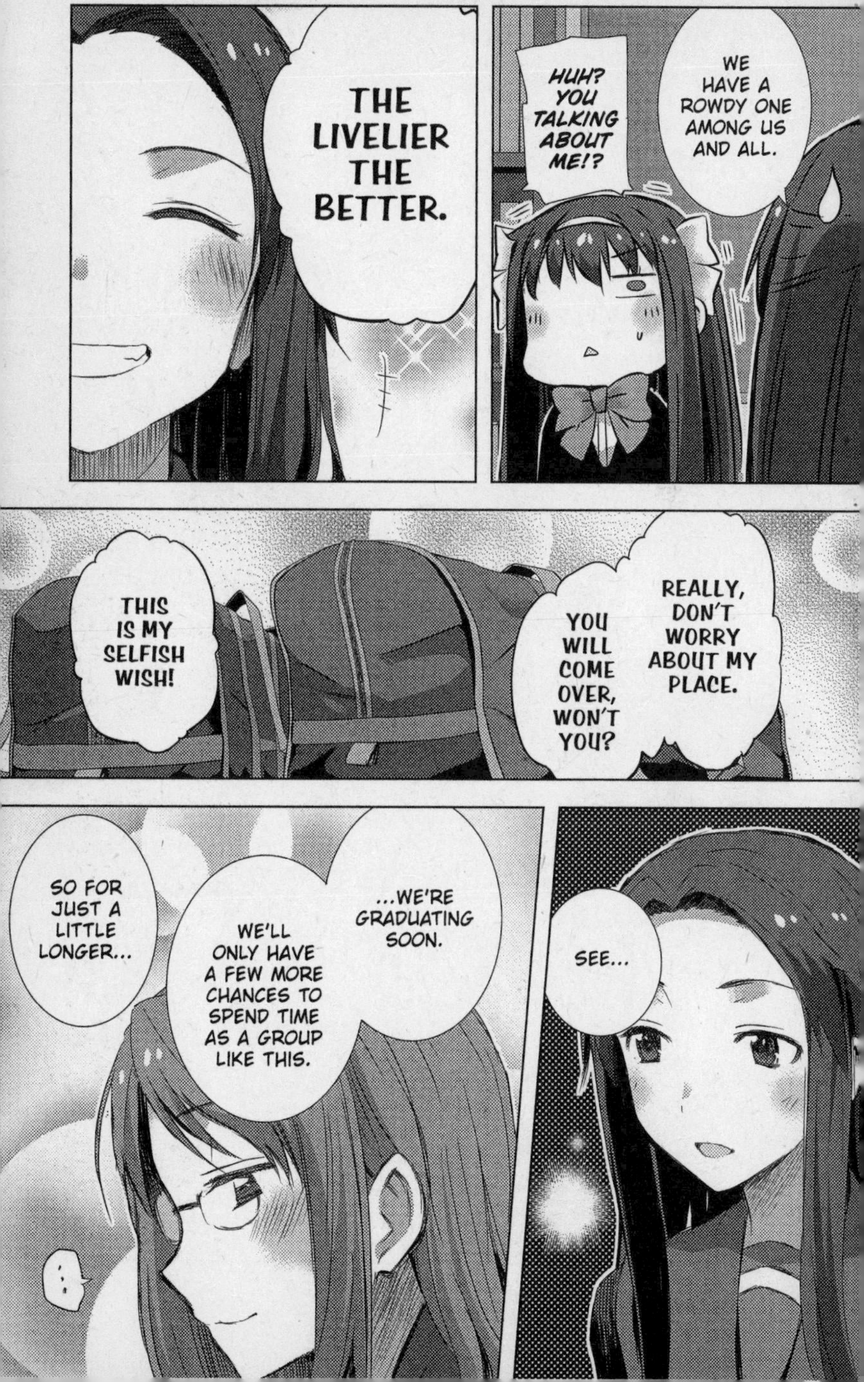
WE HAVE A ROWDY ONE AMONG US AND ALL.
HUH? YOU TALKING ABOUT ME!?
THE LIVELIER THE BETTER.
REALLY, DON'T WORRY ABOUT MY PLACE.
YOU WILL COME OVER, WON'T YOU?
THIS IS MY SELFISH WISH!
SEE...
...WE'RE GRADUATING SOON.
WE'LL ONLY HAVE A FEW MORE CHANCES TO SPEND TIME AS A GROUP LIKE THIS.
SO FOR JUST A LITTLE LONGER...
...

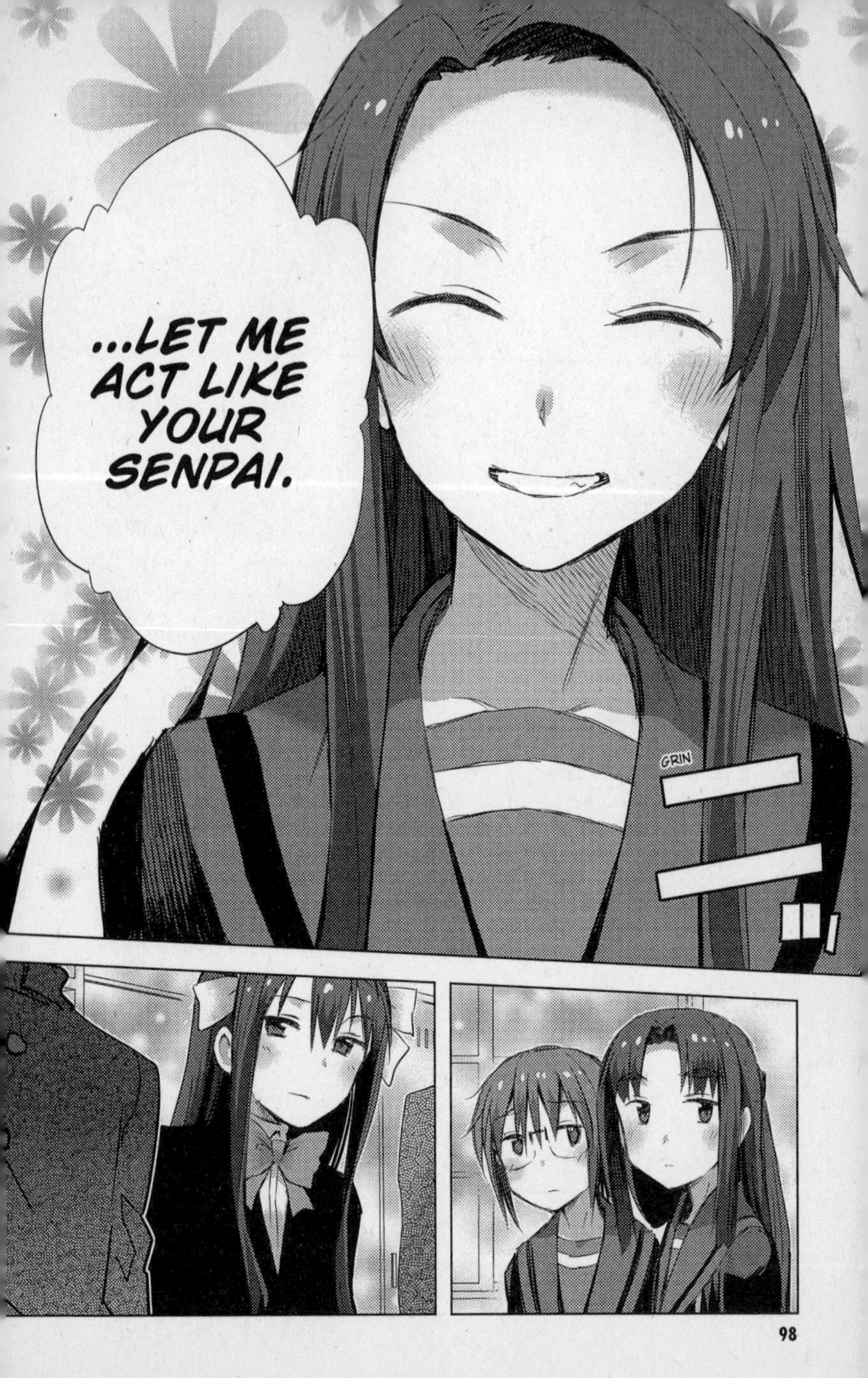
...LET ME ACT LIKE YOUR SENPAI.
GRIN

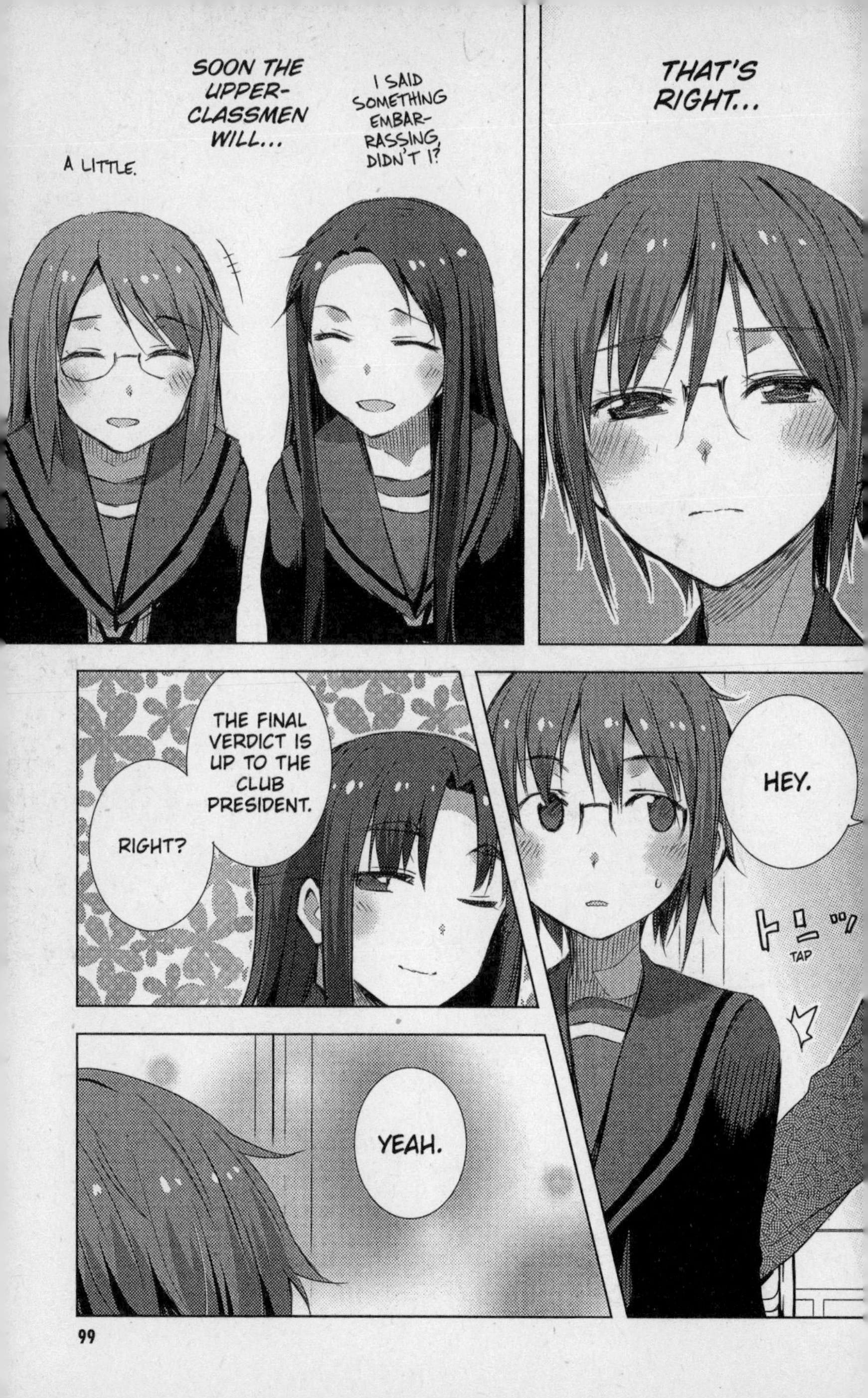

THAT'S RIGHT...
I SAID SOMETHING EMBARRASSING, DIDN'T I?
SOON THE UPPER-CLASSMEN WILL...
A LITTLE.
HEY.
TAP
THE FINAL VERDICT IS UP TO THE CLUB PRESIDENT.
RIGHT?
YEAH.

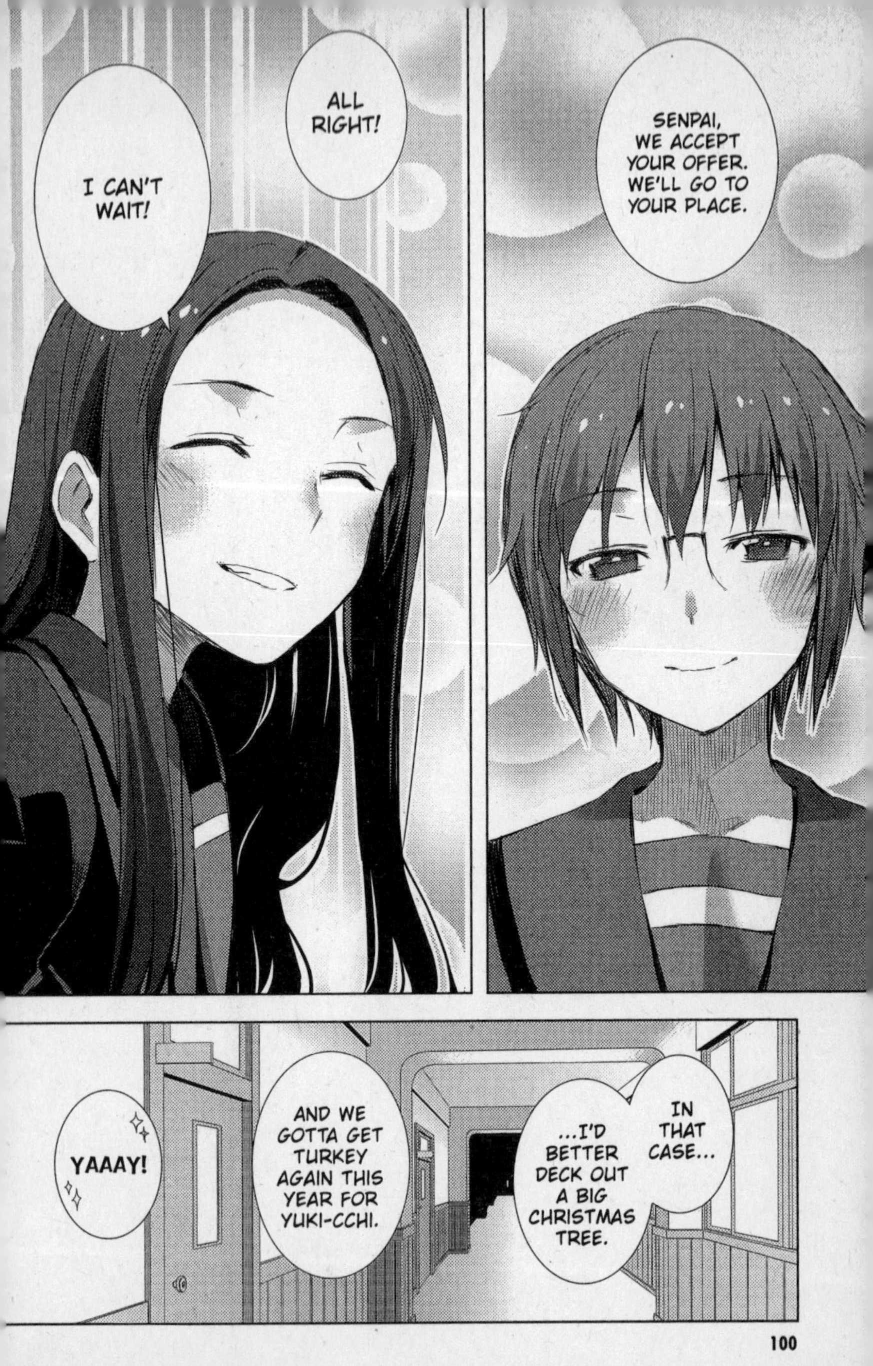
SENPAI, WE ACCEPT YOUR OFFER. WE'LL GO TO YOUR PLACE.
ALL RIGHT!
I CAN'T WAIT!
IN THAT CASE...
...I'D BETTER DECK OUT A BIG CHRISTMAS TREE.
AND WE GOTTA GET TURKEY AGAIN THIS YEAR FOR YUKI-CCHI.
YAAAY!

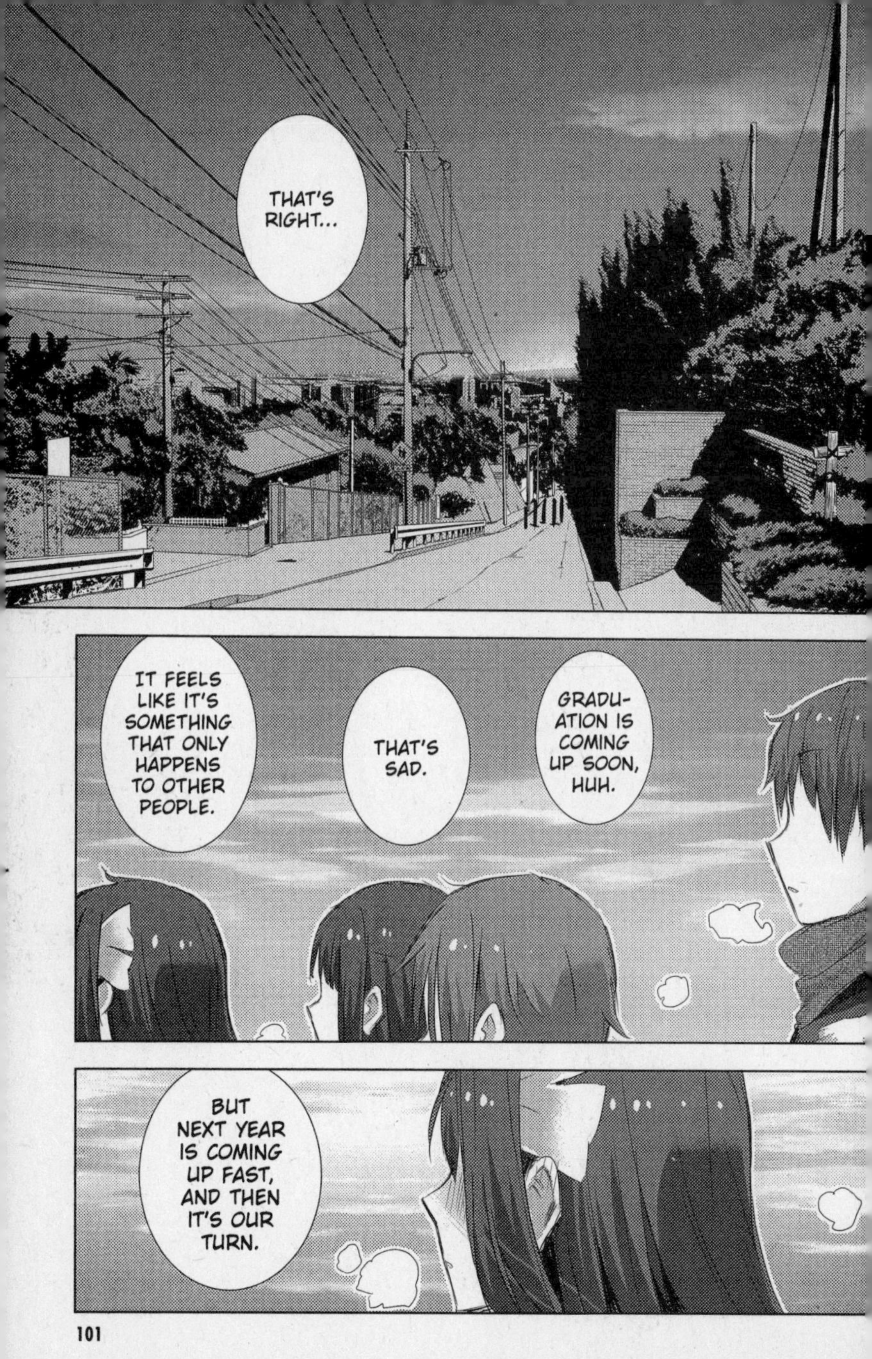
THAT'S RIGHT...
GRADU-ATION IS COMING UP SOON, HUH.
THAT'S SAD.
IT FEELS LIKE IT'S SOMETHING THAT ONLY HAPPENS TO OTHER PEOPLE.
BUT NEXT YEAR IS COMING UP FAST, AND THEN IT'S OUR TURN.

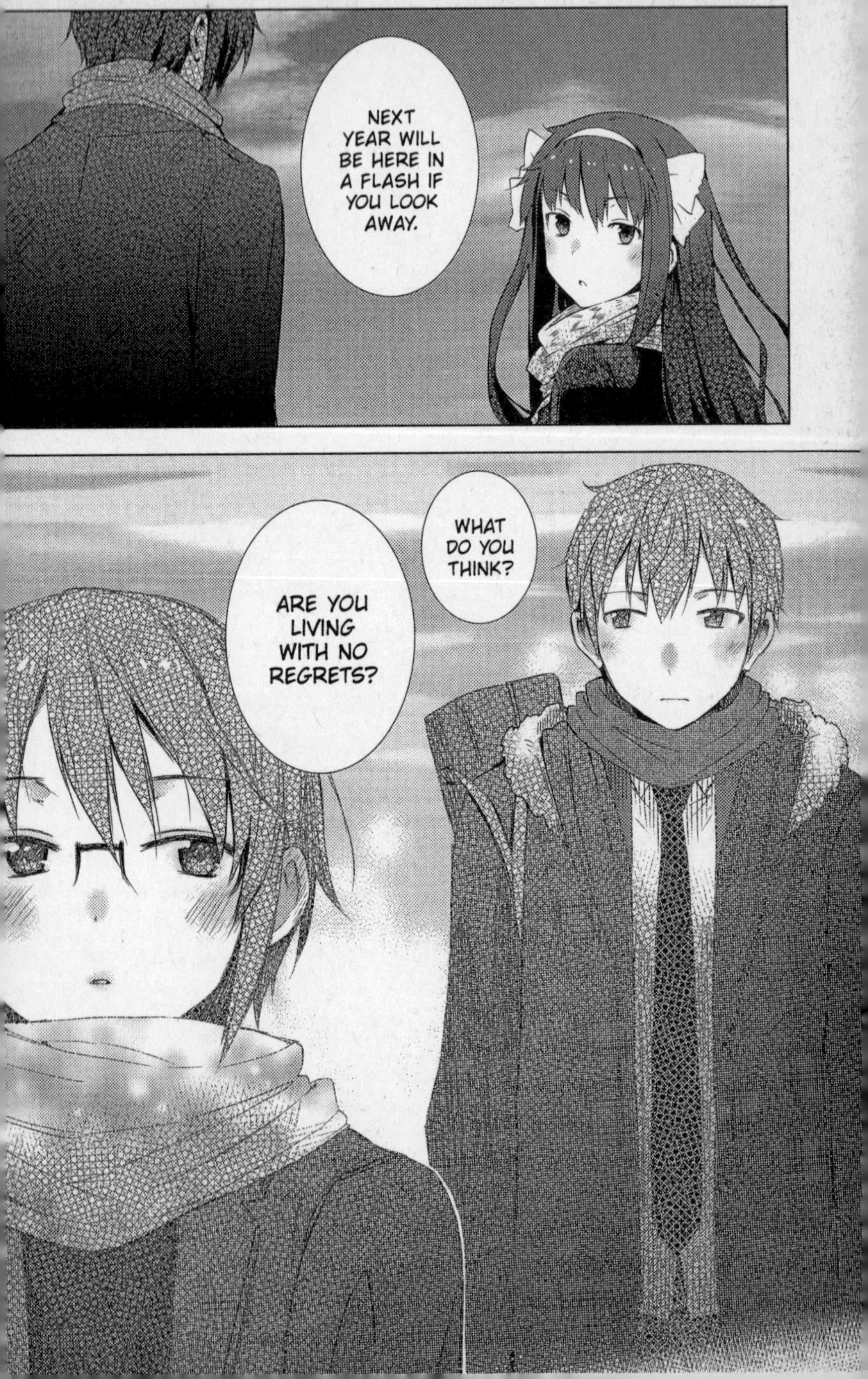
NEXT YEAR WILL BE HERE IN A FLASH IF YOU LOOK AWAY.
WHAT DO YOU THINK?
ARE YOU LIVING WITH NO REGRETS?

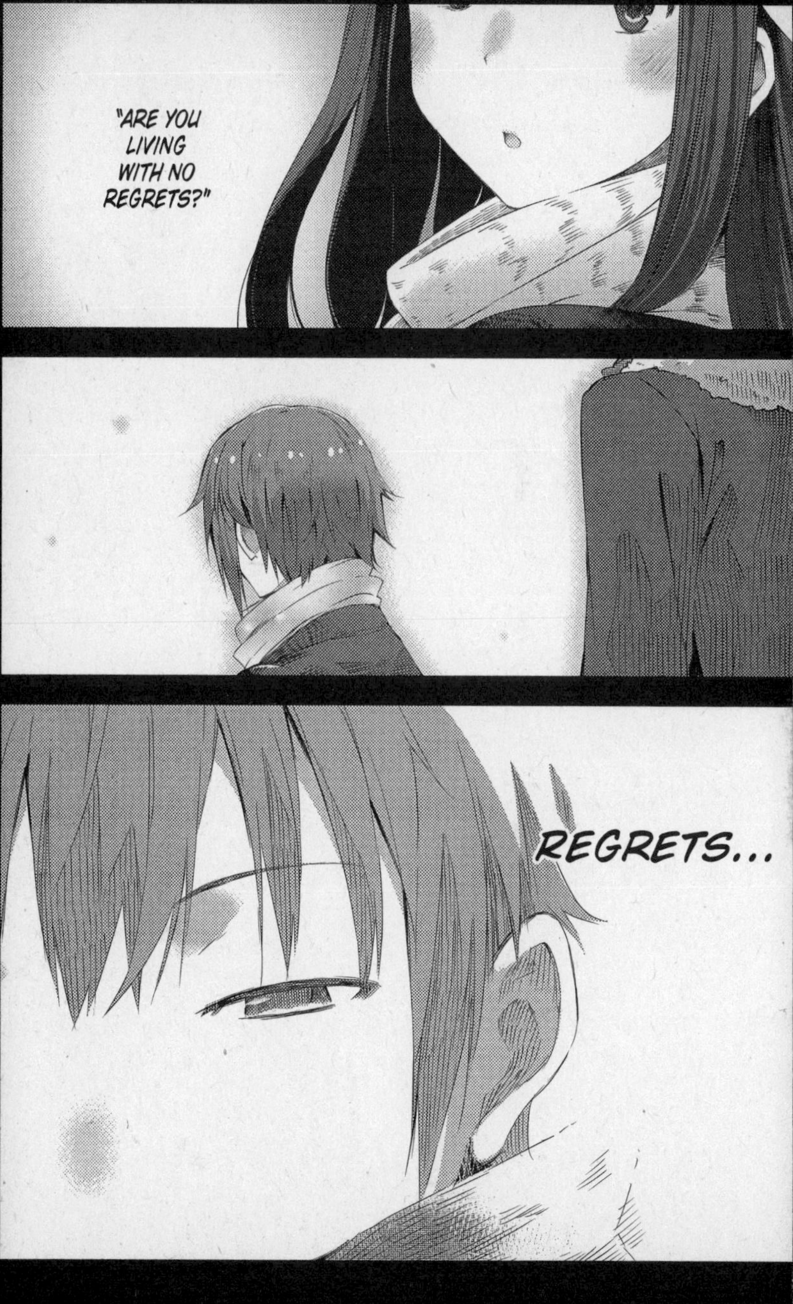
"ARE YOU LIVING WITH NO REGRETS?"
REGRETS...

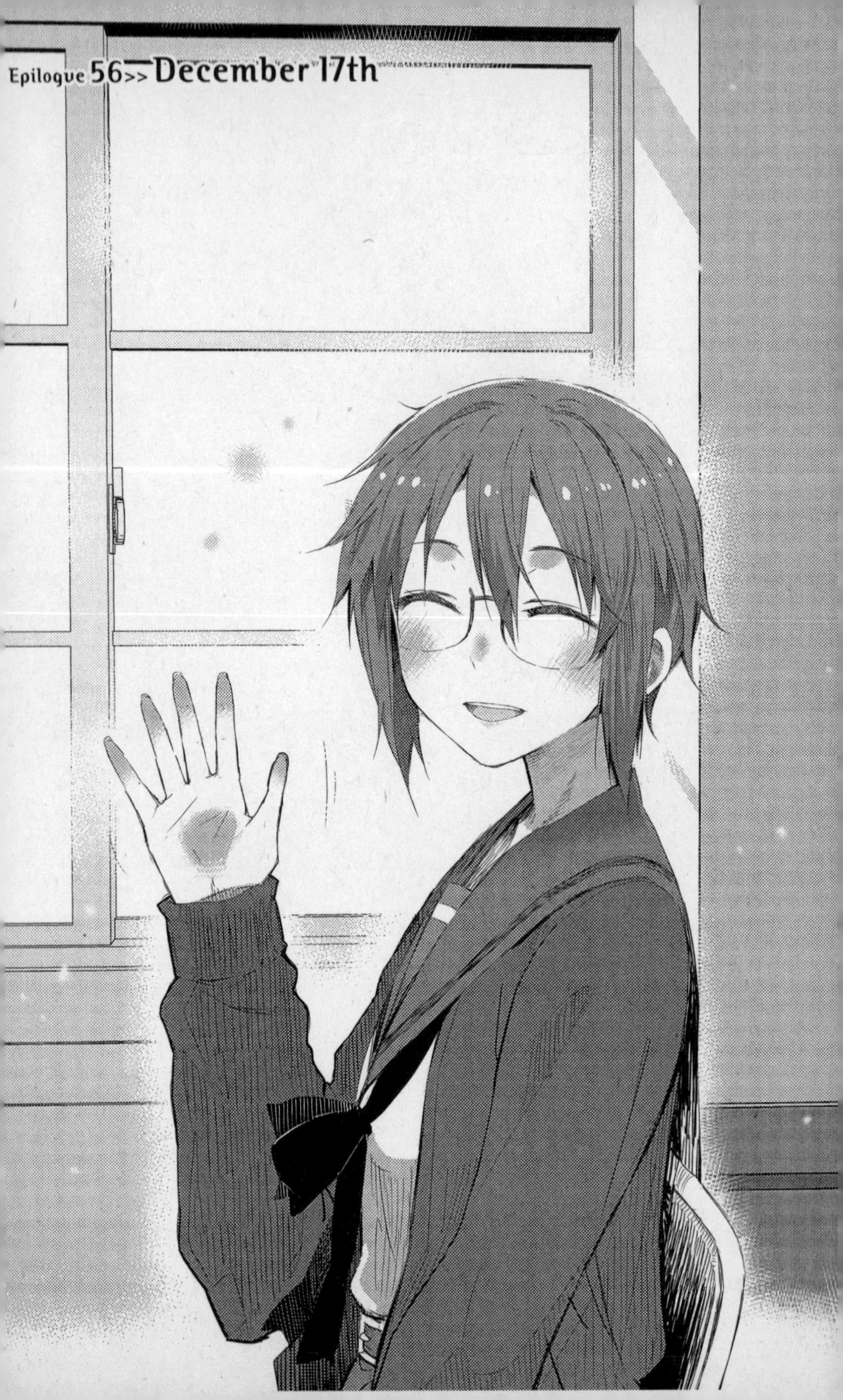
Epilogue 56>> December 17th

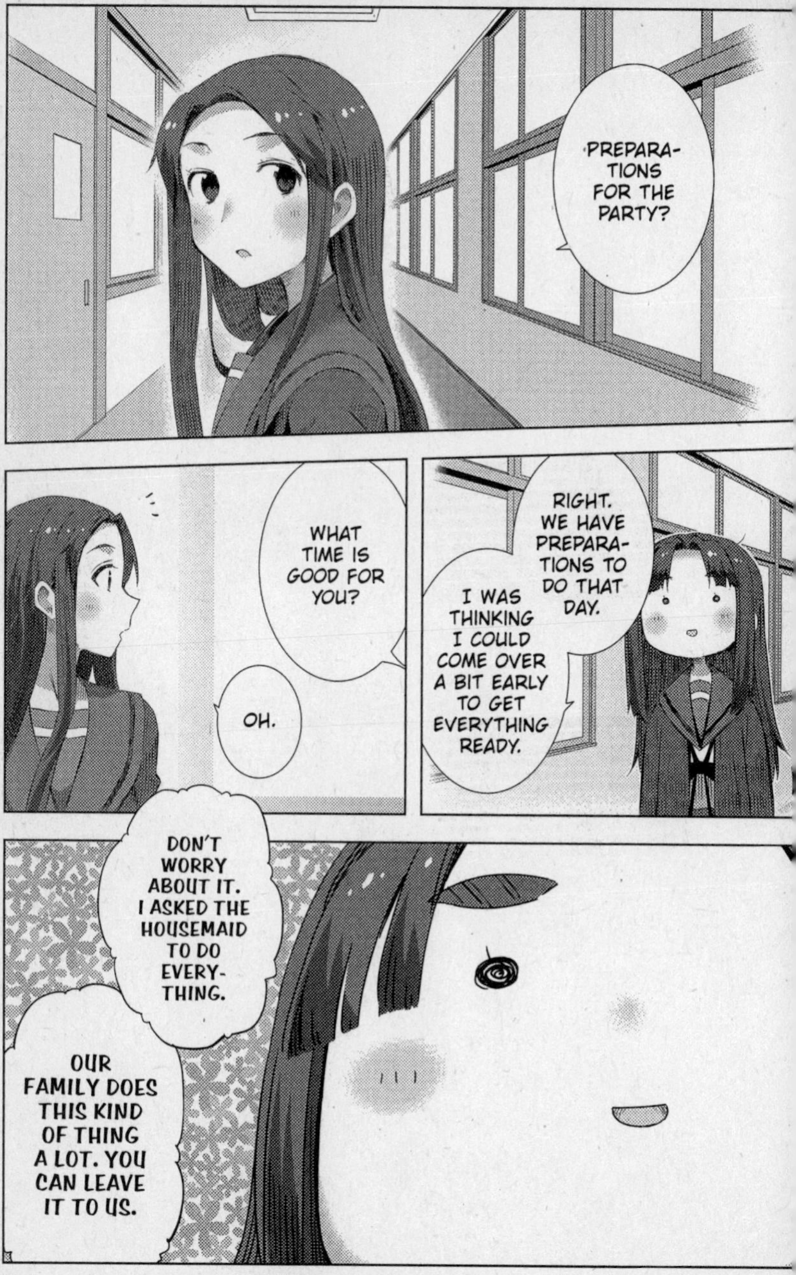
PREPARA-TIONS FOR THE PARTY?
RIGHT. WE HAVE PREPARA-TIONS TO DO THAT DAY.
I WAS THINKING I COULD COME OVER A BIT EARLY TO GET EVERYTHING READY.
WHAT TIME IS GOOD FOR YOU?
OH.
DON'T WORRY ABOUT IT. I ASKED THE HOUSEMAID TO DO EVERY-THING.
OUR FAMILY DOES THIS KIND OF THING A LOT. YOU CAN LEAVE IT TO US.

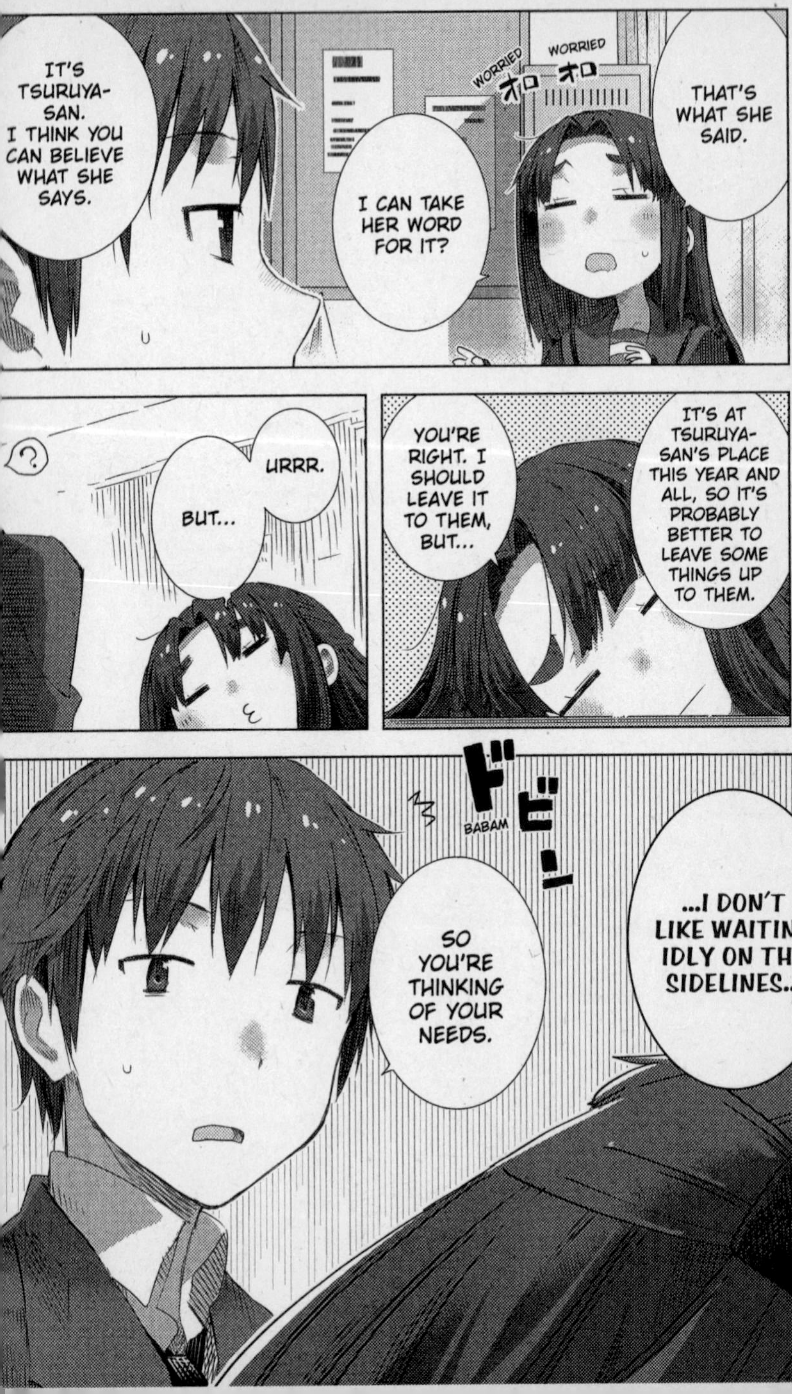
THAT'S WHAT SHE SAID.
WORRIED オロ
WORRIED オロ
I CAN TAKE HER WORD FOR IT?
IT'S TSURUYA-SAN. I THINK YOU CAN BELIEVE WHAT SHE SAYS.
IT'S AT TSURUYA-SAN'S PLACE THIS YEAR AND ALL, SO IT'S PROBABLY BETTER TO LEAVE SOME THINGS UP TO THEM.
YOU'RE RIGHT. I SHOULD LEAVE IT TO THEM, BUT...
URRR.
BUT...
?
ドビーン
BABAM
...I DON'T LIKE WAITING IDLY ON THE SIDELINES...
SO YOU'RE THINKING OF YOUR NEEDS.

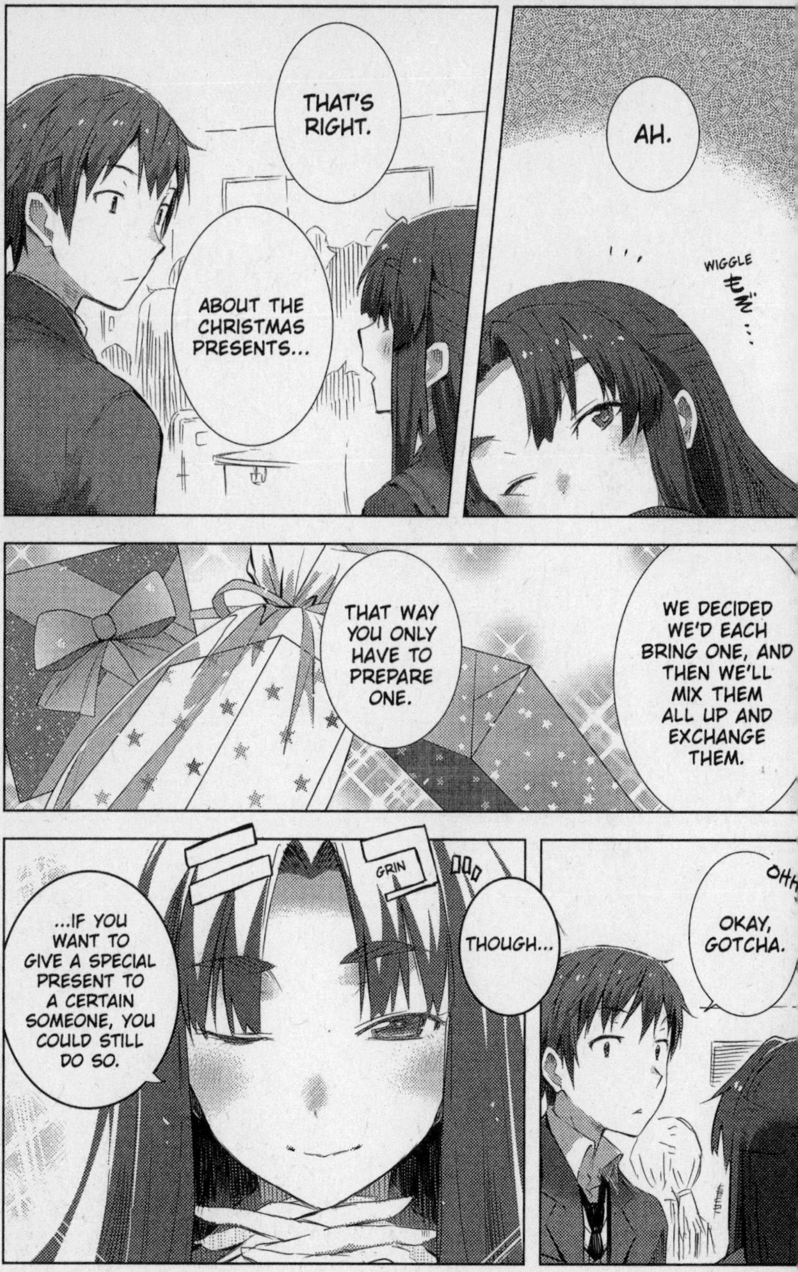
AH.
WIGGLE
THAT'S RIGHT.
ABOUT THE CHRISTMAS PRESENTS...
WE DECIDED WE'D EACH BRING ONE, AND THEN WE'LL MIX THEM ALL UP AND EXCHANGE THEM.
THAT WAY YOU ONLY HAVE TO PREPARE ONE.
OKAY, GOTCHA.
THOUGH...
GRIN
...IF YOU WANT TO GIVE A SPECIAL PRESENT TO A CERTAIN SOMEONE, YOU COULD STILL DO SO.

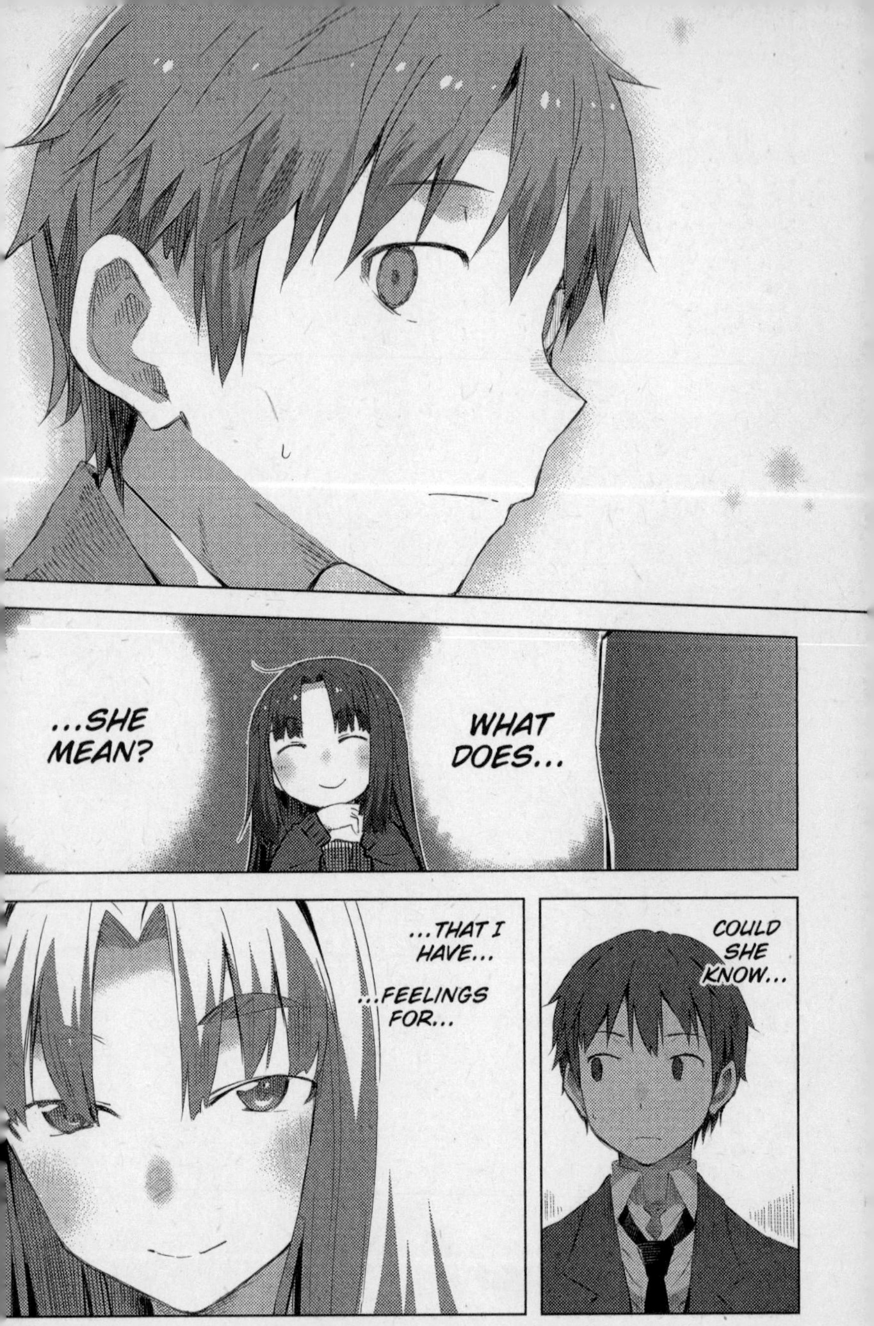
WHAT DOES...
...SHE MEAN?
COULD SHE KNOW...
...THAT I HAVE...
...FEELINGS FOR...

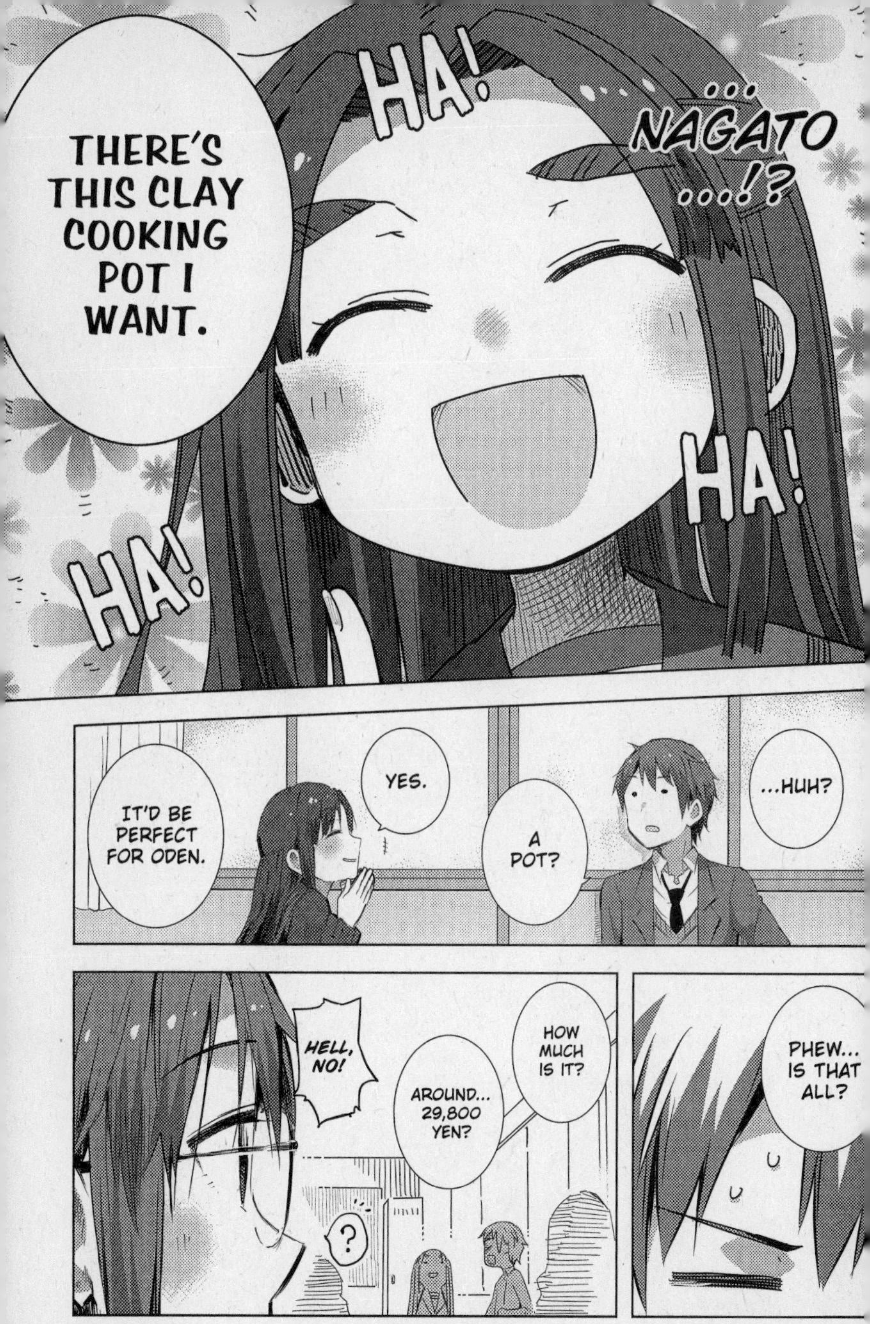
...NAGATO ...!?
HA!
HA!
THERE'S THIS CLAY COOKING POT I WANT.
HA!
...HUH?
A POT?
YES.
IT'D BE PERFECT FOR ODEN.
PHEW... IS THAT ALL?
HOW MUCH IS IT?
AROUND... 29,800 YEN?
HELL, NO!
?

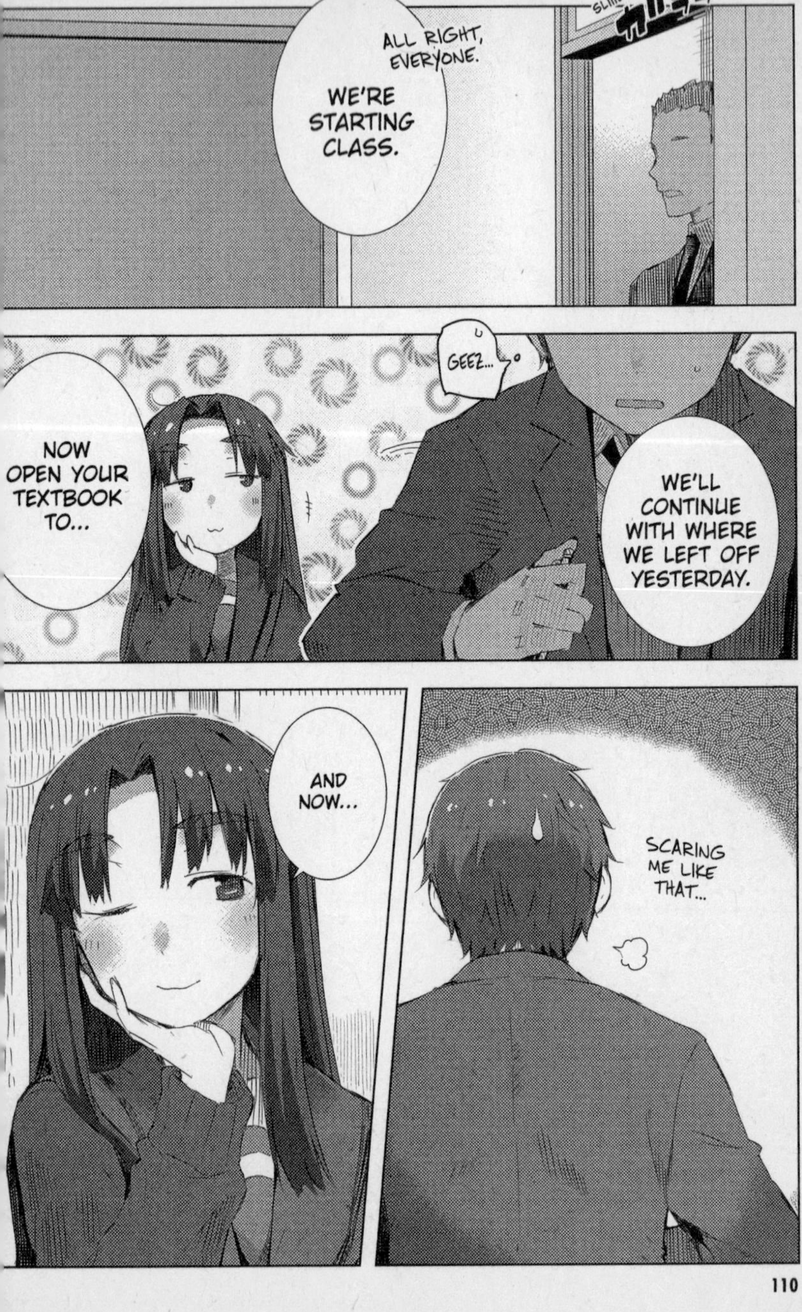
SLIIIDE
ALL RIGHT, EVERYONE.
WE'RE STARTING CLASS.
GEEZ...
WE'LL CONTINUE WITH WHERE WE LEFT OFF YESTERDAY.
NOW OPEN YOUR TEXTBOOK TO...
SCARING ME LIKE THAT...
AND NOW...

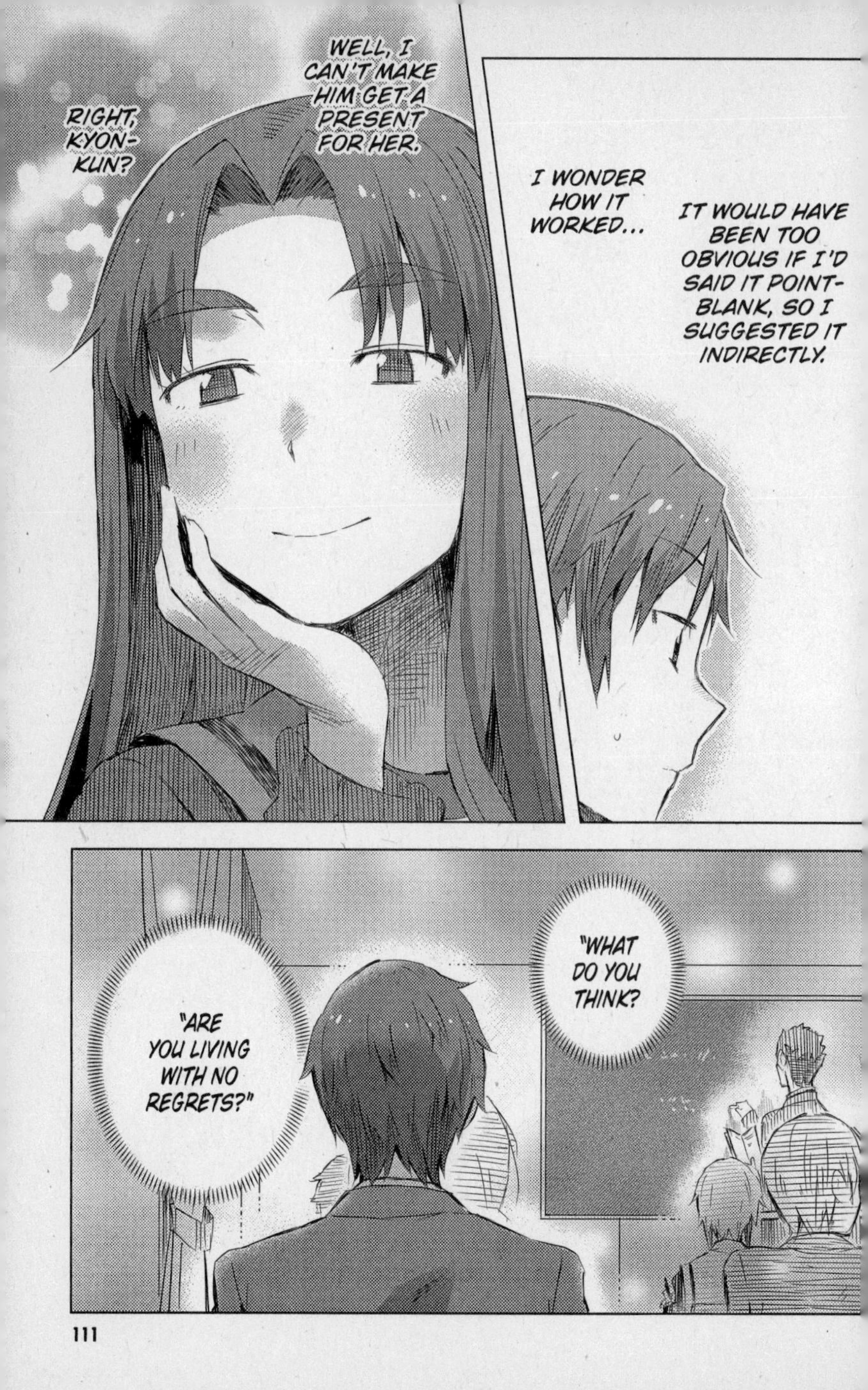
IT WOULD HAVE BEEN TOO OBVIOUS IF I'D SAID IT POINT-BLANK, SO I SUGGESTED IT INDIRECTLY.
I WONDER HOW IT WORKED...
WELL, I CAN'T MAKE HIM GET A PRESENT FOR HER.
RIGHT, KYON-KUN?
"WHAT DO YOU THINK?
"ARE YOU LIVING WITH NO REGRETS?"

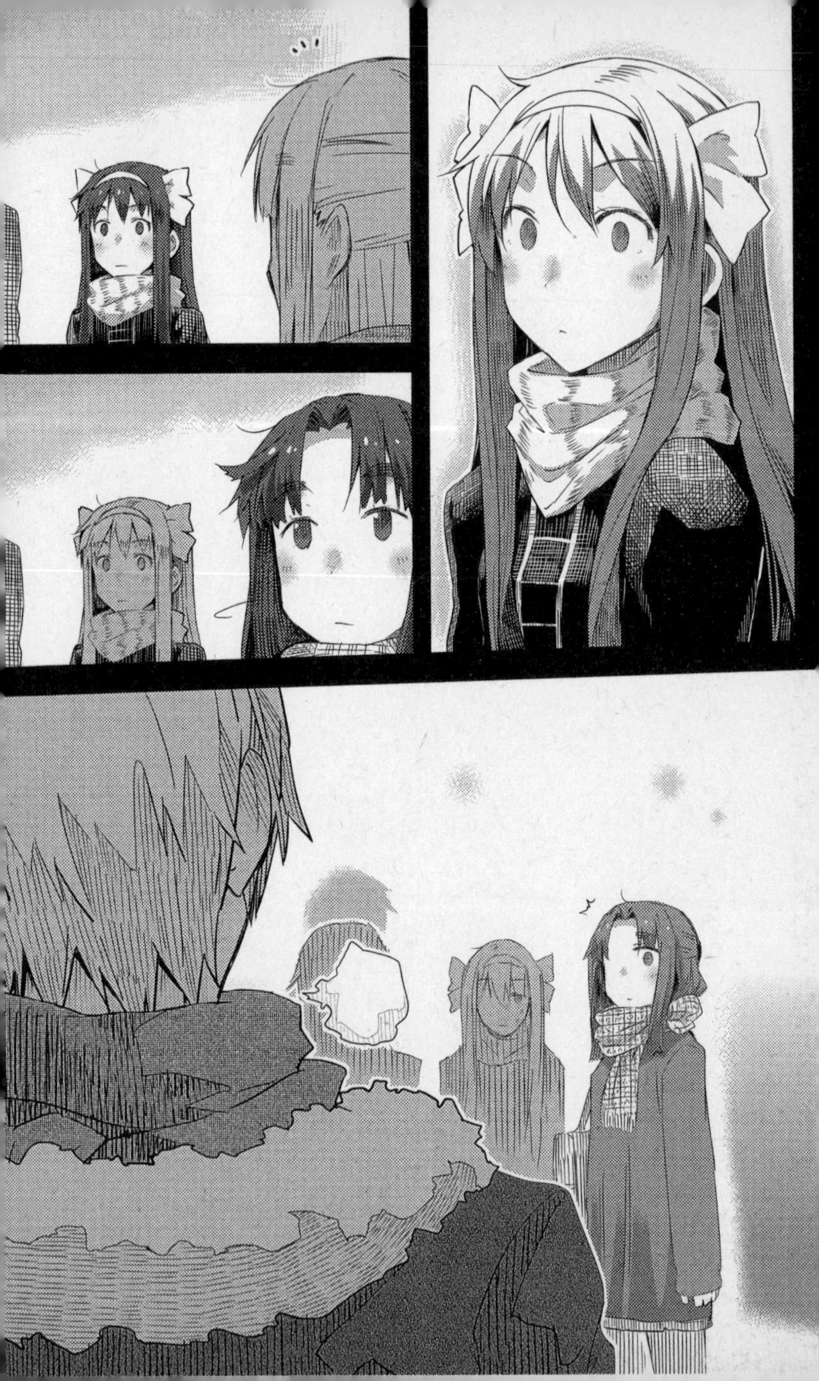

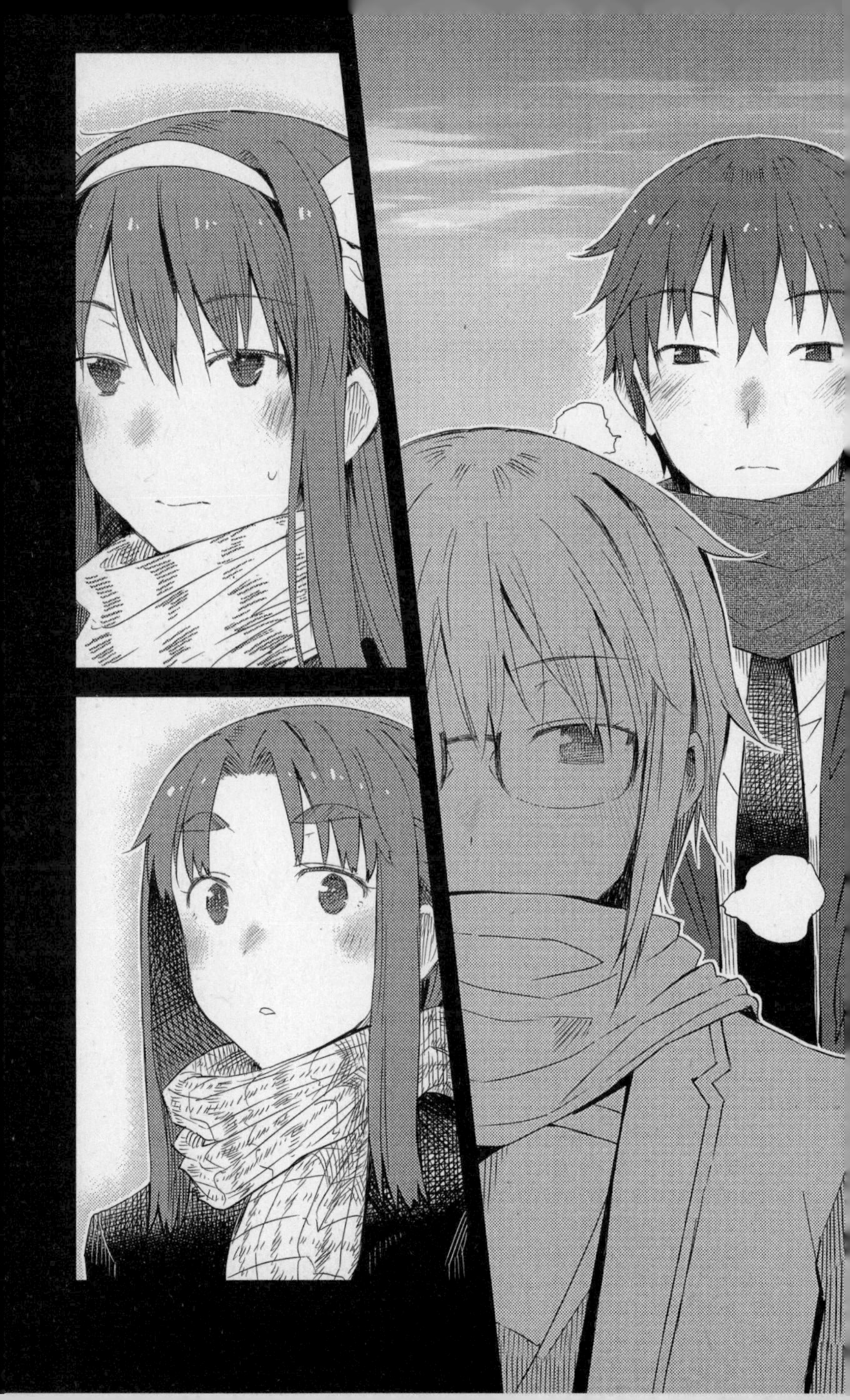

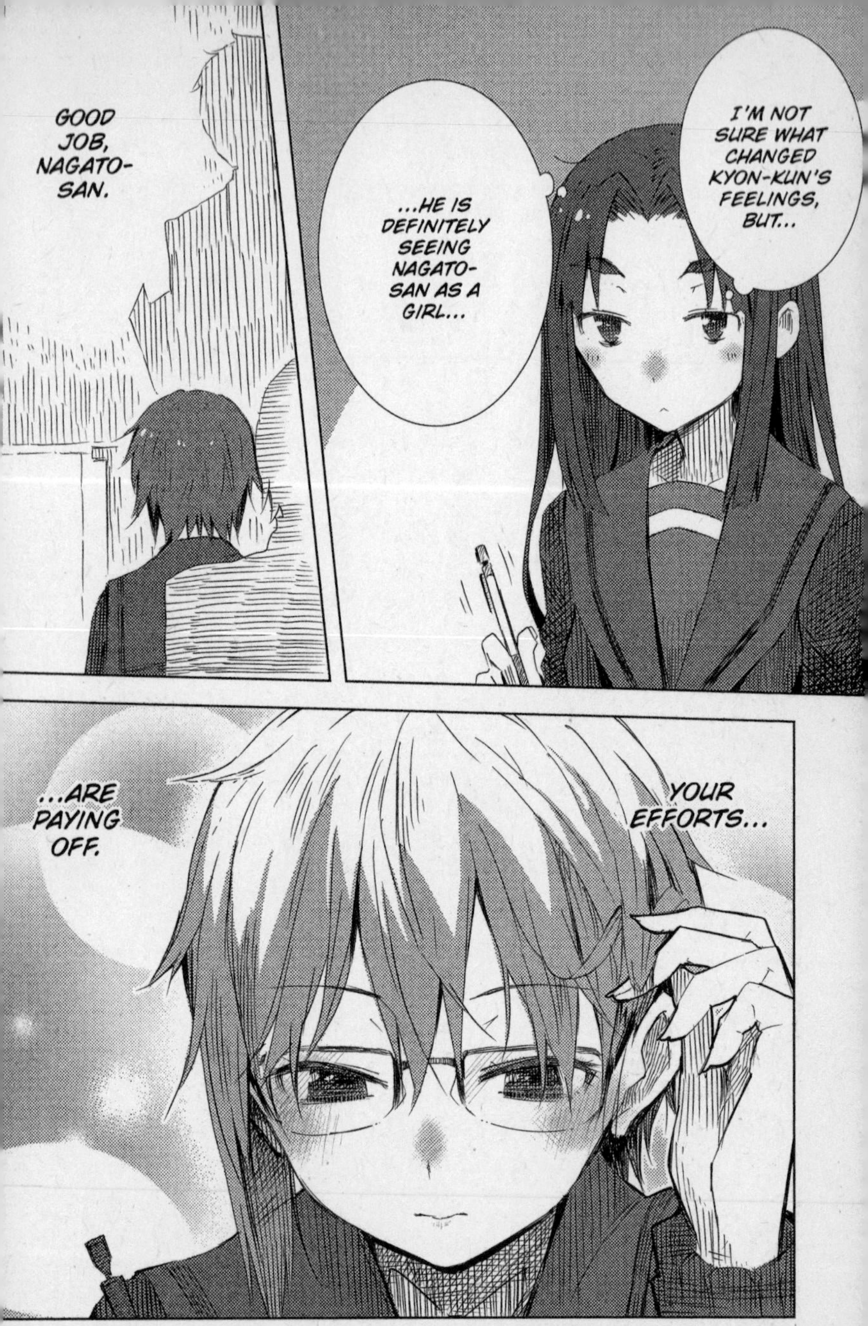
I'M NOT SURE WHAT CHANGED KYON-KUN'S FEELINGS, BUT...
...HE IS DEFINITELY SEEING NAGATO-SAN AS A GIRL...
GOOD JOB, NAGATO-SAN.
YOUR EFFORTS...
...ARE PAYING OFF.

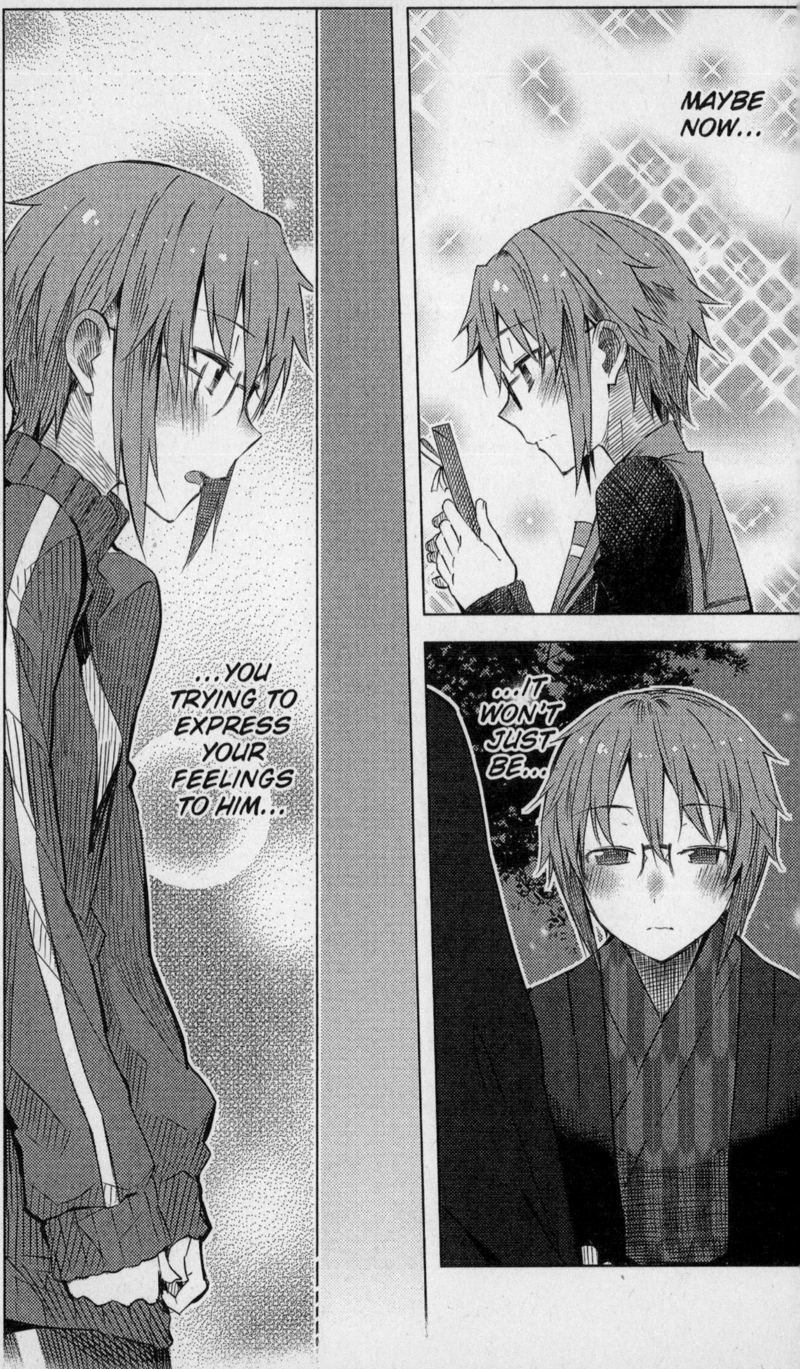
MAYBE NOW...
...IT WON'T JUST BE...
...YOU TRYING TO EXPRESS YOUR FEELINGS TO HIM...

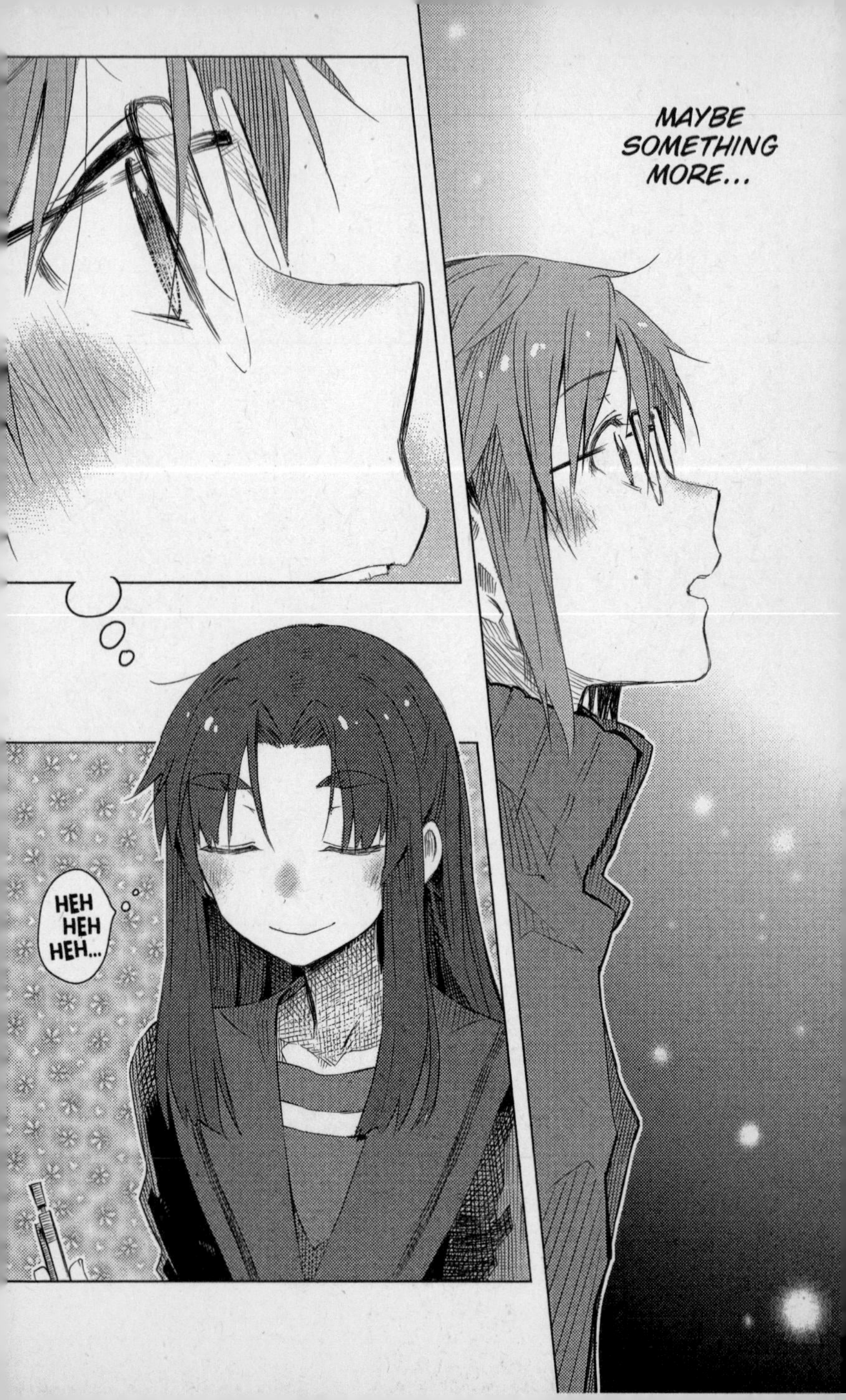
MAYBE SOMETHING MORE...
HEH HEH HEH...

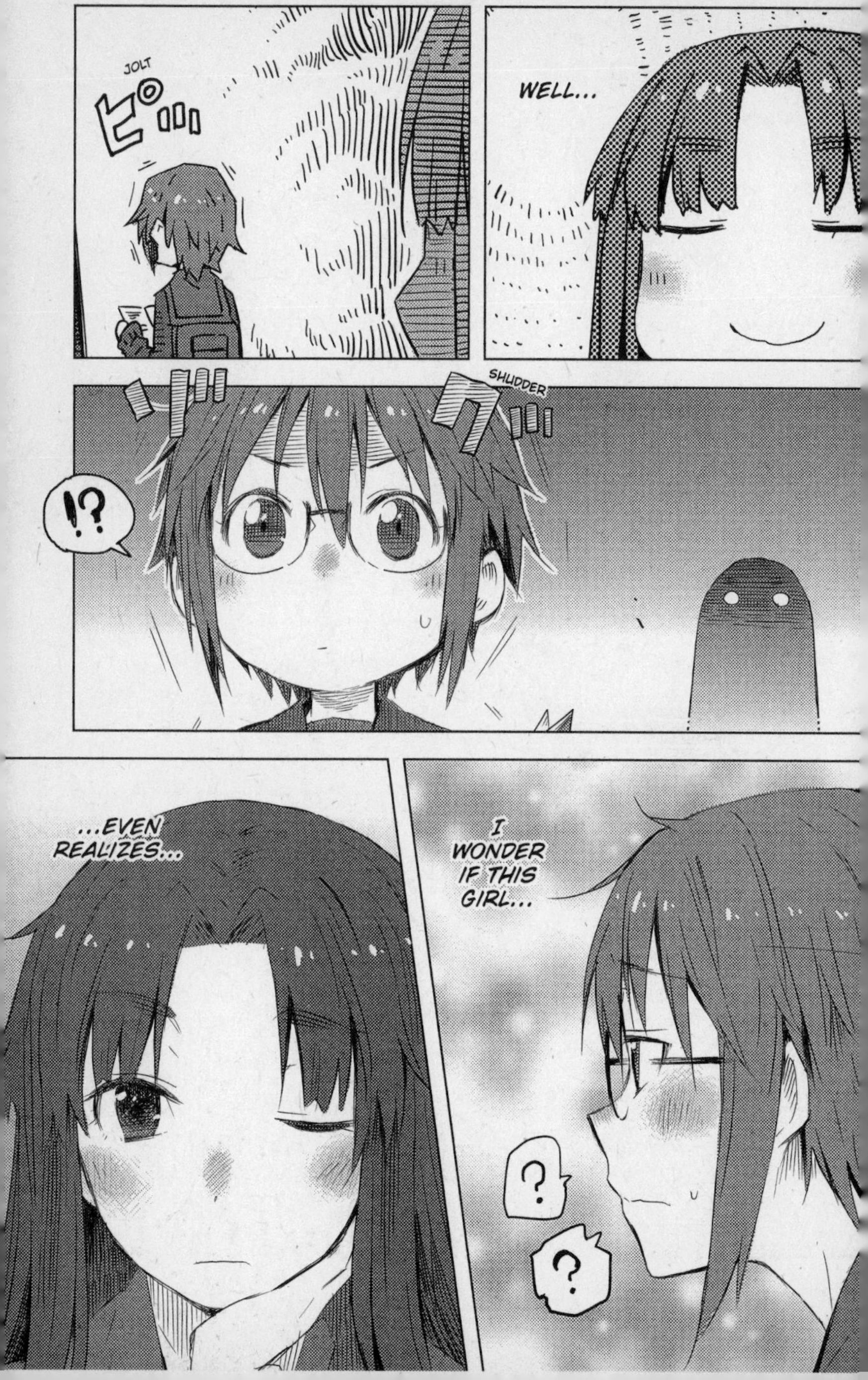

WELL...
JOLT
ビク
SHUDDER
!?
I WONDER IF THIS GIRL...
?
?
...EVEN REALIZES...

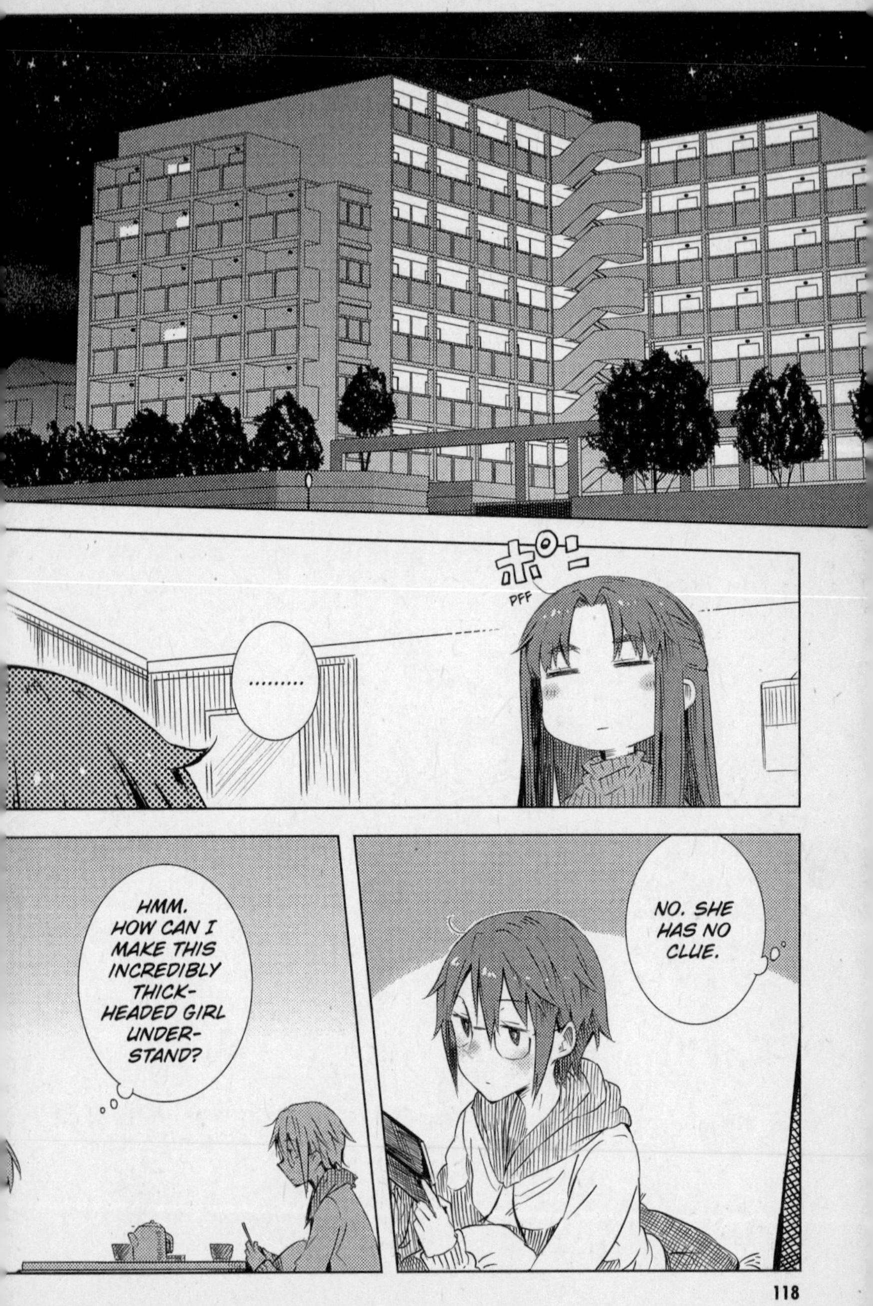
ポー
PFF
.........
NO. SHE HAS NO CLUE.
HMM. HOW CAN I MAKE THIS INCREDIBLY THICK-HEADED GIRL UNDER-STAND?

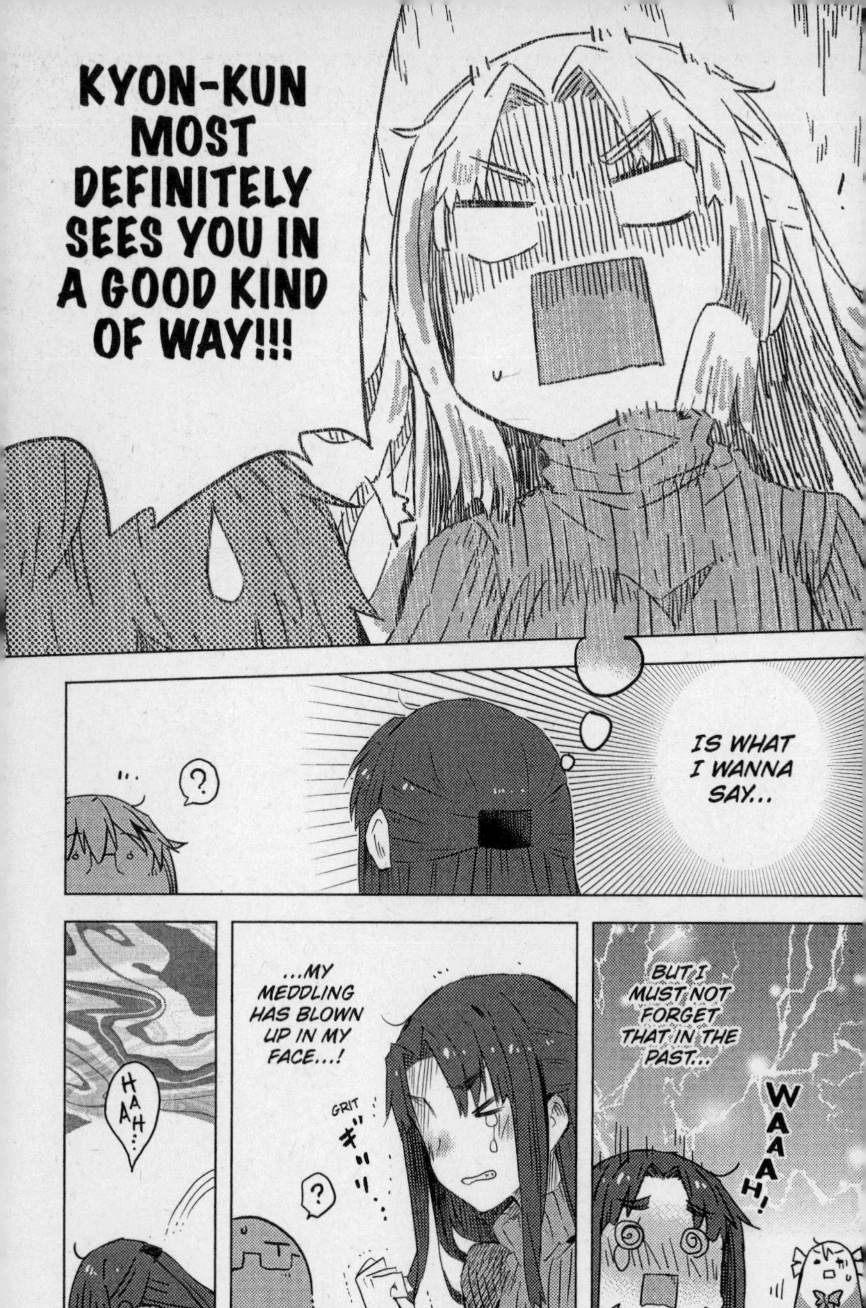
KYON-KUN MOST DEFINITELY SEES YOU IN A GOOD KIND OF WAY!!!
IS WHAT I WANNA SAY...
?
BUT I MUST NOT FORGET THAT IN THE PAST...
WAAAAH!
...MY MEDDLING HAS BLOWN UP IN MY FACE...!
GRIT
?
HAAH...

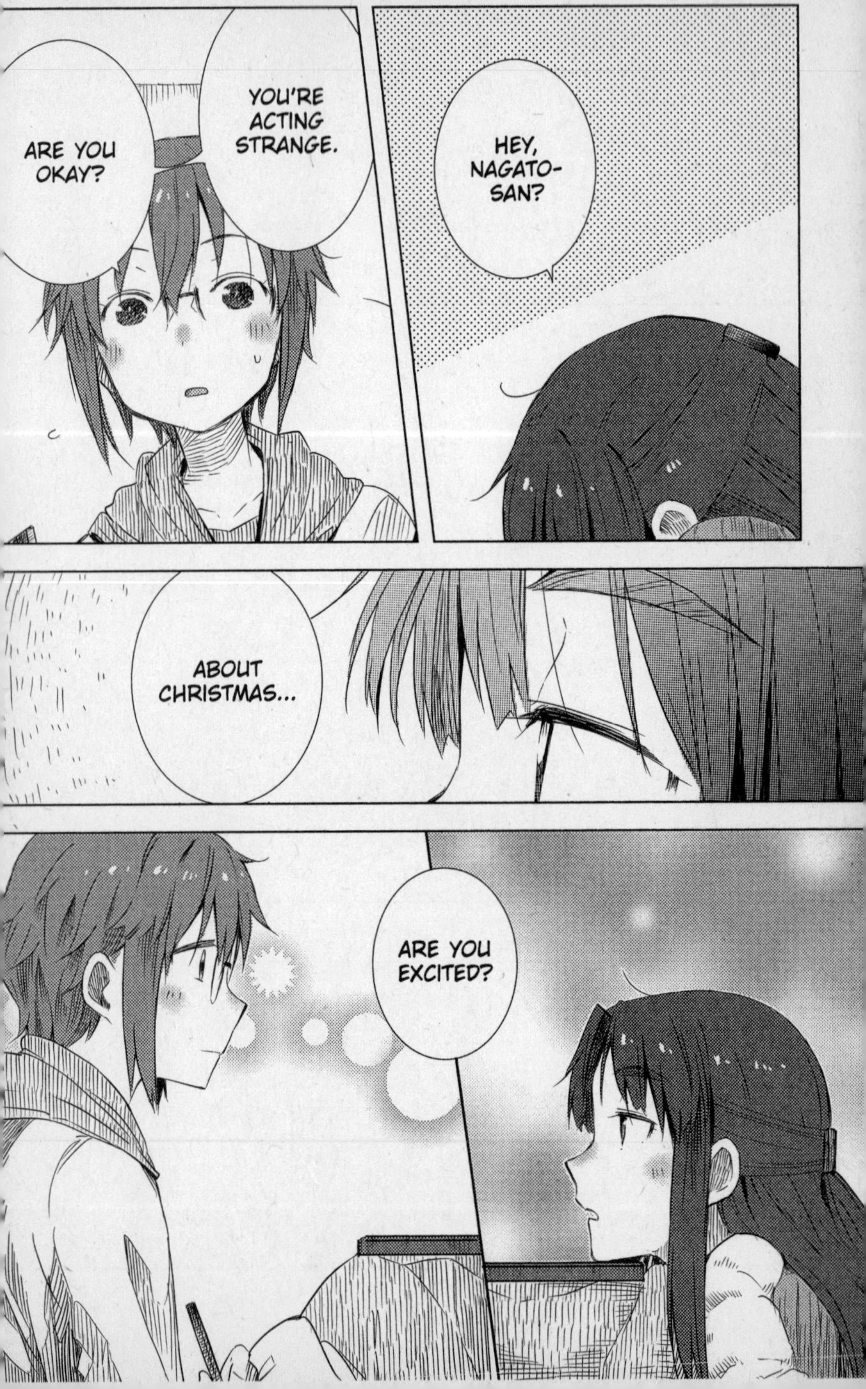
HEY, NAGATO-SAN?
YOU'RE ACTING STRANGE.
ARE YOU OKAY?
ABOUT CHRISTMAS...
ARE YOU EXCITED?

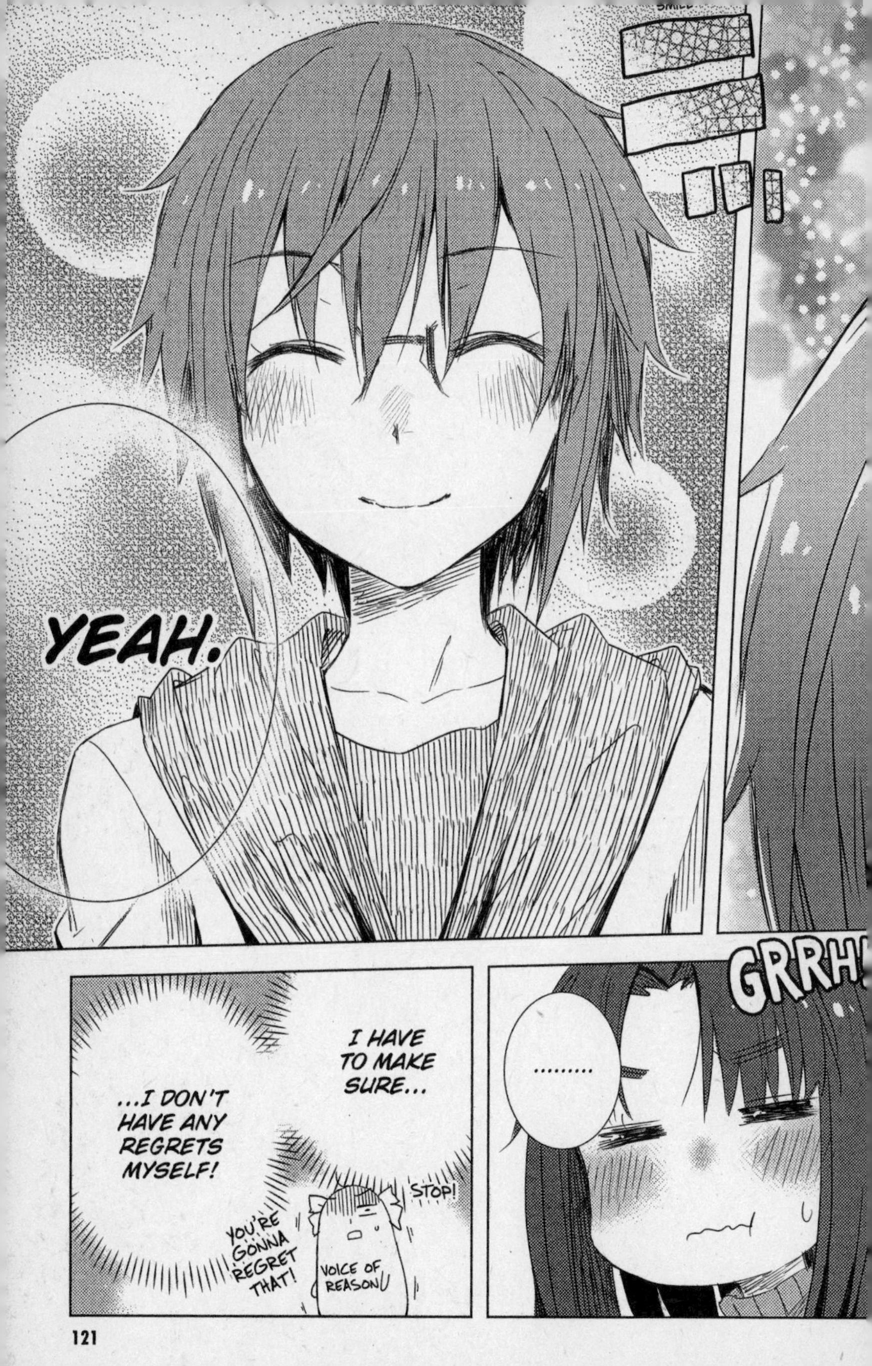
YEAH.
GRRH
.........
I HAVE TO MAKE SURE...
...I DON'T HAVE ANY REGRETS MYSELF!
STOP!
YOU'RE GONNA REGRET THAT!
VOICE OF REASON

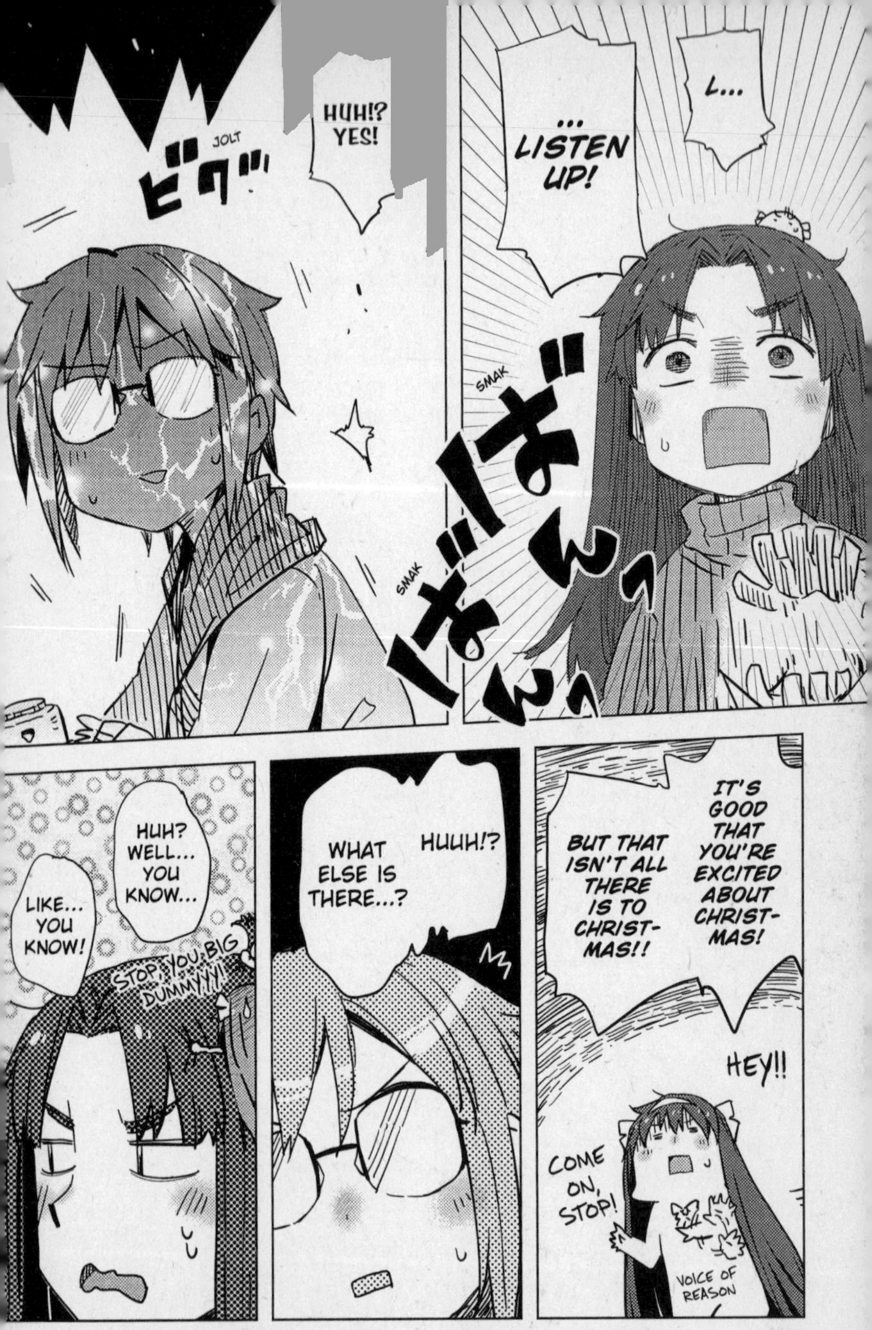
I...
...LISTEN UP!
SMAK
ばんっ
SMAK
ばんっ
JOLT
ビクッ
HUH!? YES!
IT'S GOOD THAT YOU'RE EXCITED ABOUT CHRIST-MAS!
BUT THAT ISN'T ALL THERE IS TO CHRIST-MAS!!
HEY!!
COME ON, STOP!
VOICE OF REASON
HUUH!?
WHAT ELSE IS THERE...?
HUH? WELL... YOU KNOW...
LIKE... YOU KNOW!
STOP, YOU BIG DUMMYYY!

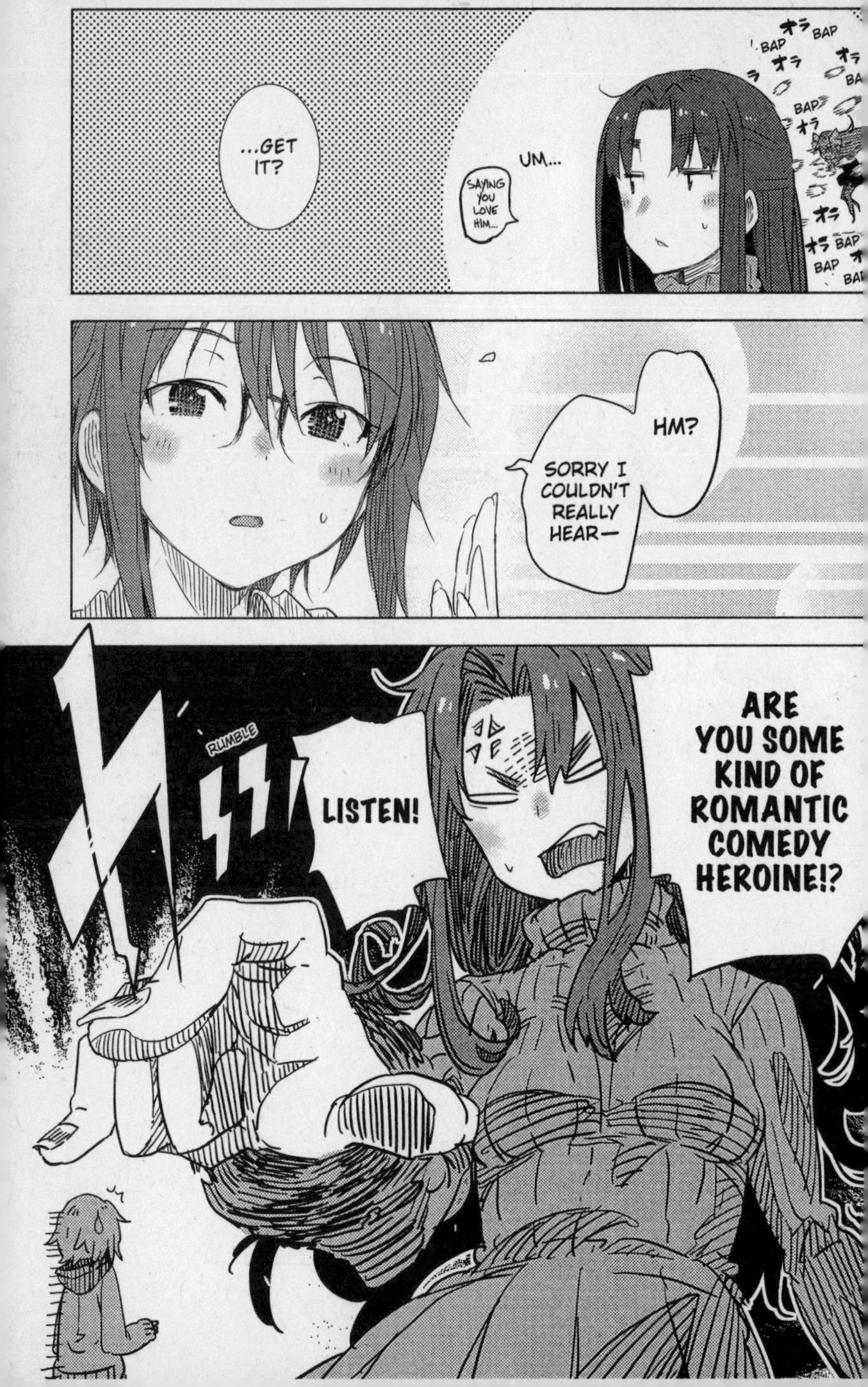
オラ BAP
BAP オラ
オラ BAP
BAP オラ
オラ BAP
BAP オラ
UM...
SAYING YOU LOVE HIM...
...GET IT?
HM?
SORRY I COULDN'T REALLY HEAR—
ARE YOU SOME KIND OF ROMANTIC COMEDY HEROINE!?
LISTEN!
RUMBLE

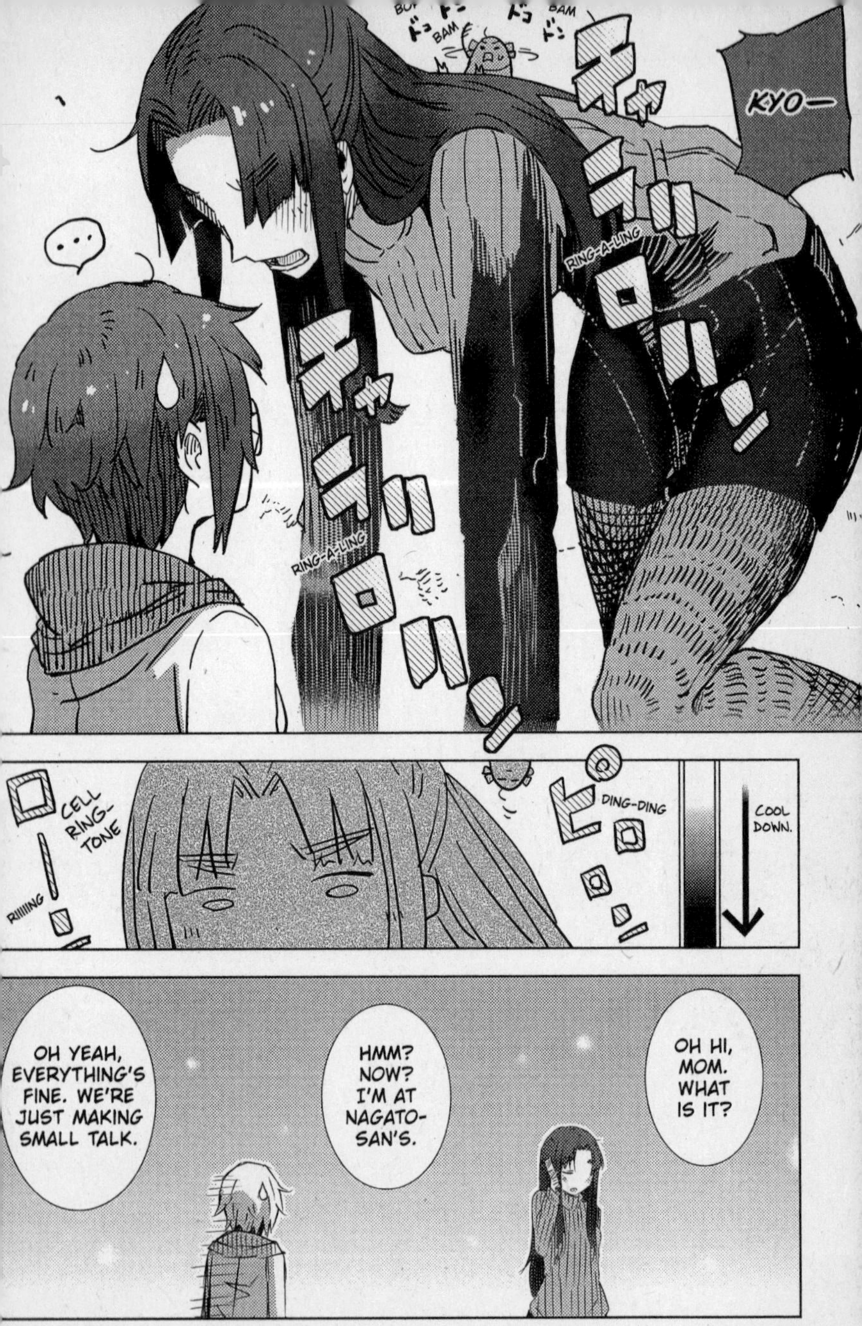
BAM
BAM
KYO—
RING-A-LING
...
RING-A-LING
COOL DOWN.
DING-DING
CELL RING-TONE
RIIIING
OH HI, MOM. WHAT IS IT?
HMM? NOW? I'M AT NAGATO-SAN'S.
OH YEAH, EVERYTHING'S FINE. WE'RE JUST MAKING SMALL TALK.

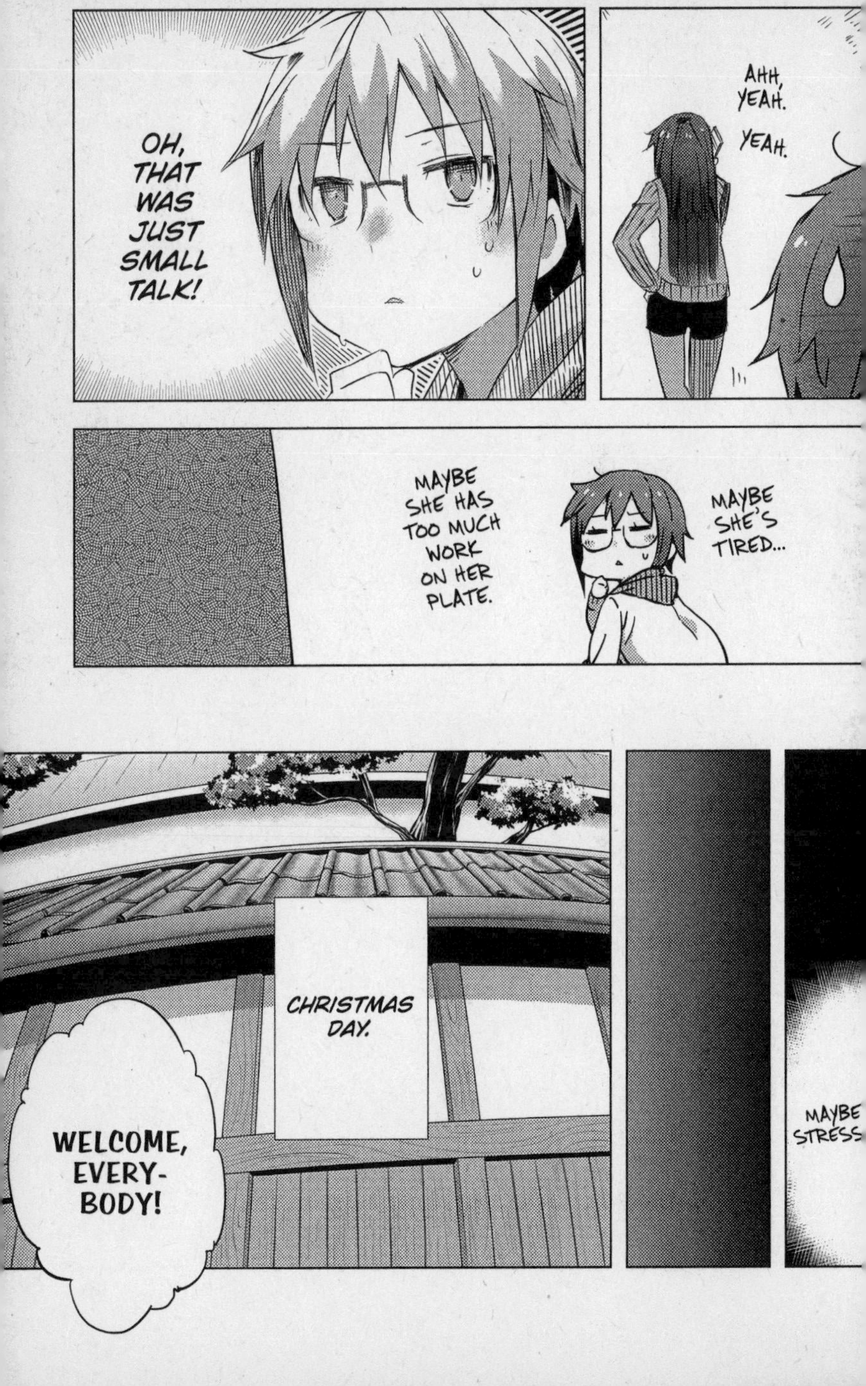
AHH, YEAH.
YEAH.
OH, THAT WAS JUST SMALL TALK!
MAYBE SHE'S TIRED...
MAYBE SHE HAS TOO MUCH WORK ON HER PLATE.
MAYBE STRESS
CHRISTMAS DAY.
WELCOME, EVERY-BODY!

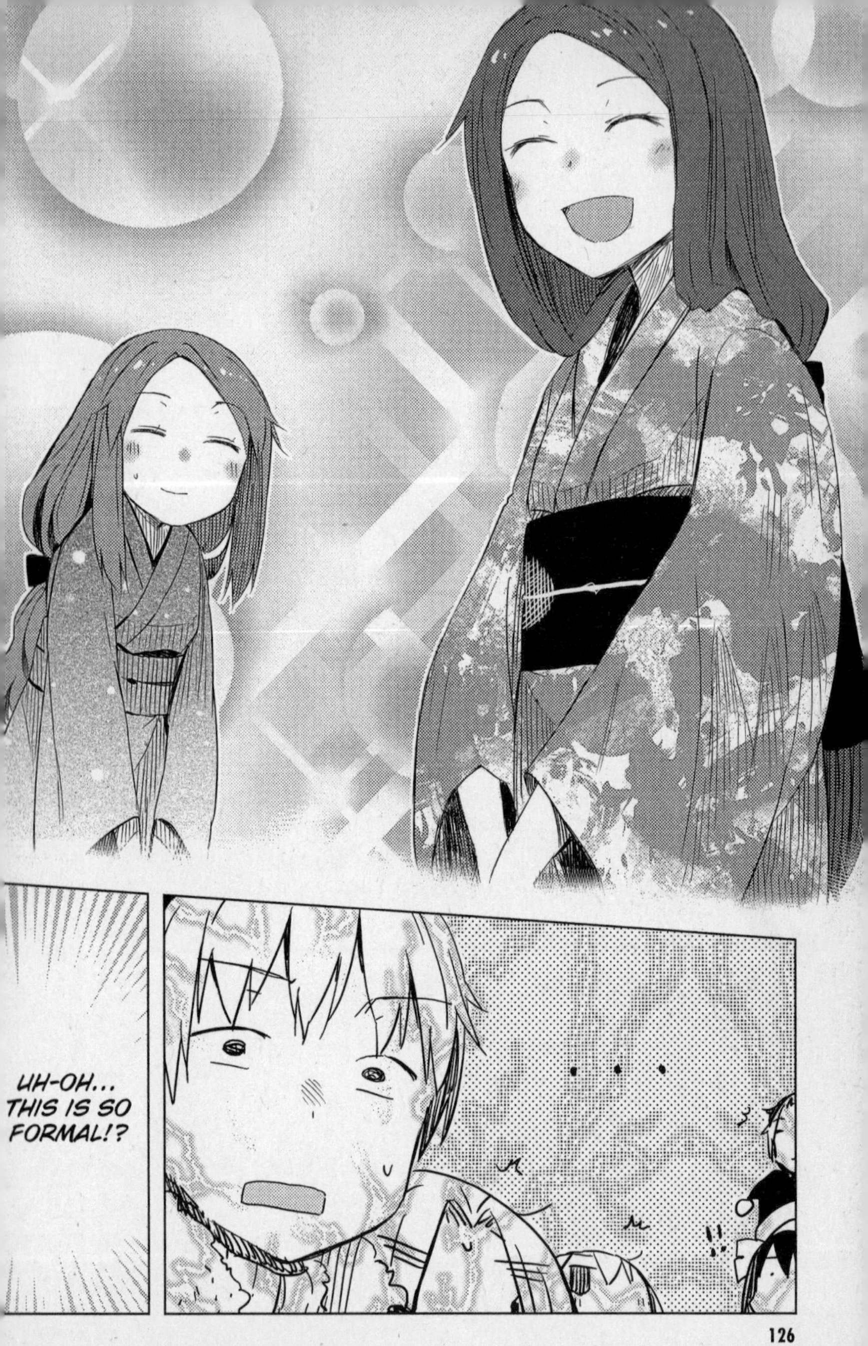
...
UH-OH... THIS IS SO FORMAL!?

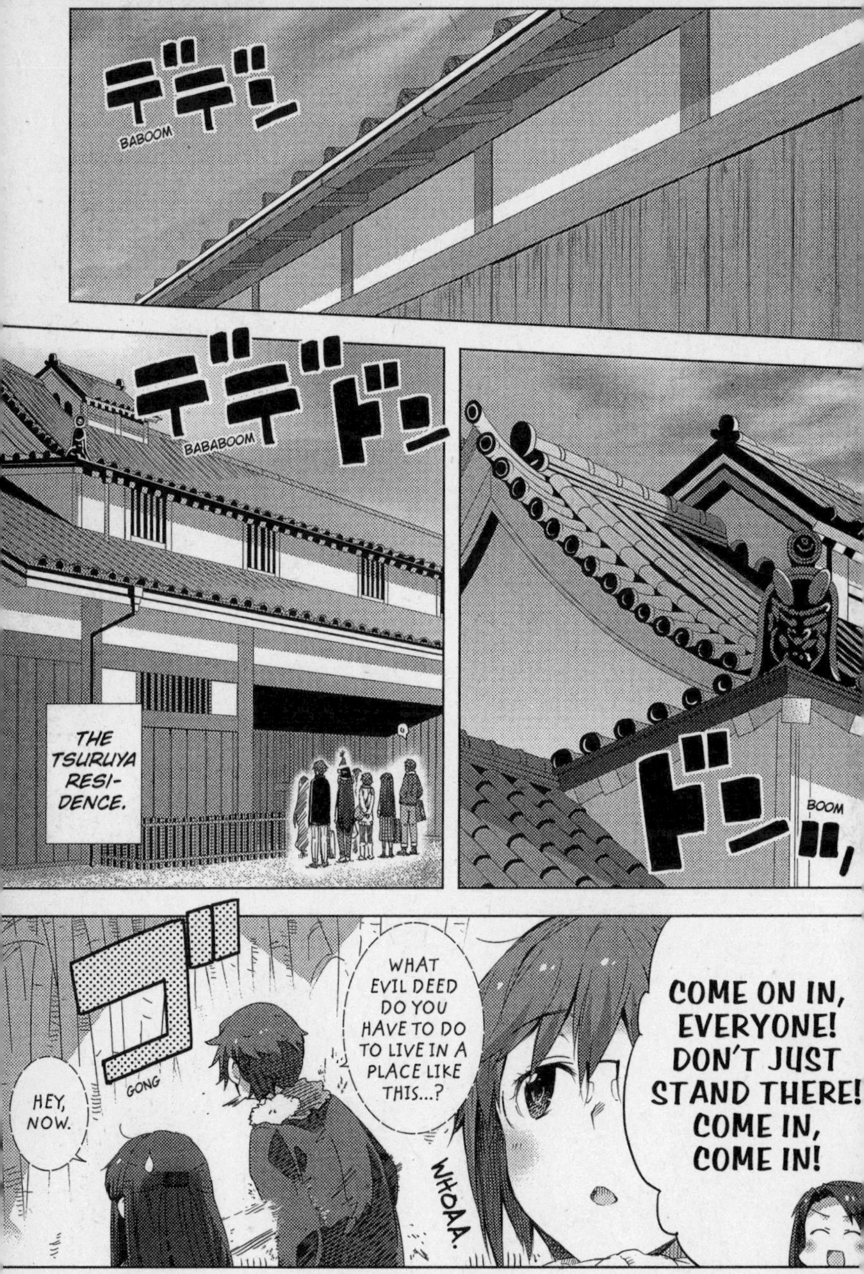
デデン
BABOOM
ドン
BOOM
デデドン
BABABOOM
THE TSURUYA RESIDENCE.
COME ON IN, EVERYONE! DON'T JUST STAND THERE! COME IN, COME IN!
WHOAA.
WHAT EVIL DEED DO YOU HAVE TO DO TO LIVE IN A PLACE LIKE THIS...?
ゴ
GONG
HEY, NOW.

## Epilogue 57>> December 24th

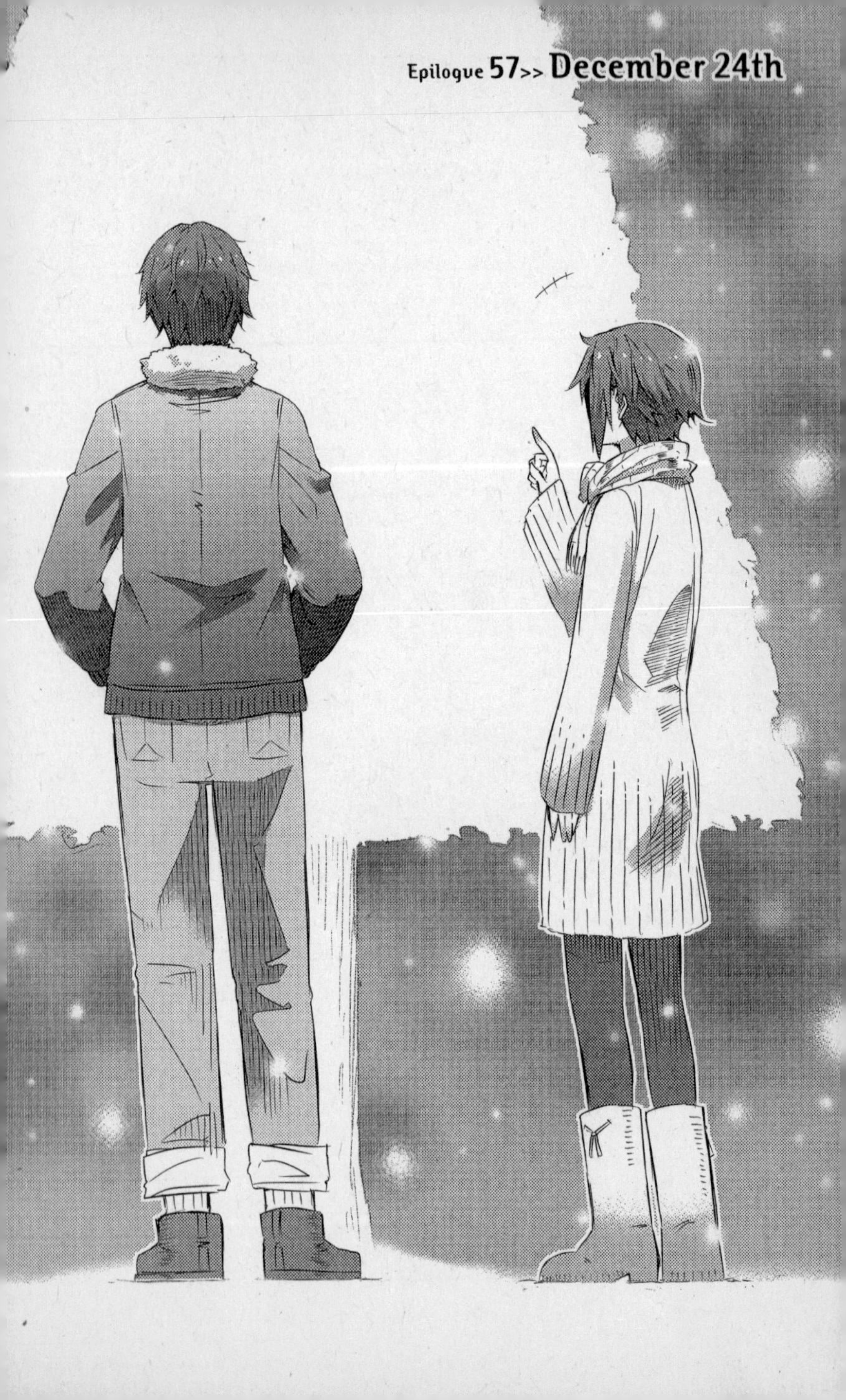

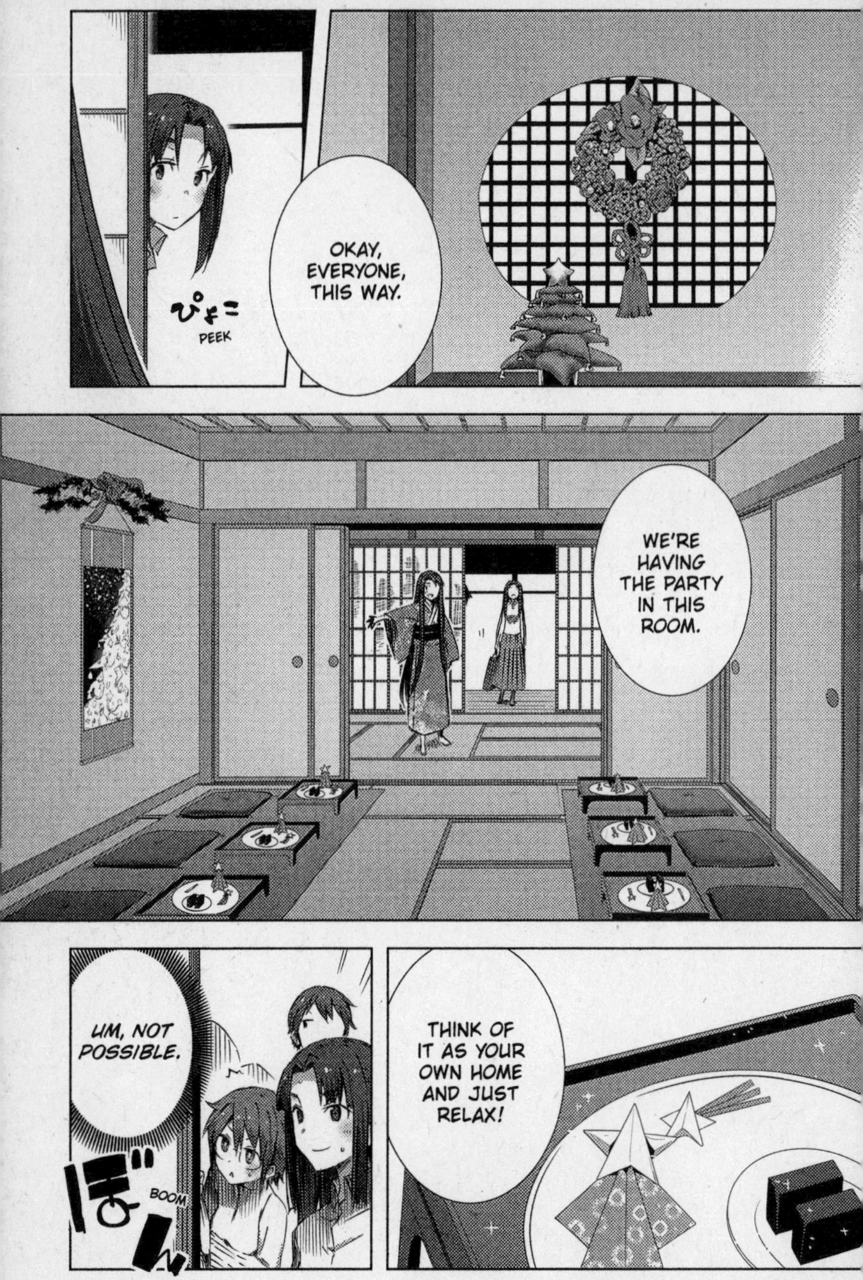
OKAY, EVERYONE, THIS WAY.
ぴょこ
PEEK
WE'RE HAVING THE PARTY IN THIS ROOM.
THINK OF IT AS YOUR OWN HOME AND JUST RELAX!
UM, NOT POSSIBLE.
ぼんっ
BOOM

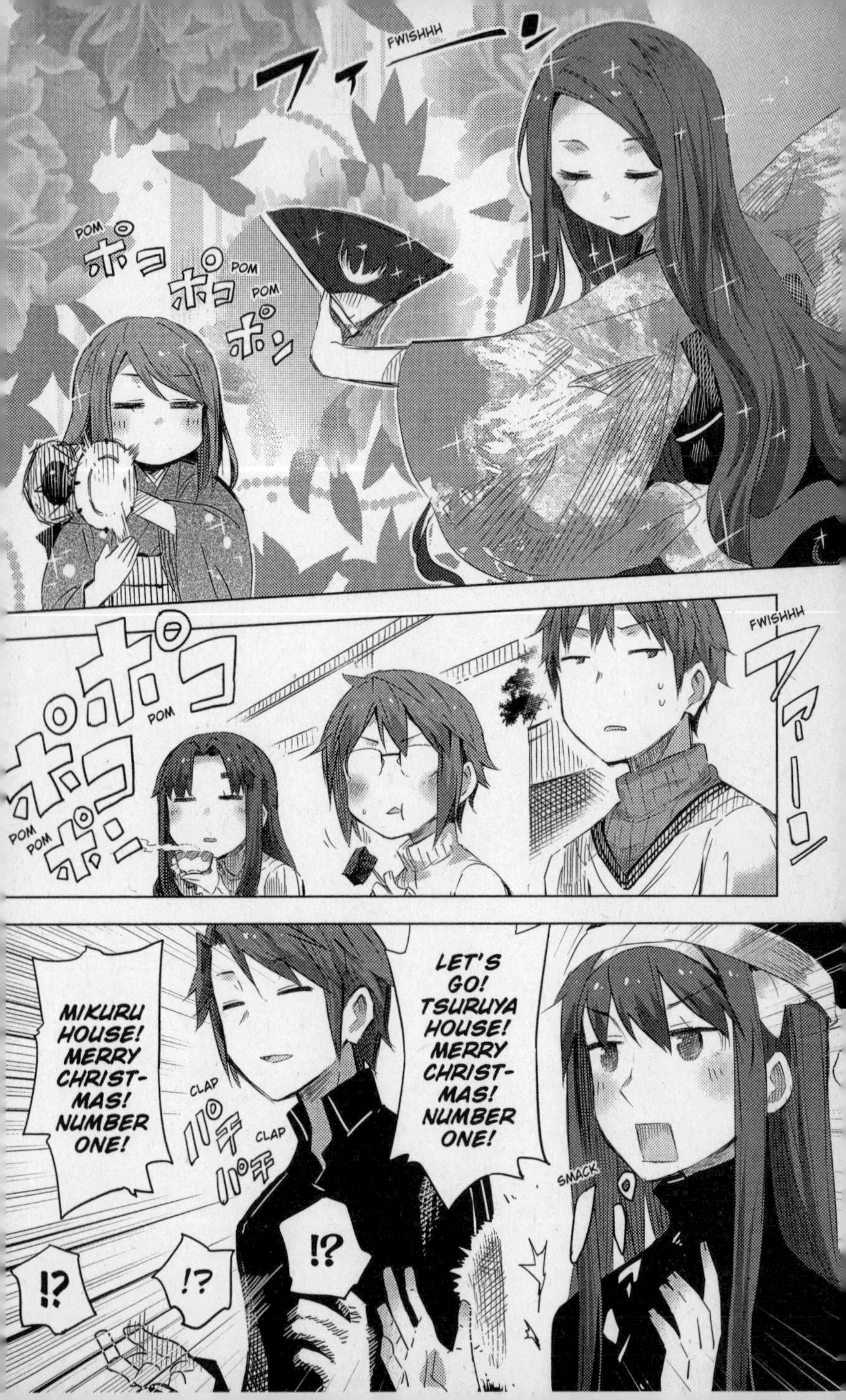
FWISHHH
POM
POM
POM
FWISHHH
POM
POM
POM
LET'S GO! TSURUYA HOUSE! MERRY CHRIST-MAS! NUMBER ONE!
SMACK
MIKURU HOUSE! MERRY CHRIST-MAS! NUMBER ONE!
CLAP
CLAP
!?
!?
!?

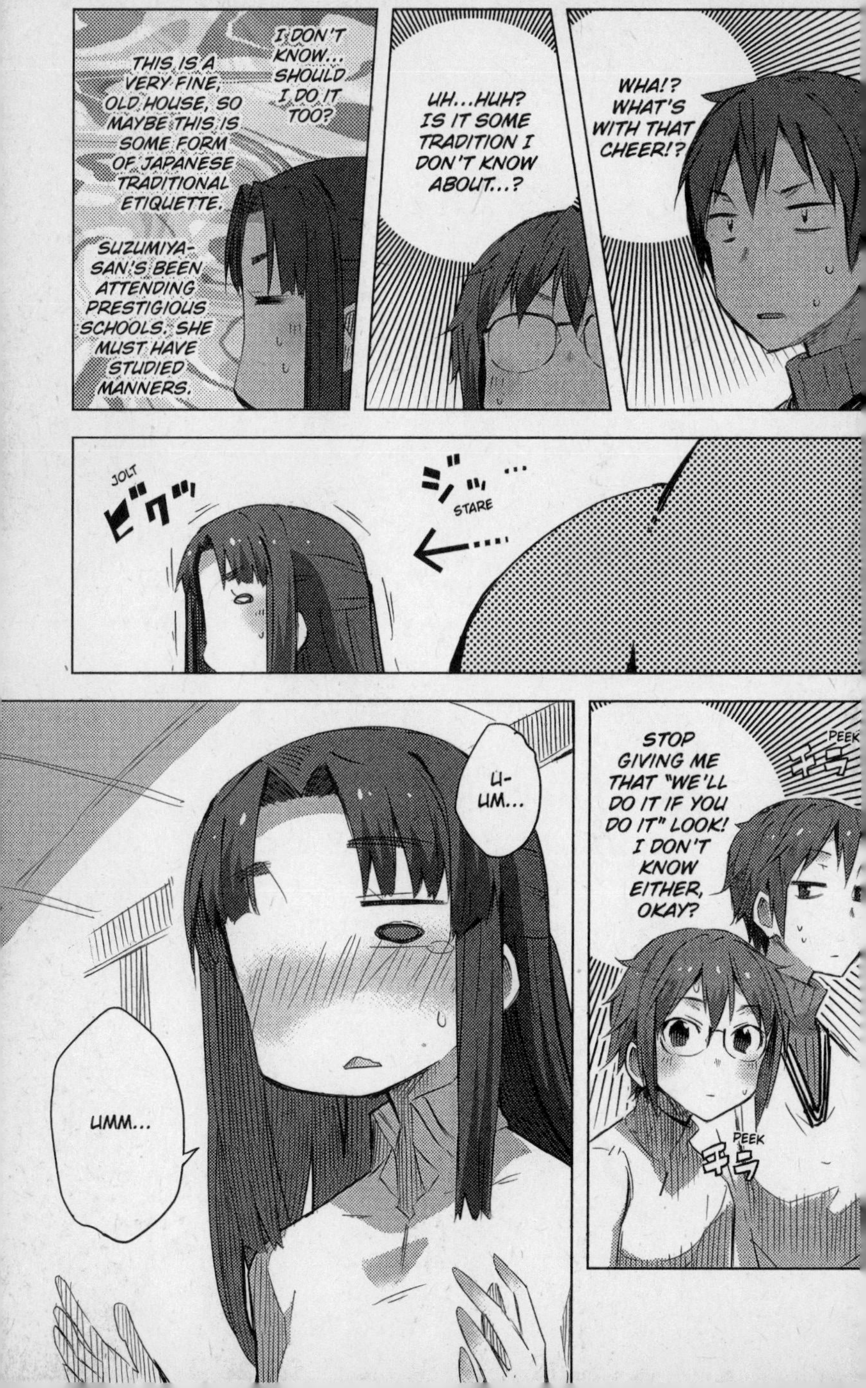
WHA!? WHAT'S WITH THAT CHEER!?
UH...HUH? IS IT SOME TRADITION I DON'T KNOW ABOUT...?
I DON'T KNOW... SHOULD I DO IT TOO?
THIS IS A VERY FINE, OLD HOUSE, SO MAYBE THIS IS SOME FORM OF JAPANESE TRADITIONAL ETIQUETTE.
SUZUMIYA-SAN'S BEEN ATTENDING PRESTIGIOUS SCHOOLS. SHE MUST HAVE STUDIED MANNERS.
...
ジッ
STARE
ビクッ
JOLT
PEEK
チラ
STOP GIVING ME THAT "WE'LL DO IT IF YOU DO IT" LOOK! I DON'T KNOW EITHER, OKAY?
PEEK
チラ
U-UM...
UMM...

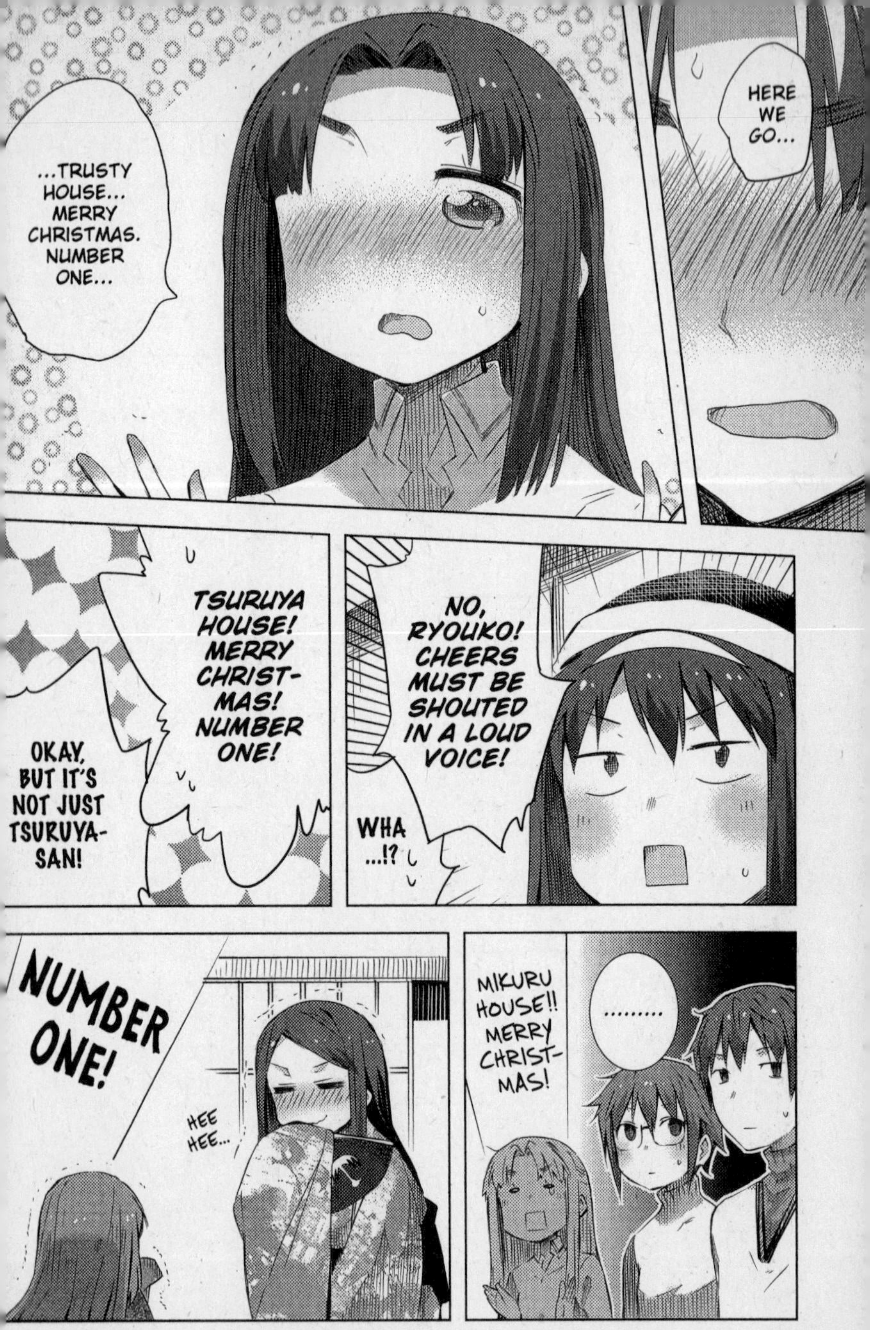
HERE WE GO...
...TRUSTY HOUSE... MERRY CHRISTMAS. NUMBER ONE...
NO, RYOUKO! CHEERS MUST BE SHOUTED IN A LOUD VOICE!
WHA ...!?
TSURUYA HOUSE! MERRY CHRIST-MAS! NUMBER ONE!
OKAY, BUT IT'S NOT JUST TSURUYA-SAN!
.........
MIKURU HOUSE!! MERRY CHRIST-MAS!
NUMBER ONE!
HEE HEE...

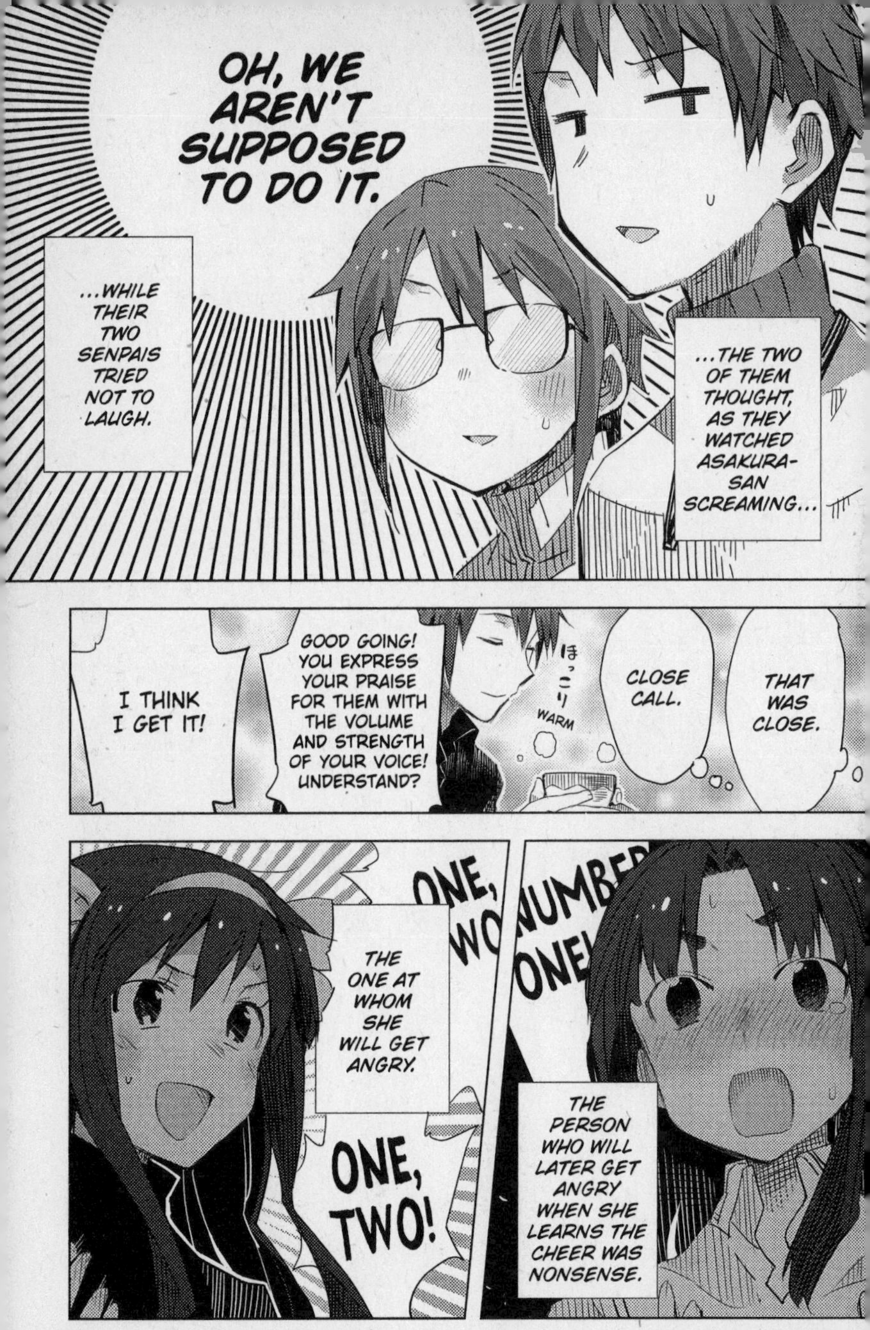
OH, WE AREN'T SUPPOSED TO DO IT.
...THE TWO OF THEM THOUGHT, AS THEY WATCHED ASAKURA-SAN SCREAMING...
...WHILE THEIR TWO SENPAIS TRIED NOT TO LAUGH.
THAT WAS CLOSE.
CLOSE CALL.
ほっこり
WARM
GOOD GOING! YOU EXPRESS YOUR PRAISE FOR THEM WITH THE VOLUME AND STRENGTH OF YOUR VOICE! UNDERSTAND?
I THINK I GET IT!
THE PERSON WHO WILL LATER GET ANGRY WHEN SHE LEARNS THE CHEER WAS NONSENSE.
THE ONE AT WHOM SHE WILL GET ANGRY.
ONE, TWO!

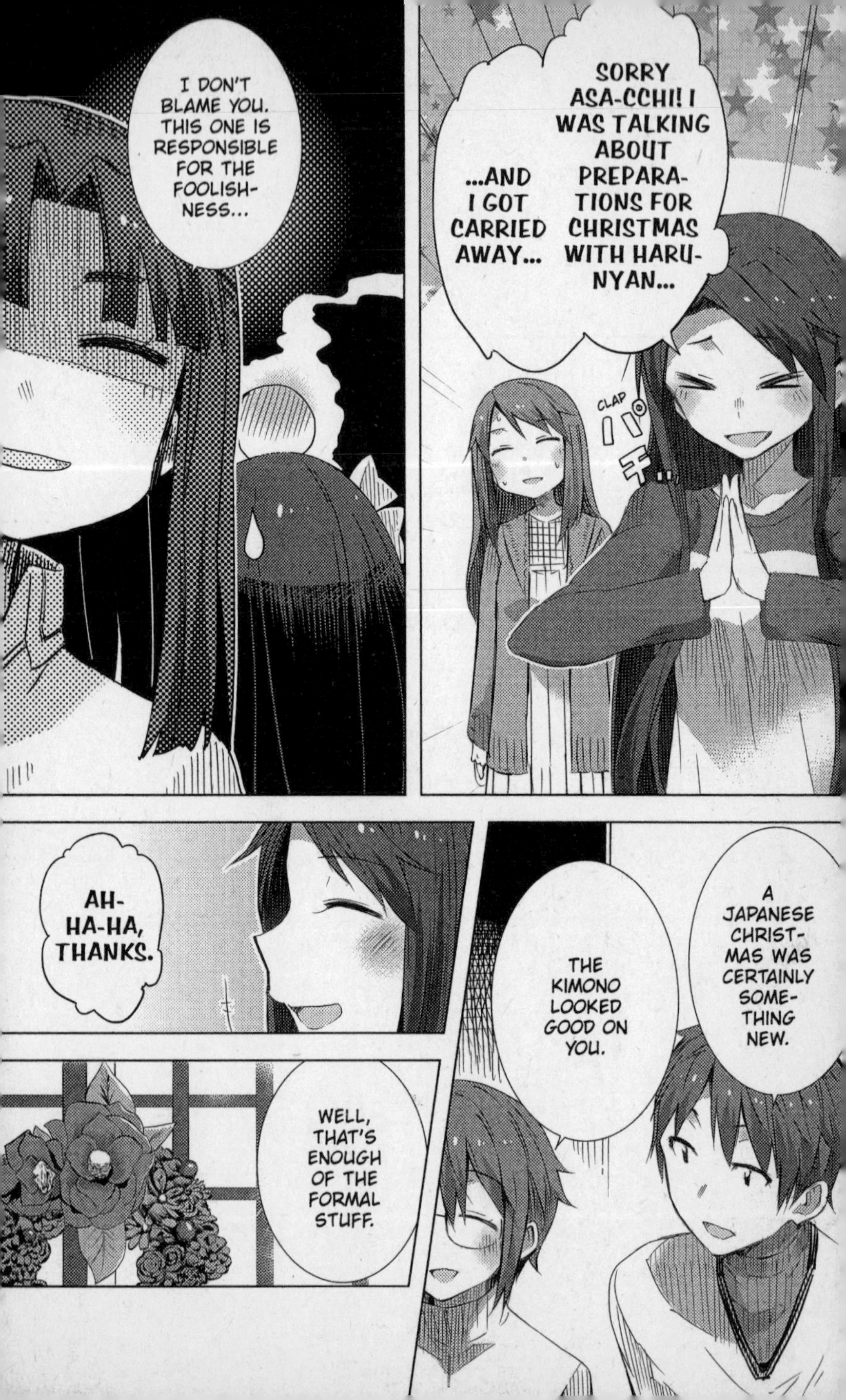
SORRY ASA-CCHI! I WAS TALKING ABOUT PREPARATIONS FOR CHRISTMAS WITH HARU-NYAN...
...AND I GOT CARRIED AWAY...
CLAP
I DON'T BLAME YOU. THIS ONE IS RESPONSIBLE FOR THE FOOLISHNESS...
A JAPANESE CHRISTMAS WAS CERTAINLY SOMETHING NEW.
THE KIMONO LOOKED GOOD ON YOU.
AH-HA-HA, THANKS.
WELL, THAT'S ENOUGH OF THE FORMAL STUFF.

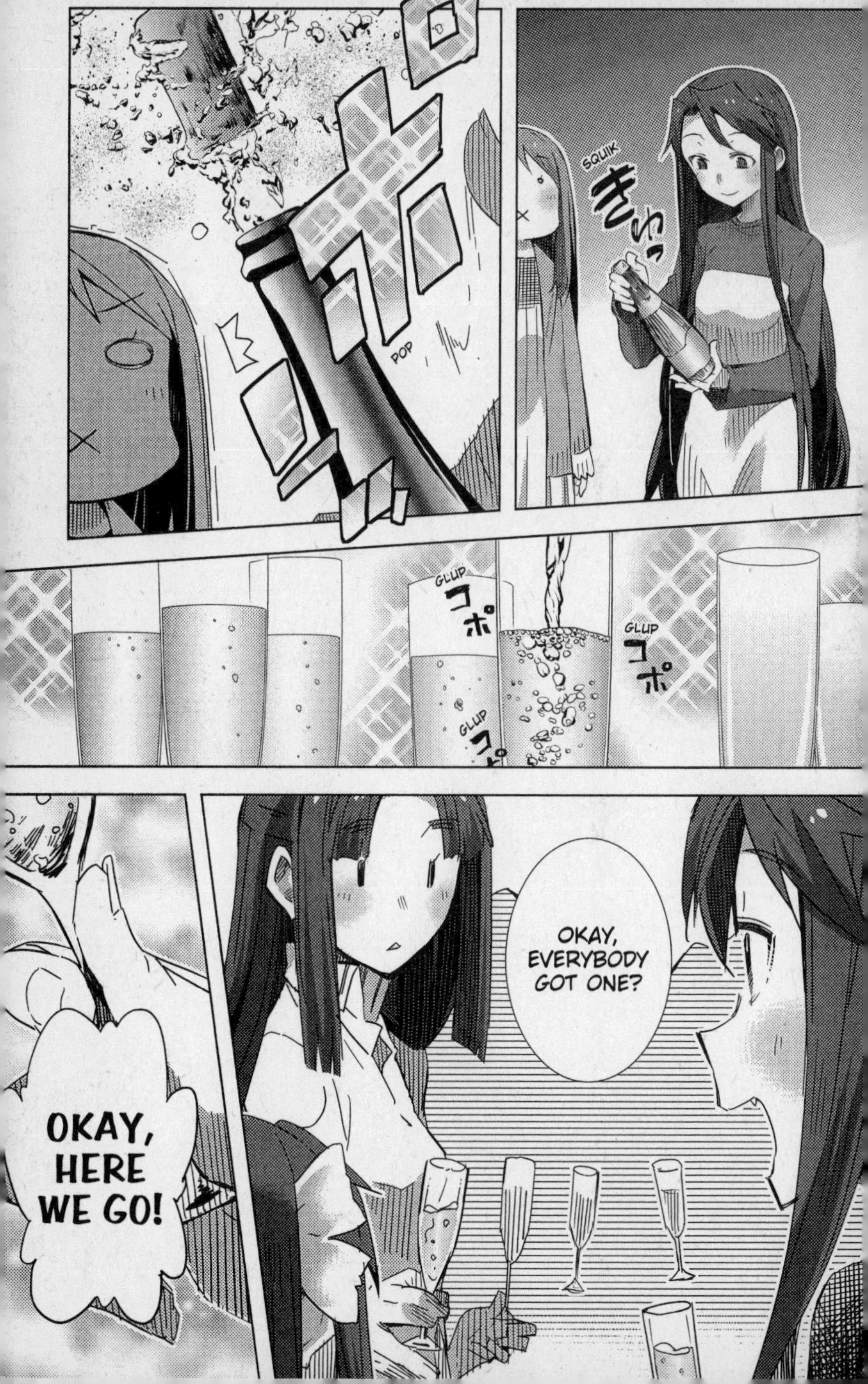
SQUIK
きゅっ
POP
GLUP
コポ
GLUP
コポ
GLUP
OKAY, EVERYBODY GOT ONE?
OKAY, HERE WE GO!

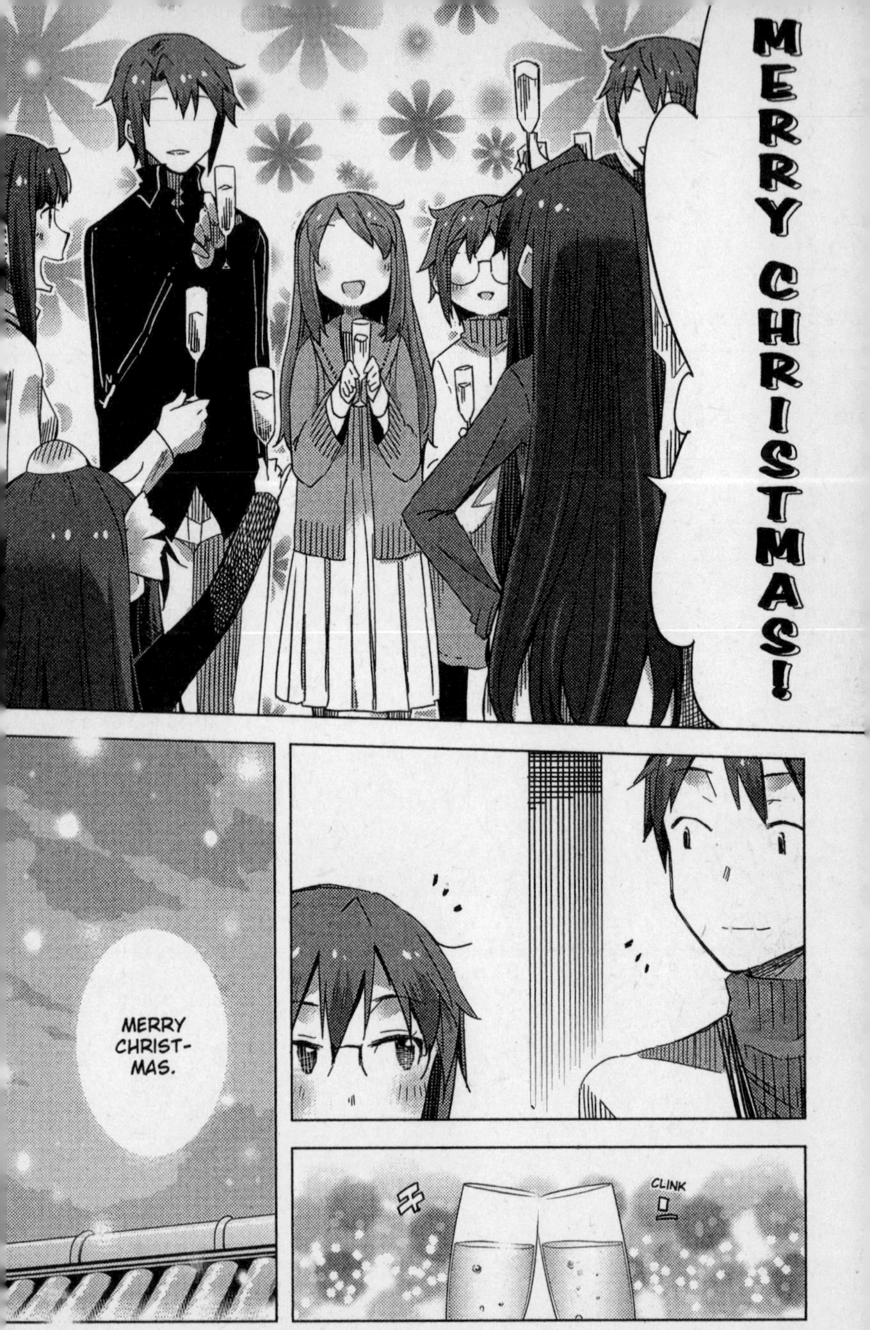
MERRY CHRISTMAS!
チ
CLINK
MERRY CHRIST-MAS.

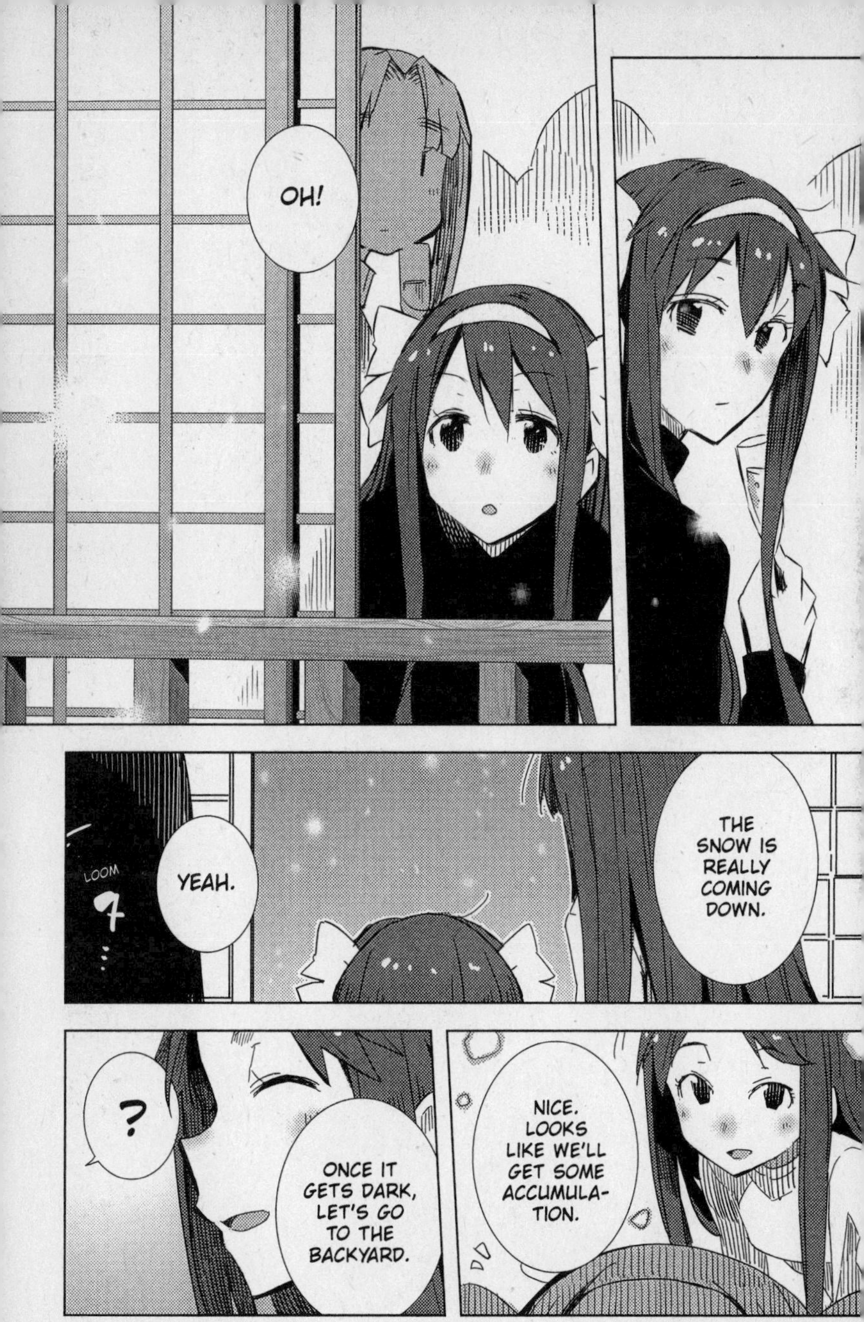
OH!
THE SNOW IS REALLY COMING DOWN.
YEAH.
LOOM
NICE. LOOKS LIKE WE'LL GET SOME ACCUMULA-TION.
ONCE IT GETS DARK, LET'S GO TO THE BACKYARD.
?

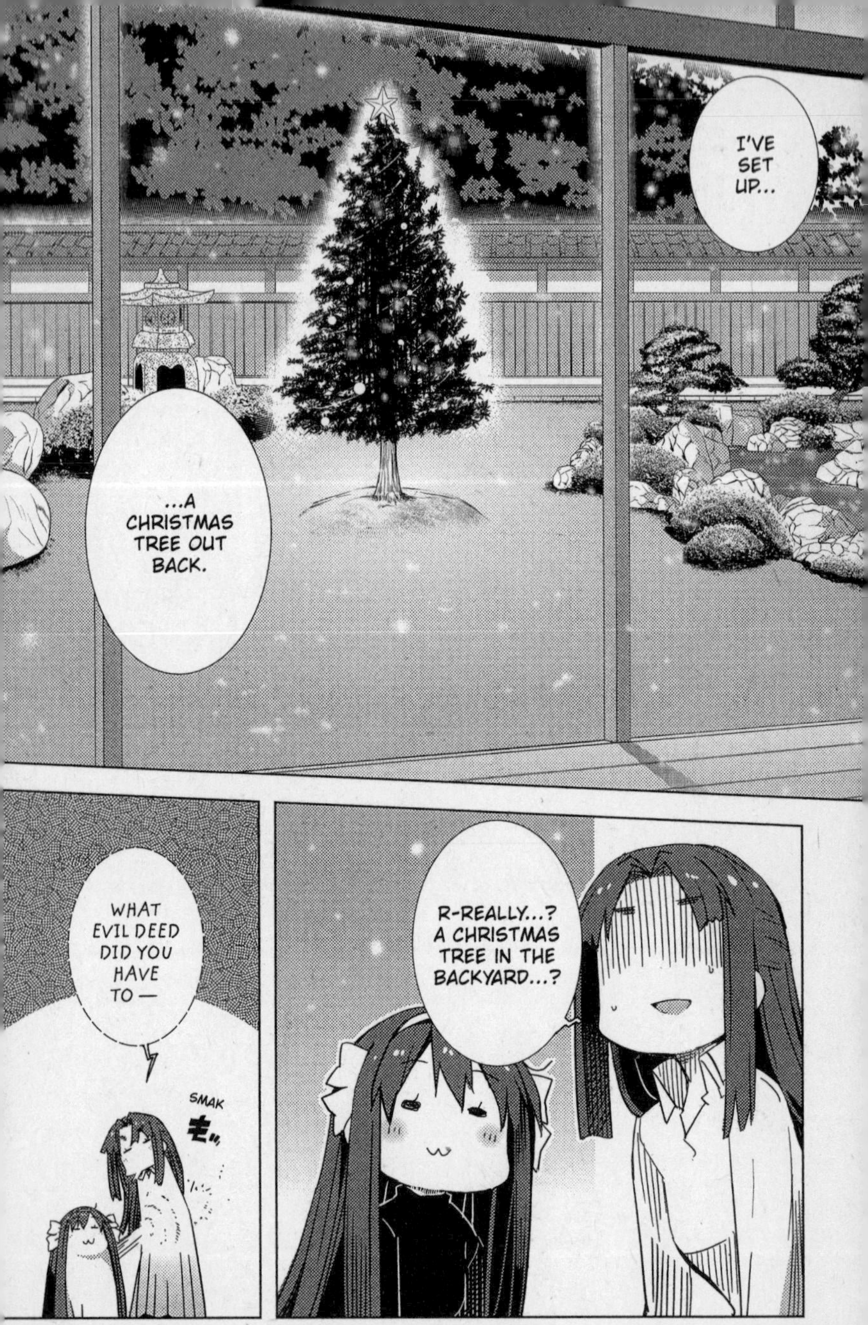
I'VE SET UP...
...A CHRISTMAS TREE OUT BACK.
R-REALLY...? A CHRISTMAS TREE IN THE BACKYARD...?
WHAT EVIL DEED DID YOU HAVE TO—
SMAK

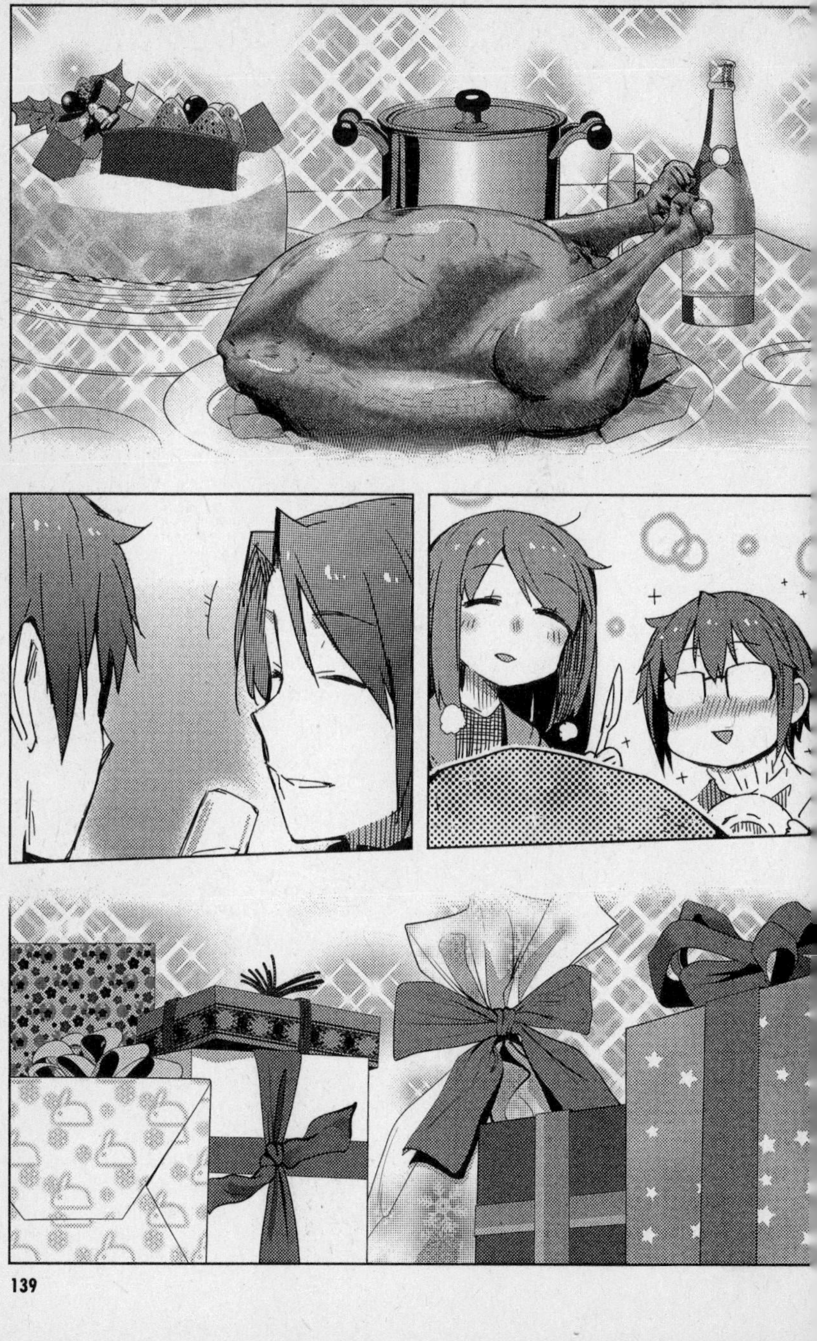

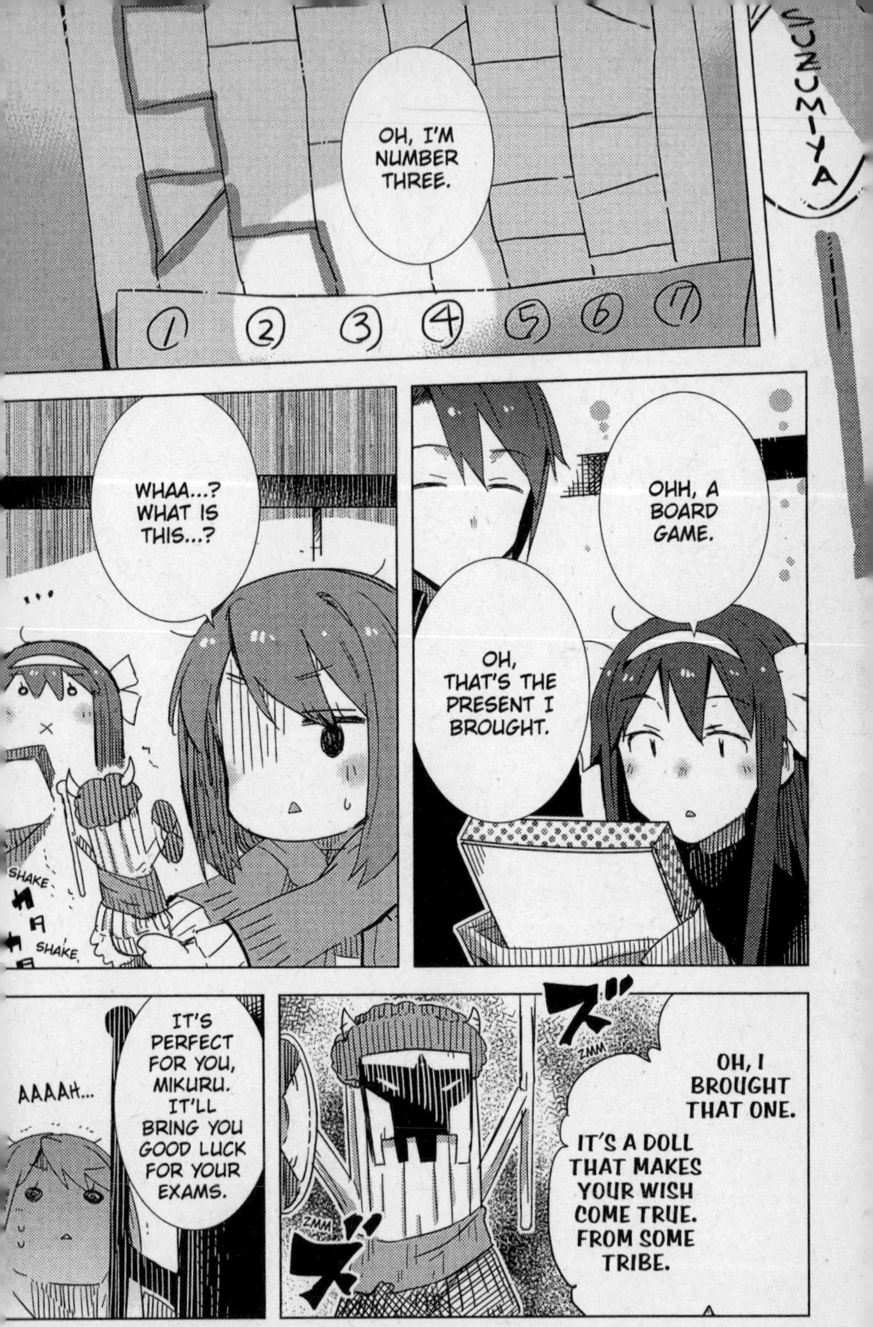
SUZUMIYA
OH, I'M NUMBER THREE.
OHH, A BOARD GAME.
OH, THAT'S THE PRESENT I BROUGHT.
WHAA...? WHAT IS THIS...?
...
SHAKE
SHAKE
ZMM
OH, I BROUGHT THAT ONE.
IT'S A DOLL THAT MAKES YOUR WISH COME TRUE. FROM SOME TRIBE.
ZMM
IT'S PERFECT FOR YOU, MIKURU. IT'LL BRING YOU GOOD LUCK FOR YOUR EXAMS.
AAAAH...

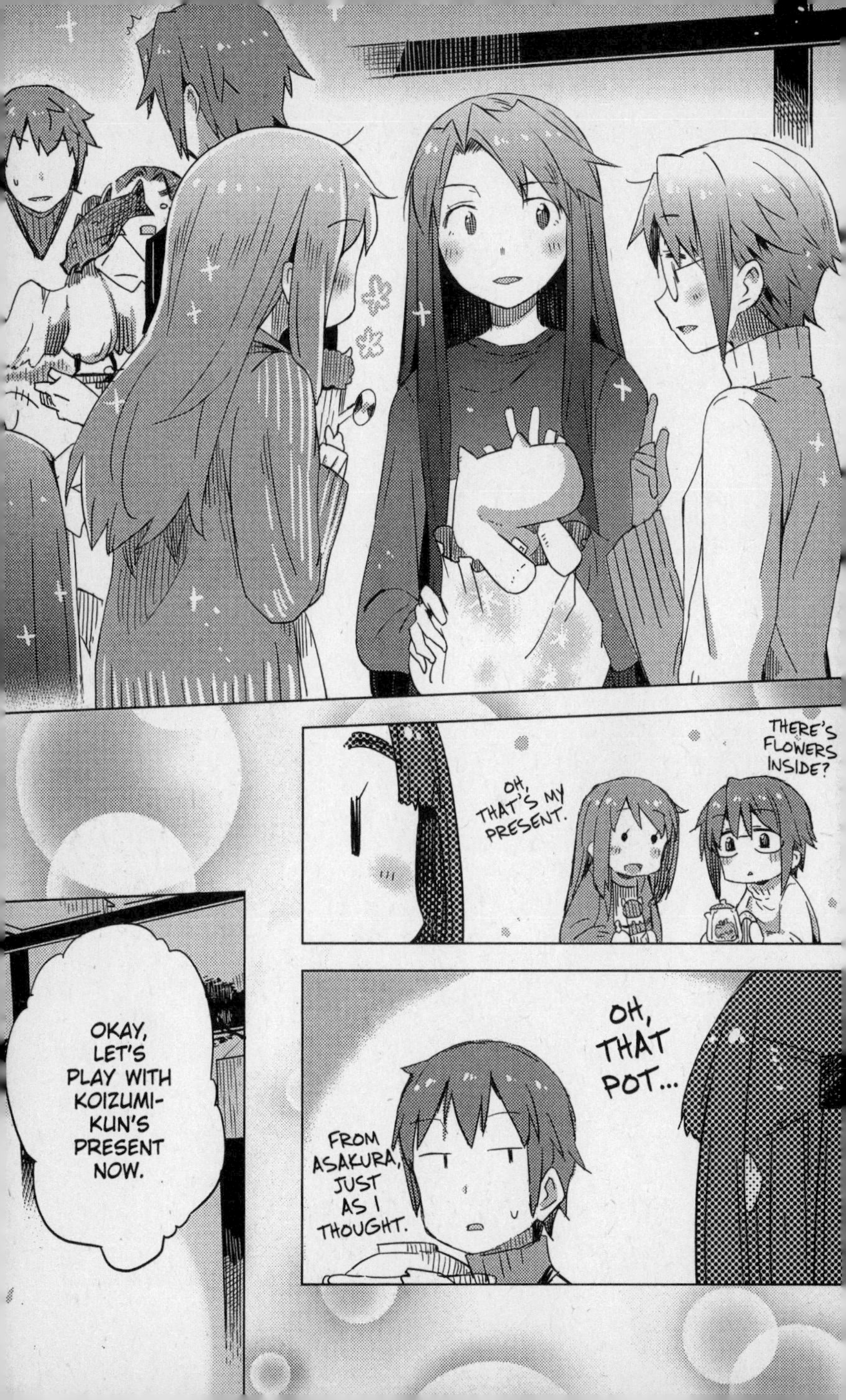
THERE'S FLOWERS INSIDE?
OH, THAT'S MY PRESENT.
OH, THAT POT...
FROM ASAKURA, JUST AS I THOUGHT.
OKAY, LET'S PLAY WITH KOIZUMI-KUN'S PRESENT NOW.

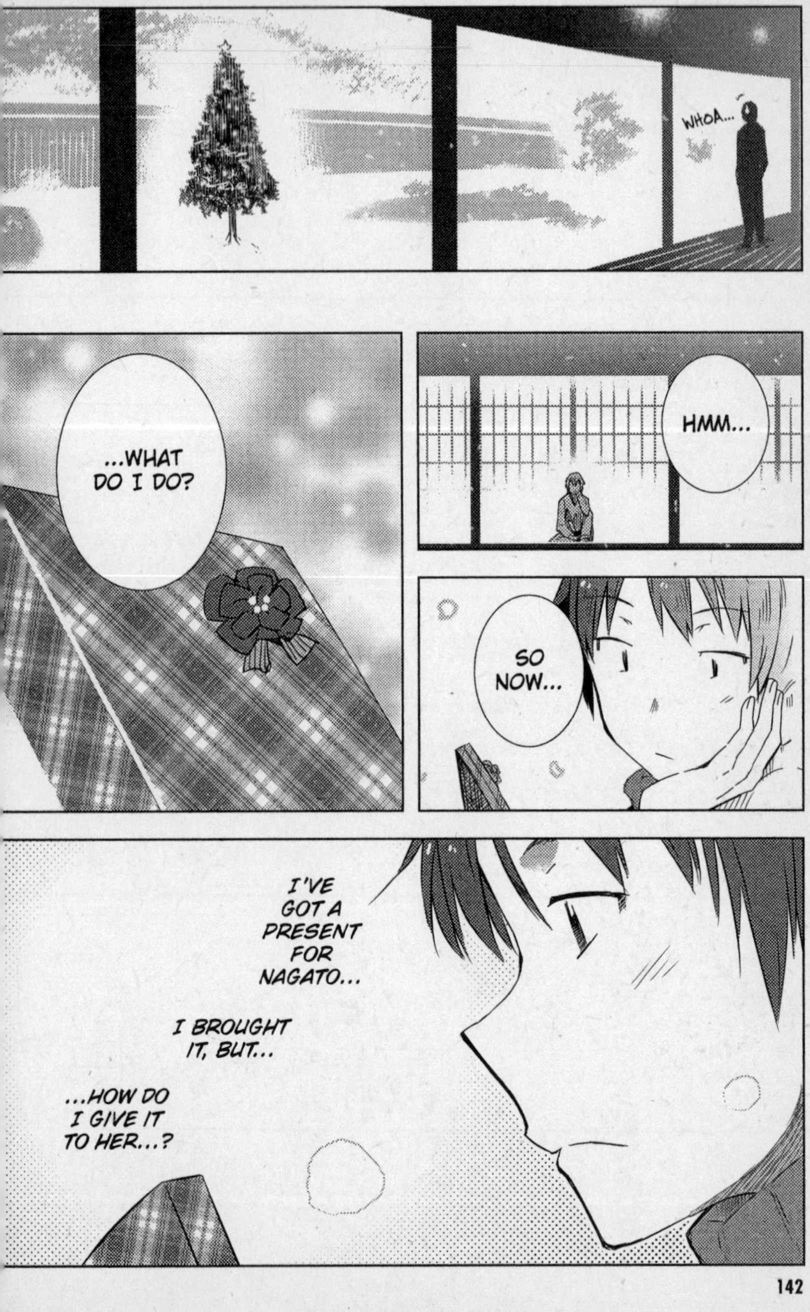
WHOA...
HMM...
SO NOW...
...WHAT DO I DO?
I'VE GOT A PRESENT FOR NAGATO...
I BROUGHT IT, BUT...
...HOW DO I GIVE IT TO HER...?

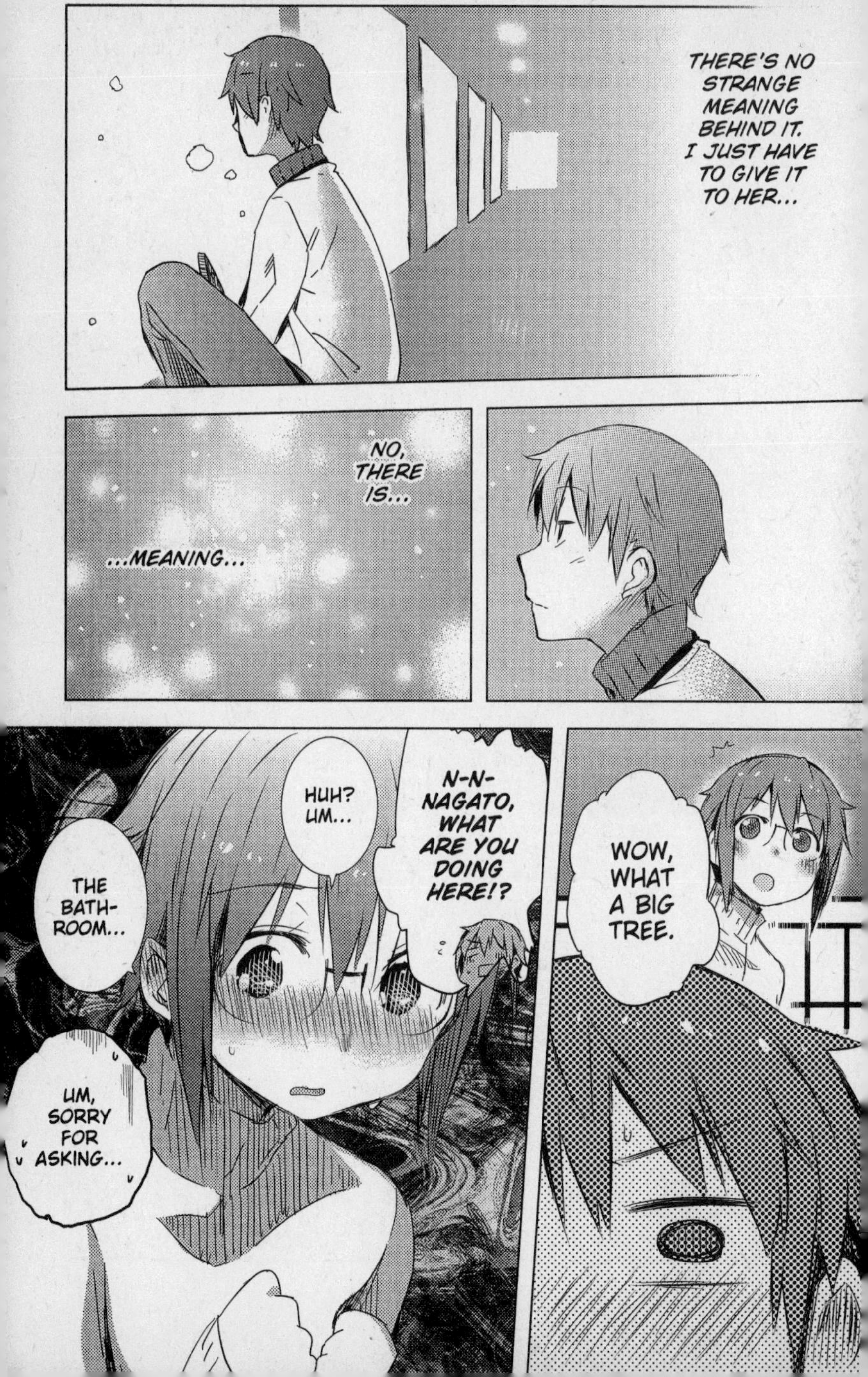
THERE'S NO STRANGE MEANING BEHIND IT. I JUST HAVE TO GIVE IT TO HER...
NO, THERE IS...
...MEANING...
WOW, WHAT A BIG TREE.
N-N-NAGATO, WHAT ARE YOU DOING HERE!?
HUH? UM...
THE BATHROOM...
UM, SORRY FOR ASKING...

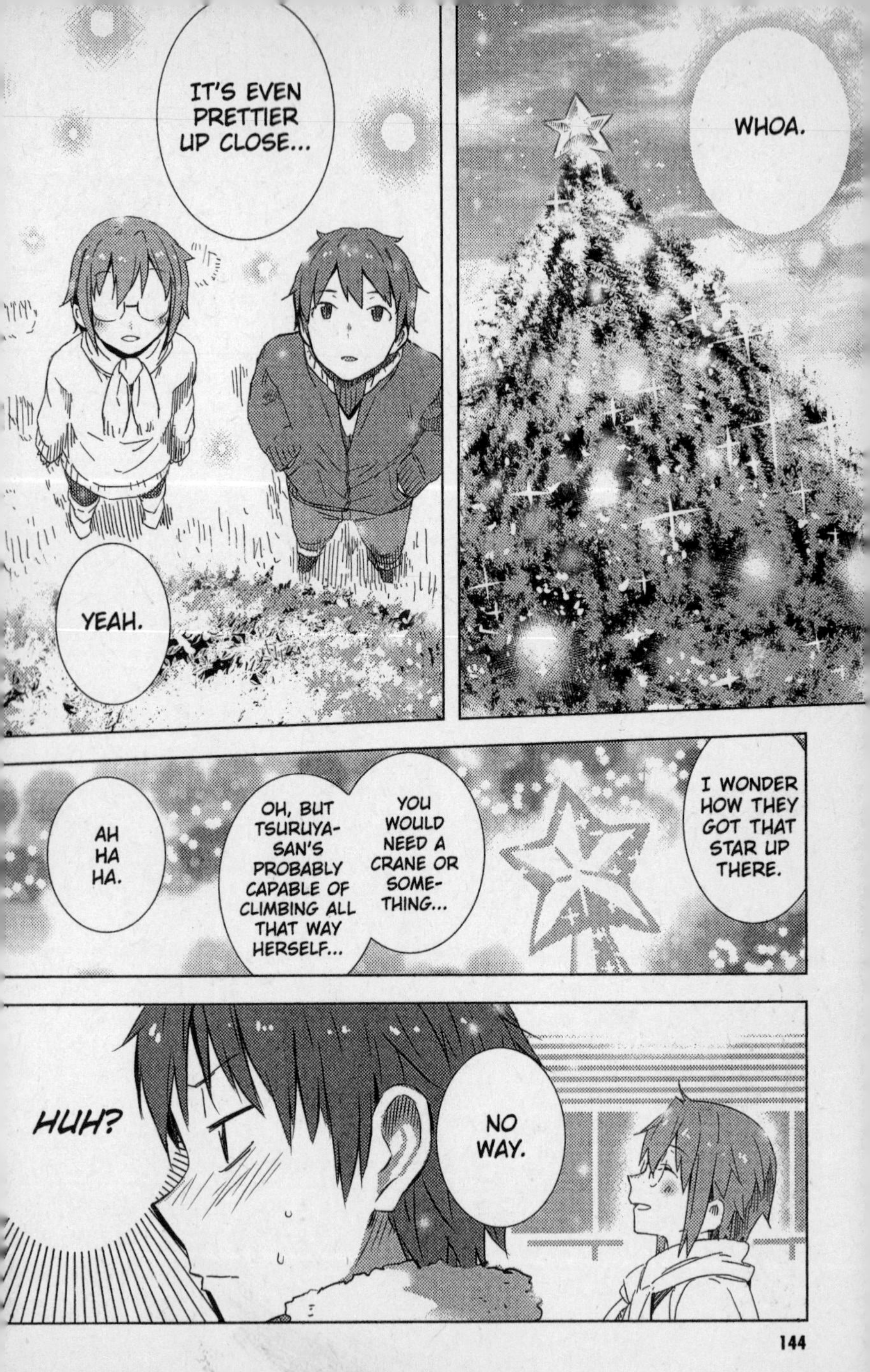
WHOA.
IT'S EVEN PRETTIER UP CLOSE...
YEAH.
I WONDER HOW THEY GOT THAT STAR UP THERE.
YOU WOULD NEED A CRANE OR SOME-THING...
OH, BUT TSURUYA-SAN'S PROBABLY CAPABLE OF CLIMBING ALL THAT WAY HERSELF...
AH HA HA.
NO WAY.
HUH?

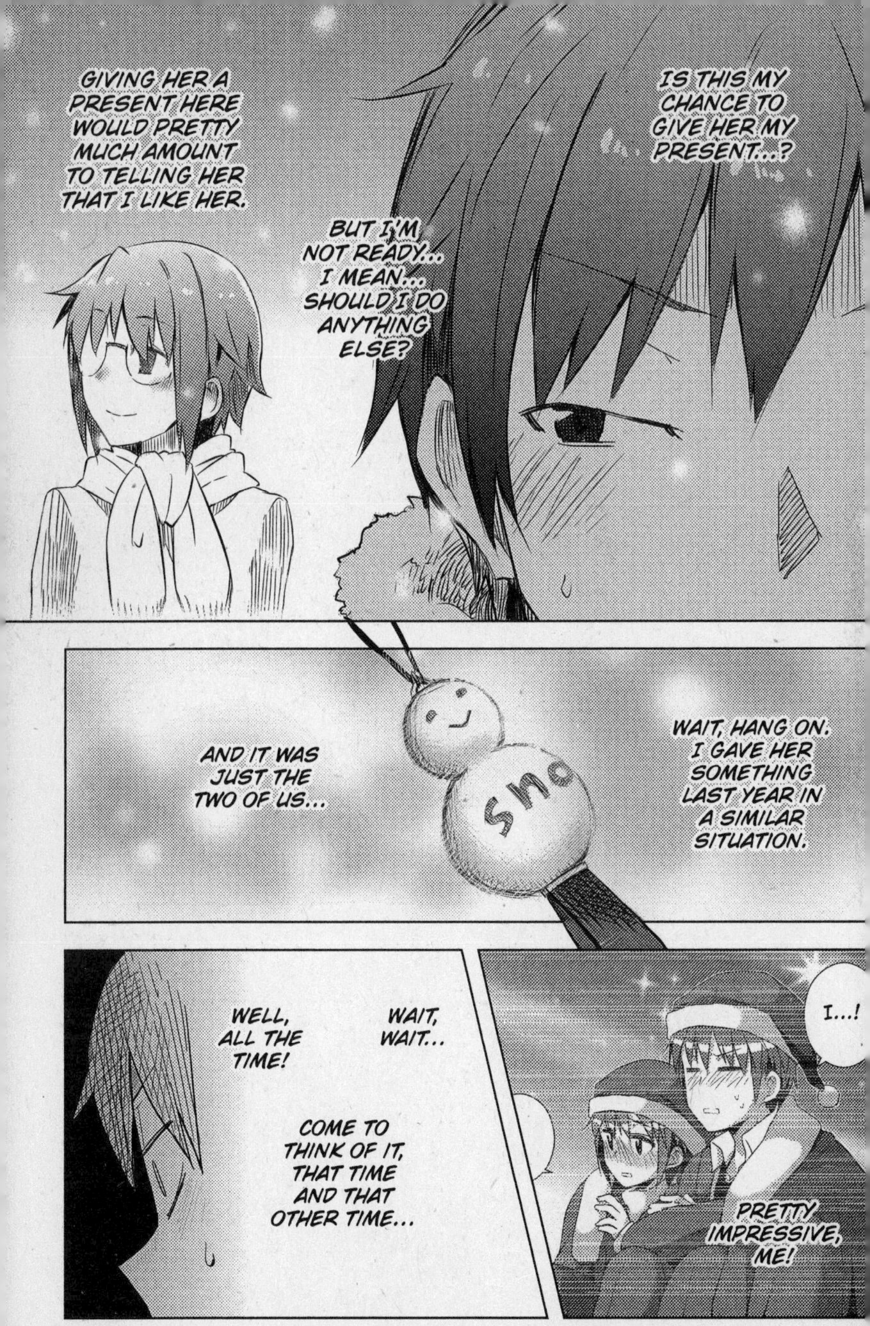
IS THIS MY CHANCE TO GIVE HER MY PRESENT...?
GIVING HER A PRESENT HERE WOULD PRETTY MUCH AMOUNT TO TELLING HER THAT I LIKE HER.
BUT I'M NOT READY... I MEAN... SHOULD I DO ANYTHING ELSE?
WAIT, HANG ON. I GAVE HER SOMETHING LAST YEAR IN A SIMILAR SITUATION.
AND IT WAS JUST THE TWO OF US...
I...!
PRETTY IMPRESSIVE, ME!
WAIT, WAIT...
WELL, ALL THE TIME!
COME TO THINK OF IT, THAT TIME AND THAT OTHER TIME...

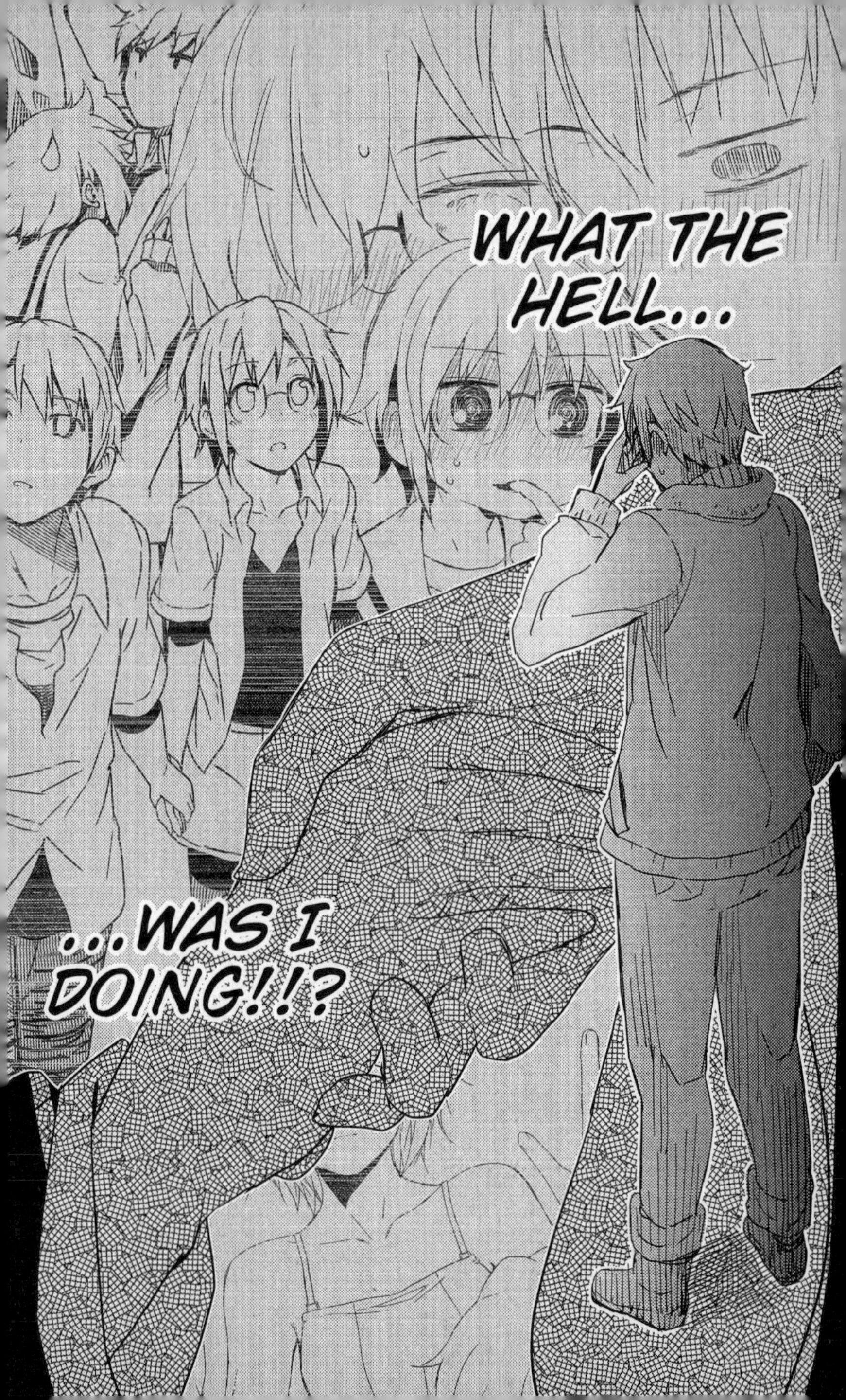
WHAT THE HELL...
...WAS I DOING!!?

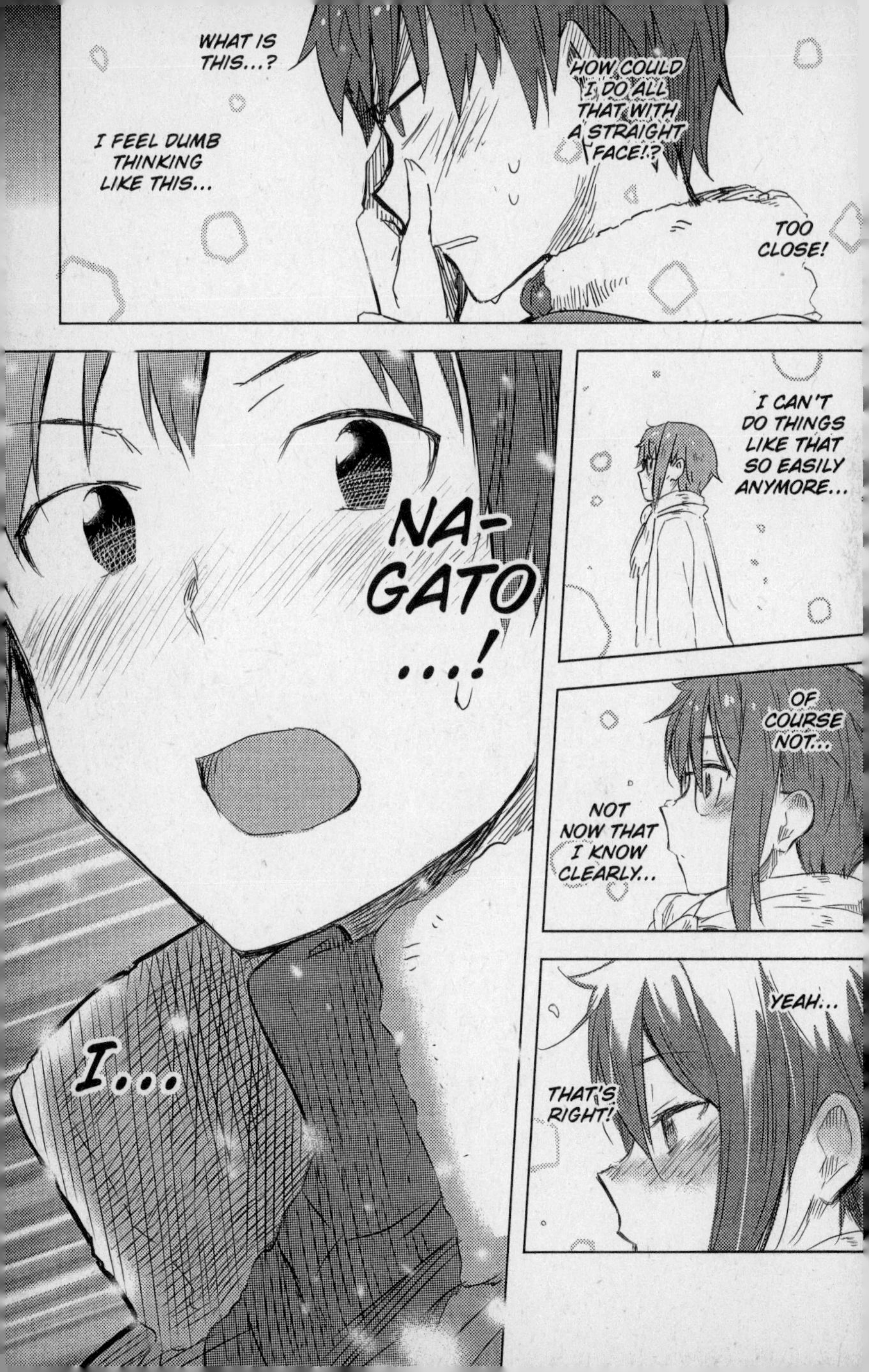
HOW COULD I DO ALL THAT WITH A STRAIGHT FACE!?
WHAT IS THIS...?
TOO CLOSE!
I FEEL DUMB THINKING LIKE THIS...
I CAN'T DO THINGS LIKE THAT SO EASILY ANYMORE...
OF COURSE NOT...
NOT NOW THAT I KNOW CLEARLY...
YEAH...
THAT'S RIGHT!
NA-GATO...!
I...

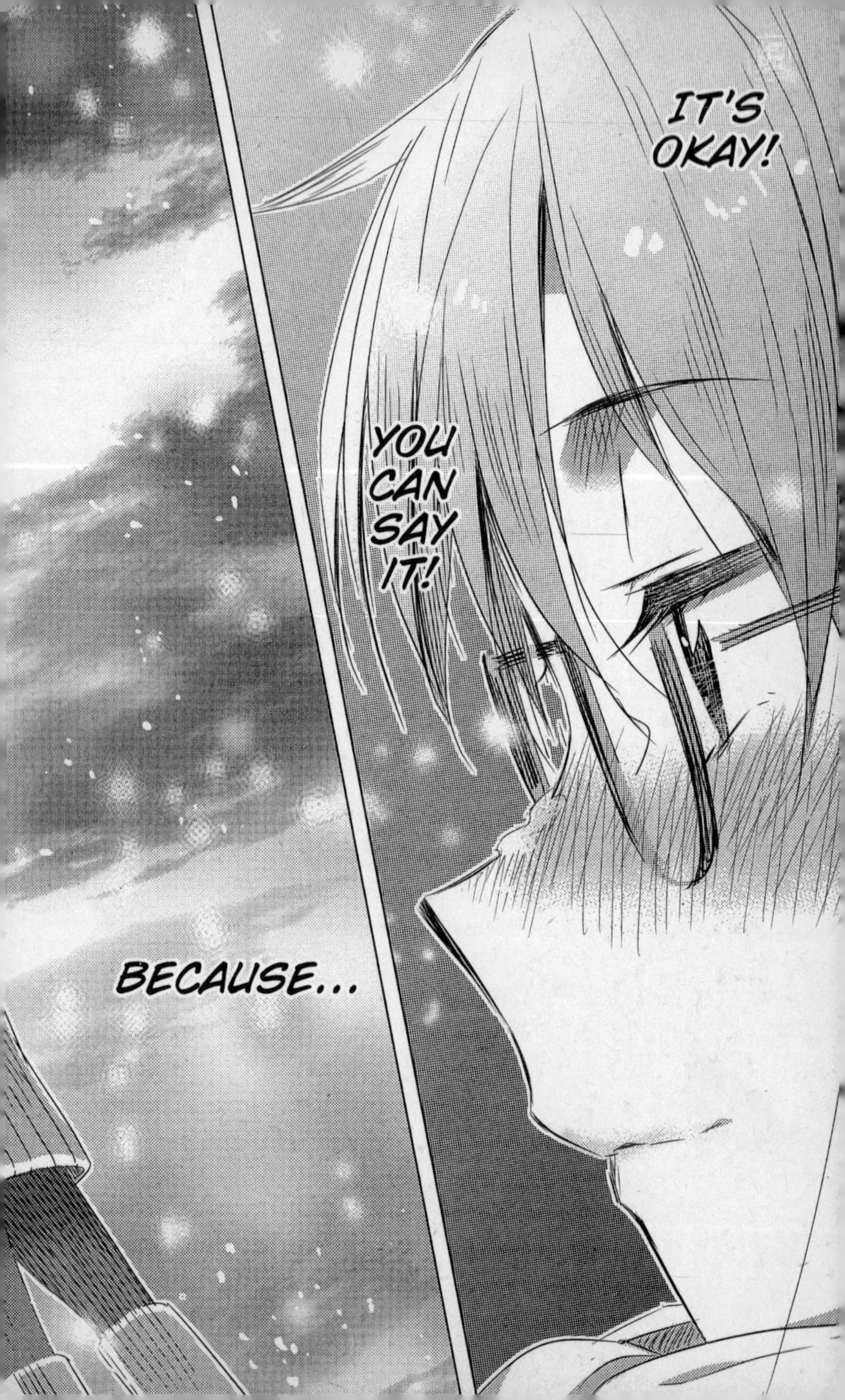
IT'S OKAY!
YOU CAN SAY IT!
BECAUSE...

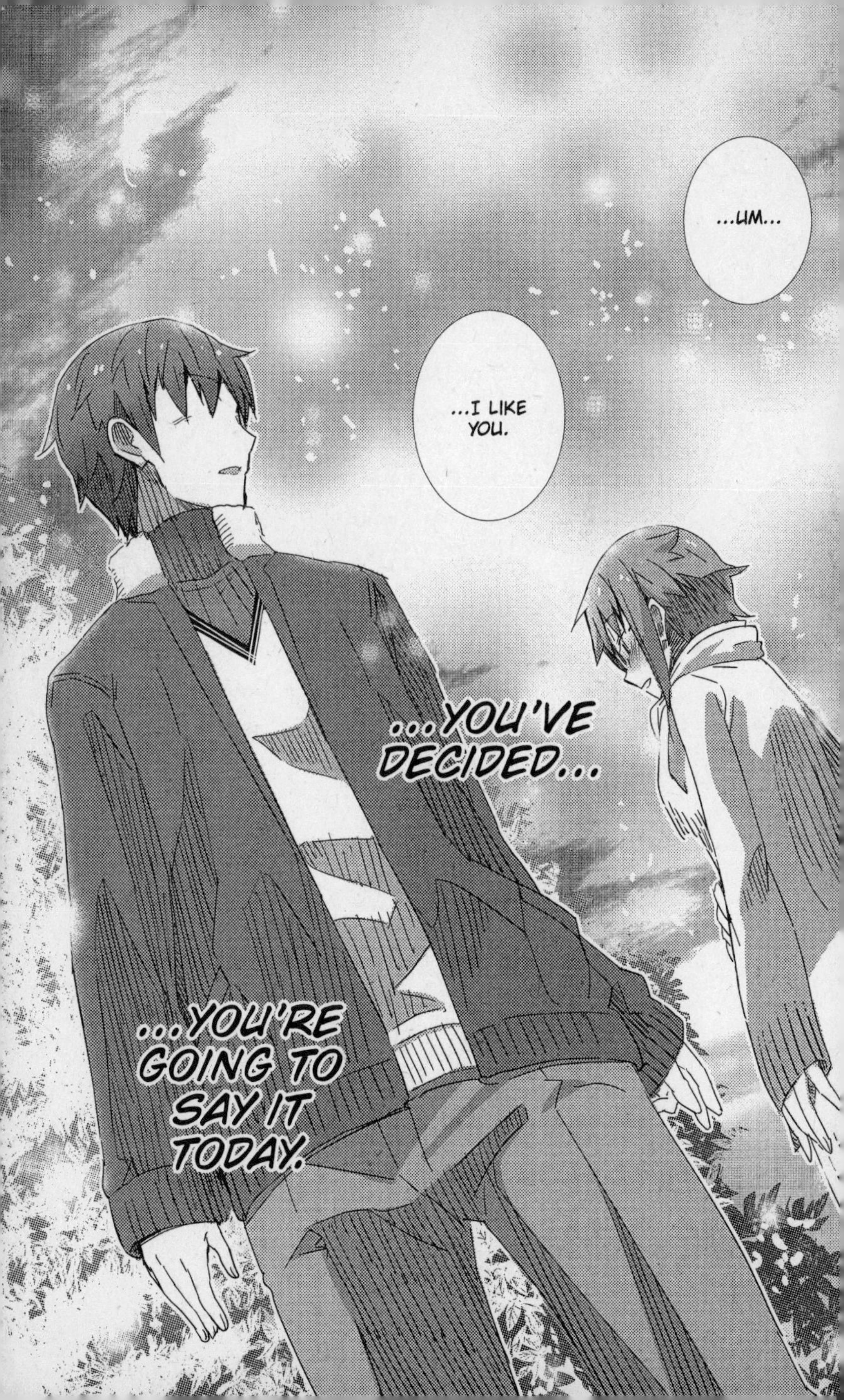
...UM...
...I LIKE YOU.
...YOU'VE DECIDED...
...YOU'RE GOING TO SAY IT TODAY.

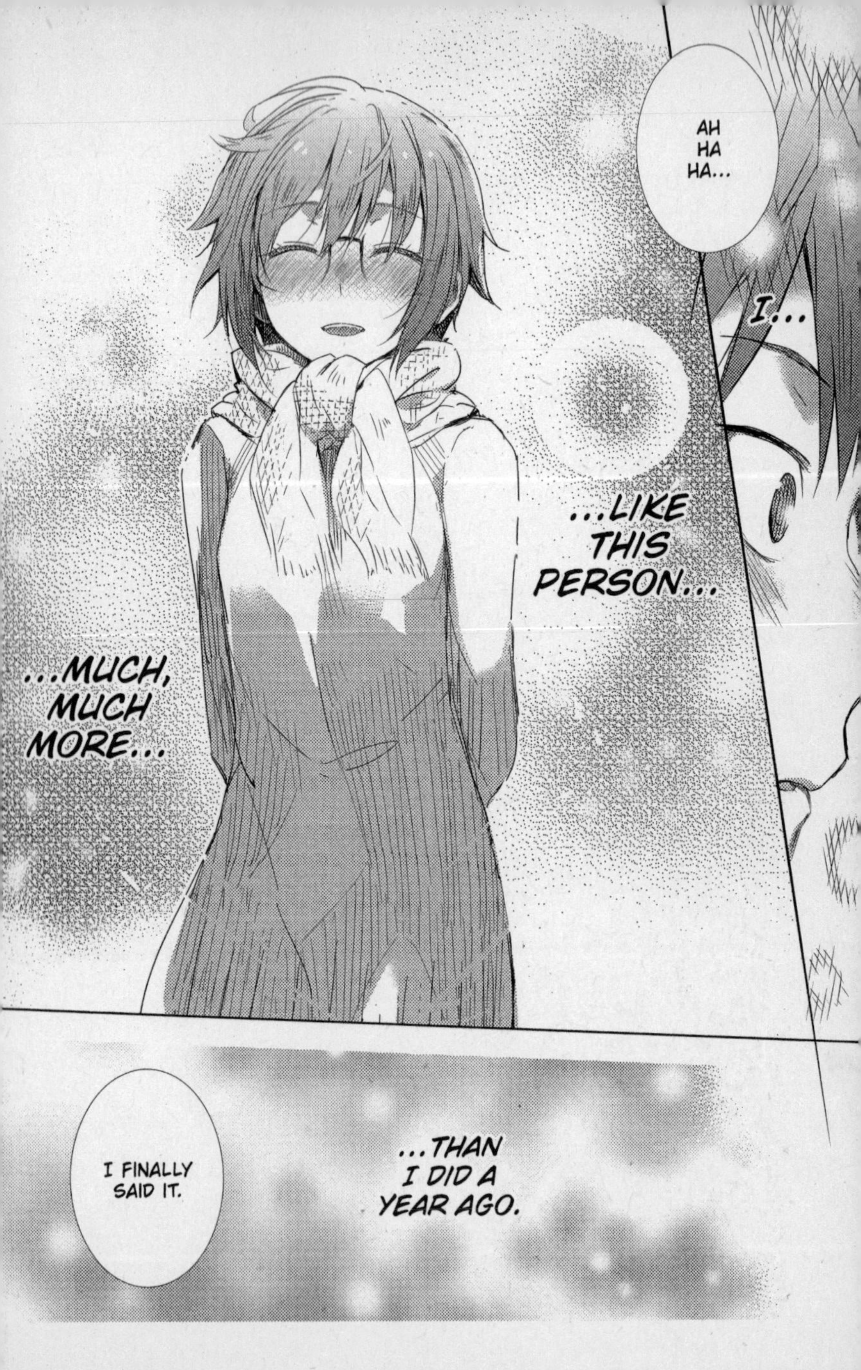
AH HA HA...
I...
...LIKE THIS PERSON...
...MUCH, MUCH MORE...
...THAN I DID A YEAR AGO.
I FINALLY SAID IT.

CONTINUED IN THE
NEXT VOLUME.

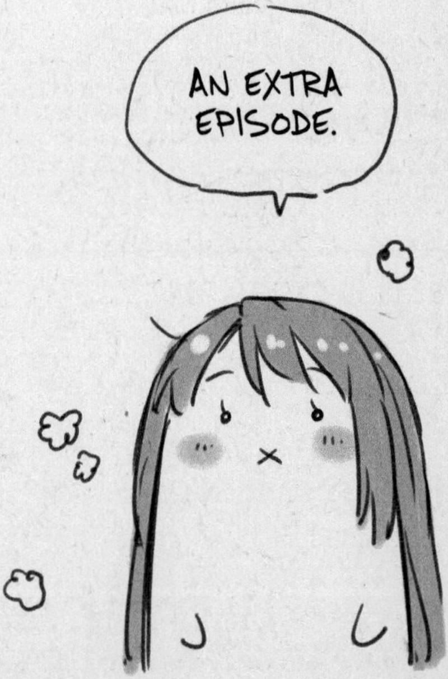
AN EXTRA EPISODE.

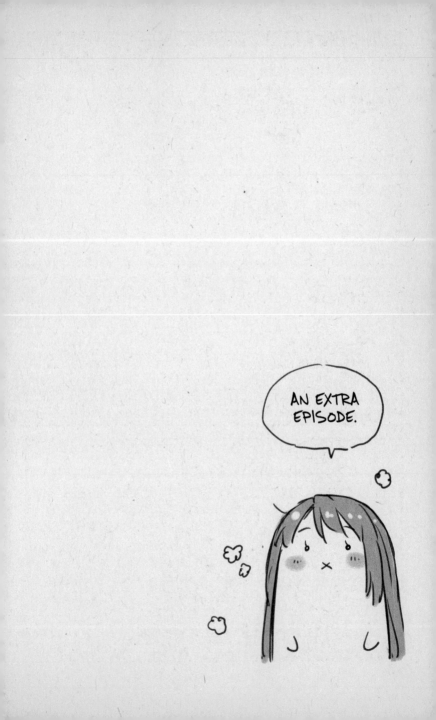

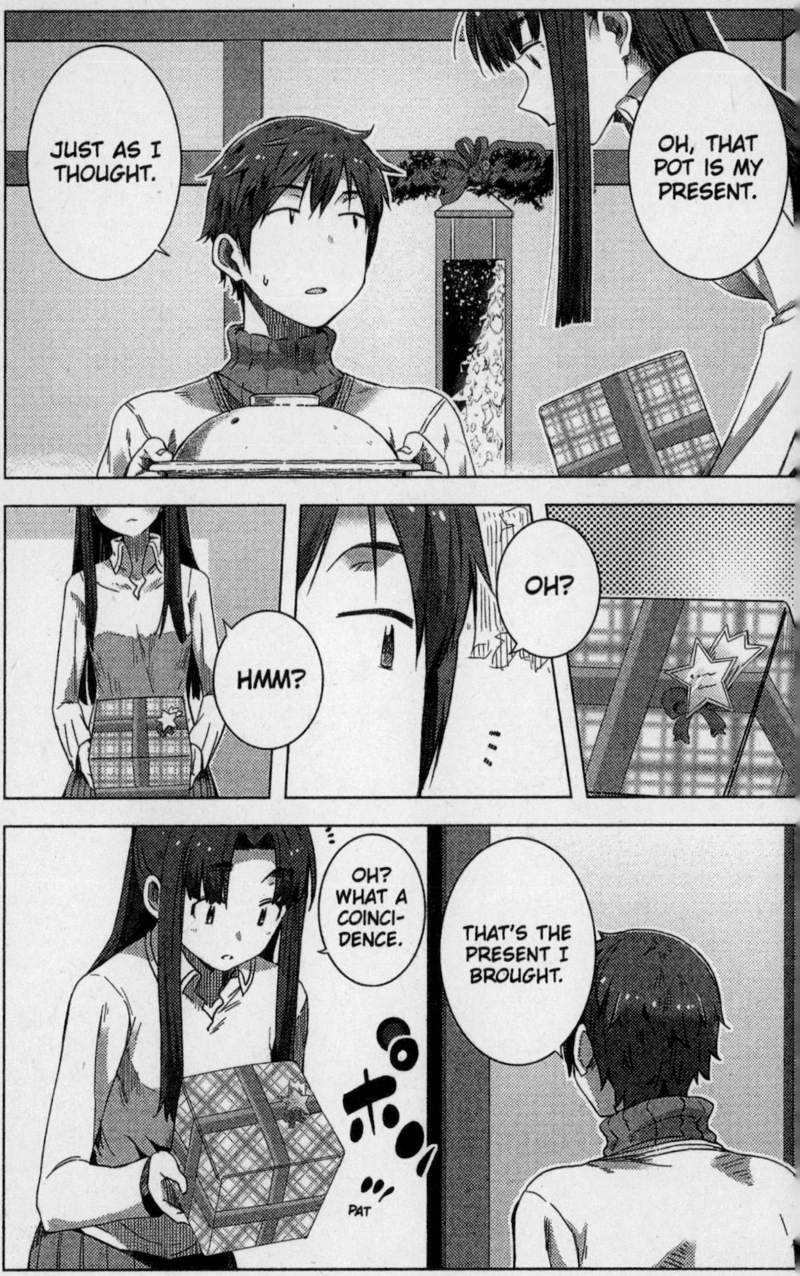
OH, THAT POT IS MY PRESENT.
JUST AS I THOUGHT.
OH?
HMM?
THAT'S THE PRESENT I BROUGHT.
OH? WHAT A COINCIDENCE.
PAT

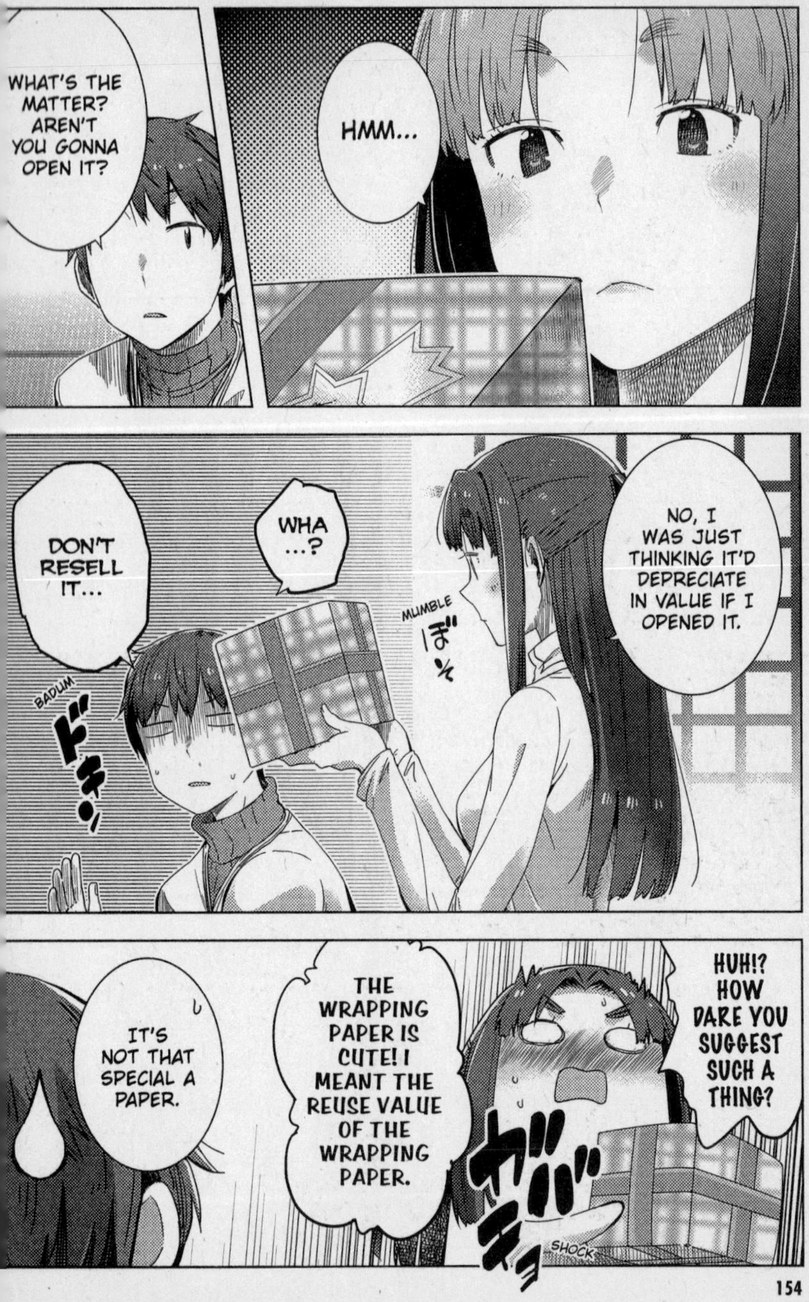
HMM...
WHAT'S THE MATTER? AREN'T YOU GONNA OPEN IT?
NO, I WAS JUST THINKING IT'D DEPRECIATE IN VALUE IF I OPENED IT.
MUMBLE
ぼそ
WHA ...?
DON'T RESELL IT...
BADUM
ドキ
HUH!? HOW DARE YOU SUGGEST SUCH A THING?
SHOCK
THE WRAPPING PAPER IS CUTE! I MEANT THE REUSE VALUE OF THE WRAPPING PAPER.
IT'S NOT THAT SPECIAL A PAPER.

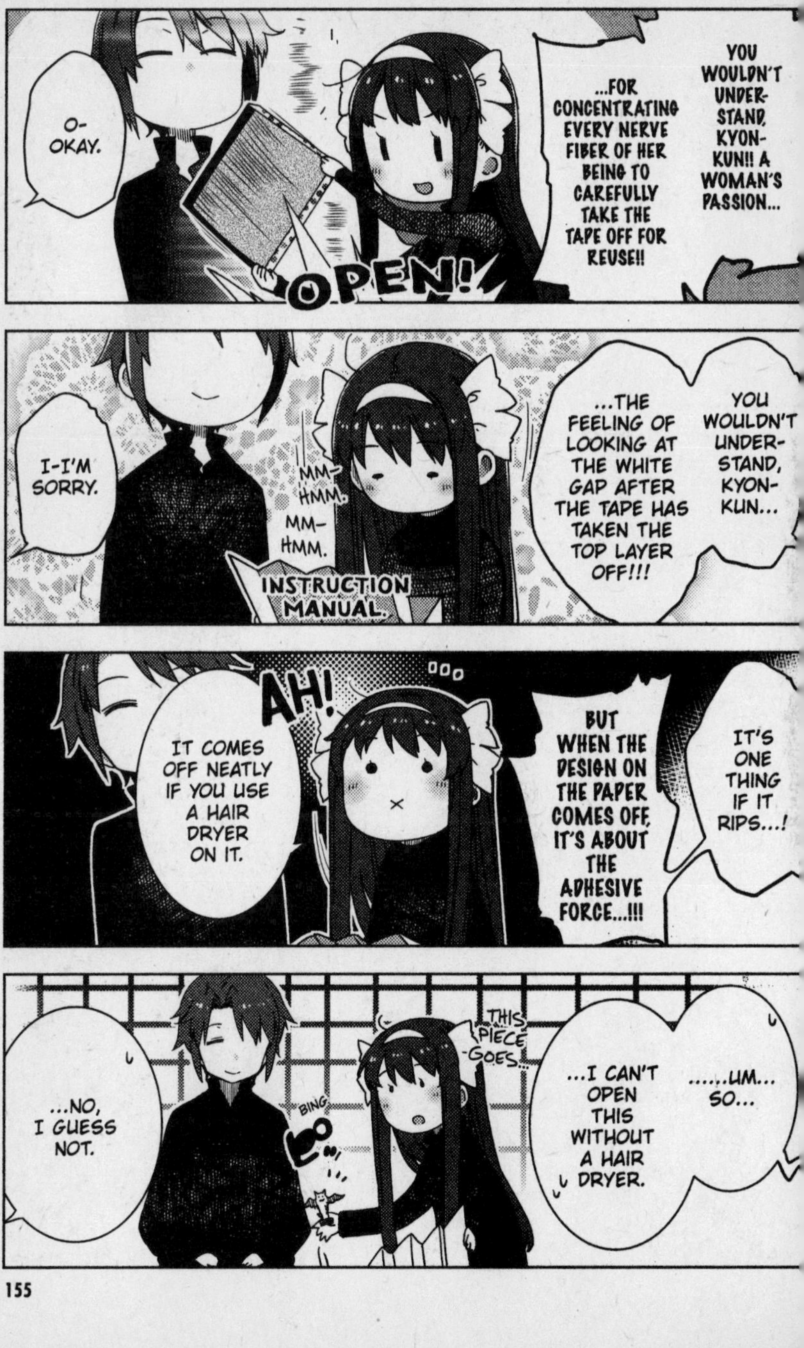
YOU WOULDN'T UNDERSTAND, KYON-KUN!! A WOMAN'S PASSION...
...FOR CONCENTRATING EVERY NERVE FIBER OF HER BEING TO CAREFULLY TAKE THE TAPE OFF FOR REUSE!!
OPEN!
O-OKAY.
YOU WOULDN'T UNDERSTAND, KYON-KUN...
...THE FEELING OF LOOKING AT THE WHITE GAP AFTER THE TAPE HAS TAKEN THE TOP LAYER OFF!!!
MM-HMM.
MM-HMM.
INSTRUCTION MANUAL.
I-I'M SORRY.
IT'S ONE THING IF IT RIPS...!
BUT WHEN THE DESIGN ON THE PAPER COMES OFF, IT'S ABOUT THE ADHESIVE FORCE...!!!
AH!
IT COMES OFF NEATLY IF YOU USE A HAIR DRYER ON IT.
......UM... SO...
...I CAN'T OPEN THIS WITHOUT A HAIR DRYER.
THIS PIECE GOES...
BING
...NO, I GUESS NOT.

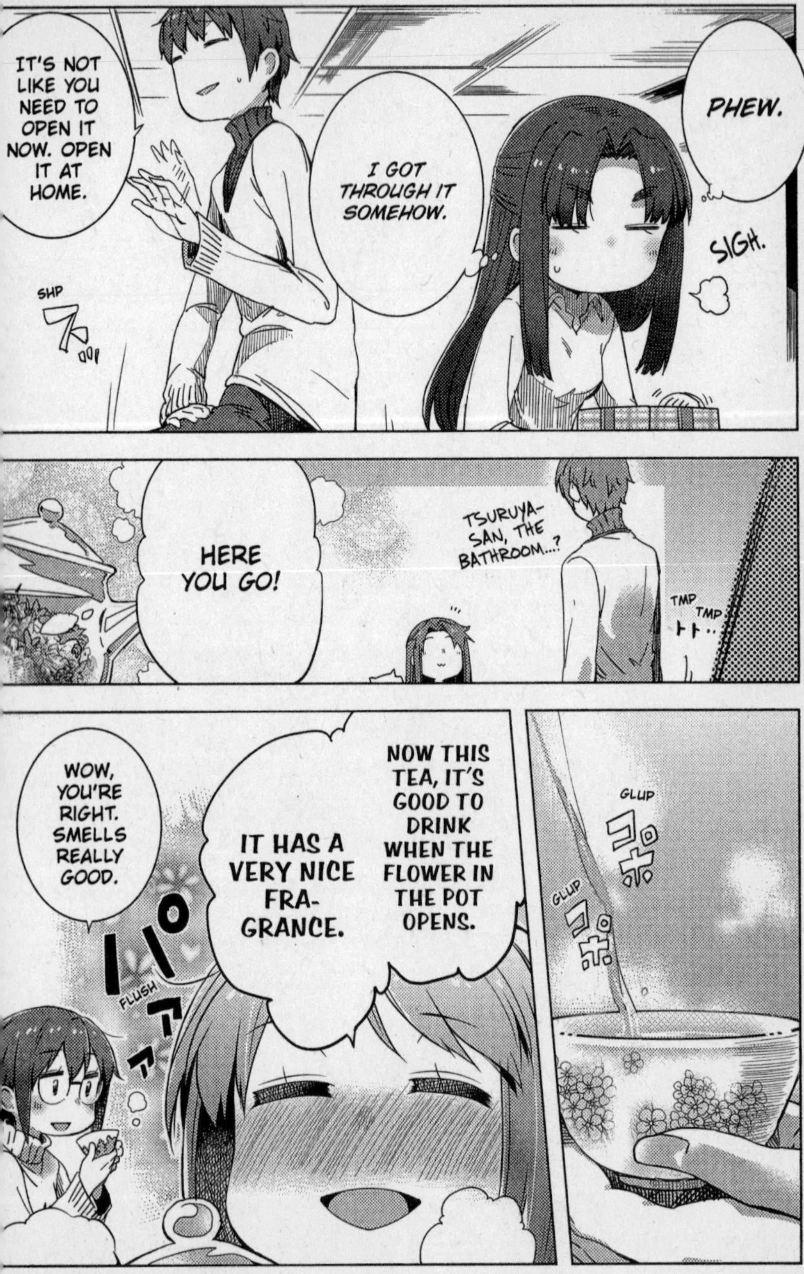
PHEW.
I GOT THROUGH IT SOMEHOW.
IT'S NOT LIKE YOU NEED TO OPEN IT NOW. OPEN IT AT HOME.
SIGH.
SHP
TSURUYA-SAN, THE BATHROOM...?
TMP TMP
HERE YOU GO!
GLUP
GLUP
NOW THIS TEA, IT'S GOOD TO DRINK WHEN THE FLOWER IN THE POT OPENS.
IT HAS A VERY NICE FRA-GRANCE.
WOW, YOU'RE RIGHT. SMELLS REALLY GOOD.
FLUSH

OHHHH?
THIS TEA CHANGES FLAVOR EVERY TIME YOU POUR.
SMILE SMILE SMILE
OH, I'M SORRY, YOU SHOULD HAVE SOME TOO, SENPA—
NO, NO.
THIS IS A PRESENT FOR YOU, NAGATO-SAN.
BUT THERE'S SO MUCH TEA LEFT...
THERE IS.
SO DRINK UP!
FLINCH
UMM...
SHE COULD NOT SAY NO IN THE FACE OF THAT INNOCENT, UNWAVERING LOVE.

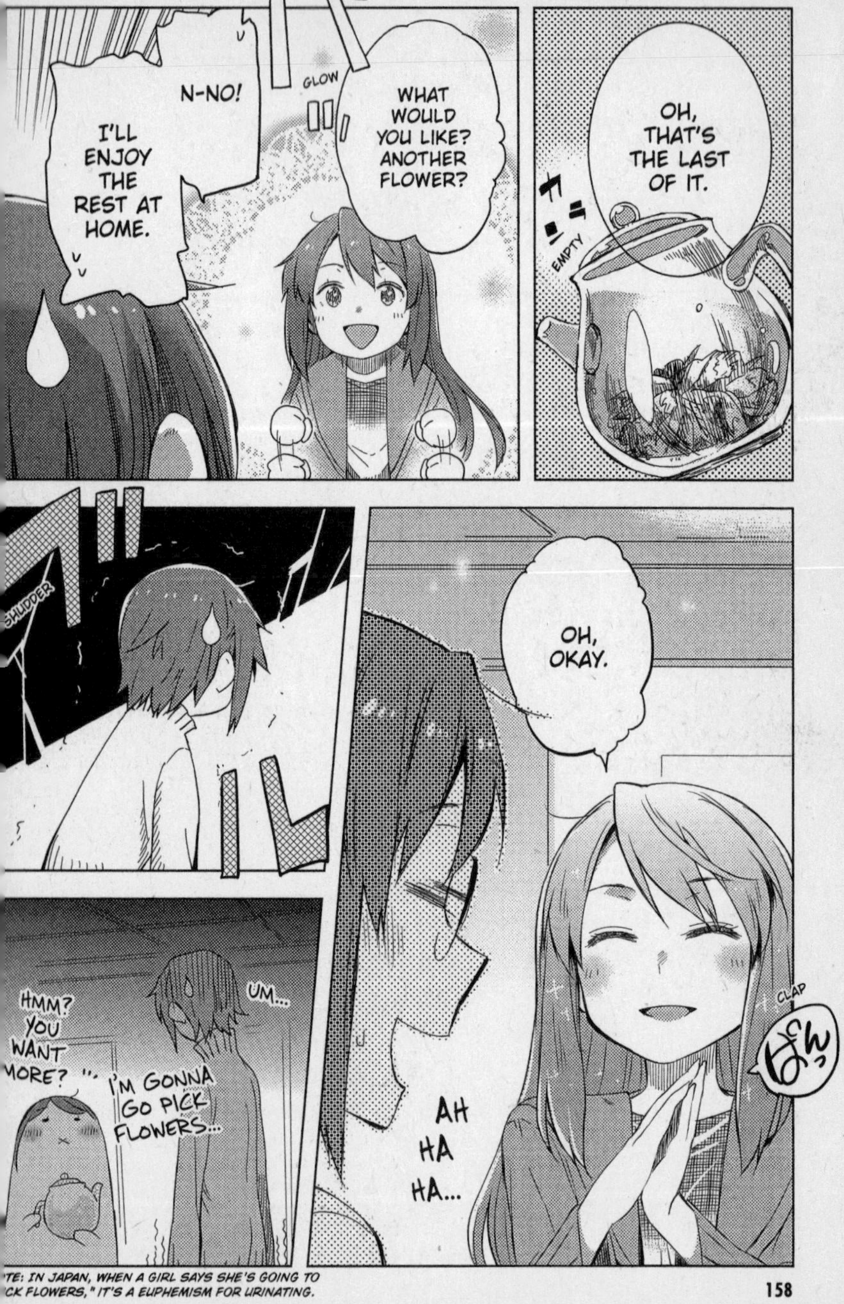
OH, THAT'S THE LAST OF IT.
EMPTY
GLOW
WHAT WOULD YOU LIKE? ANOTHER FLOWER?
N-NO!
I'LL ENJOY THE REST AT HOME.
OH, OKAY.
CLAP
ぱんっ
AH HA HA...
SHUDDER
UM...
HMM? YOU WANT MORE?
I'M GONNA GO PICK FLOWERS...

TE: IN JAPAN, WHEN A GIRL SAYS SHE'S GOING TO
CK FLOWERS," IT'S A EUPHEMISM FOR URINATING.

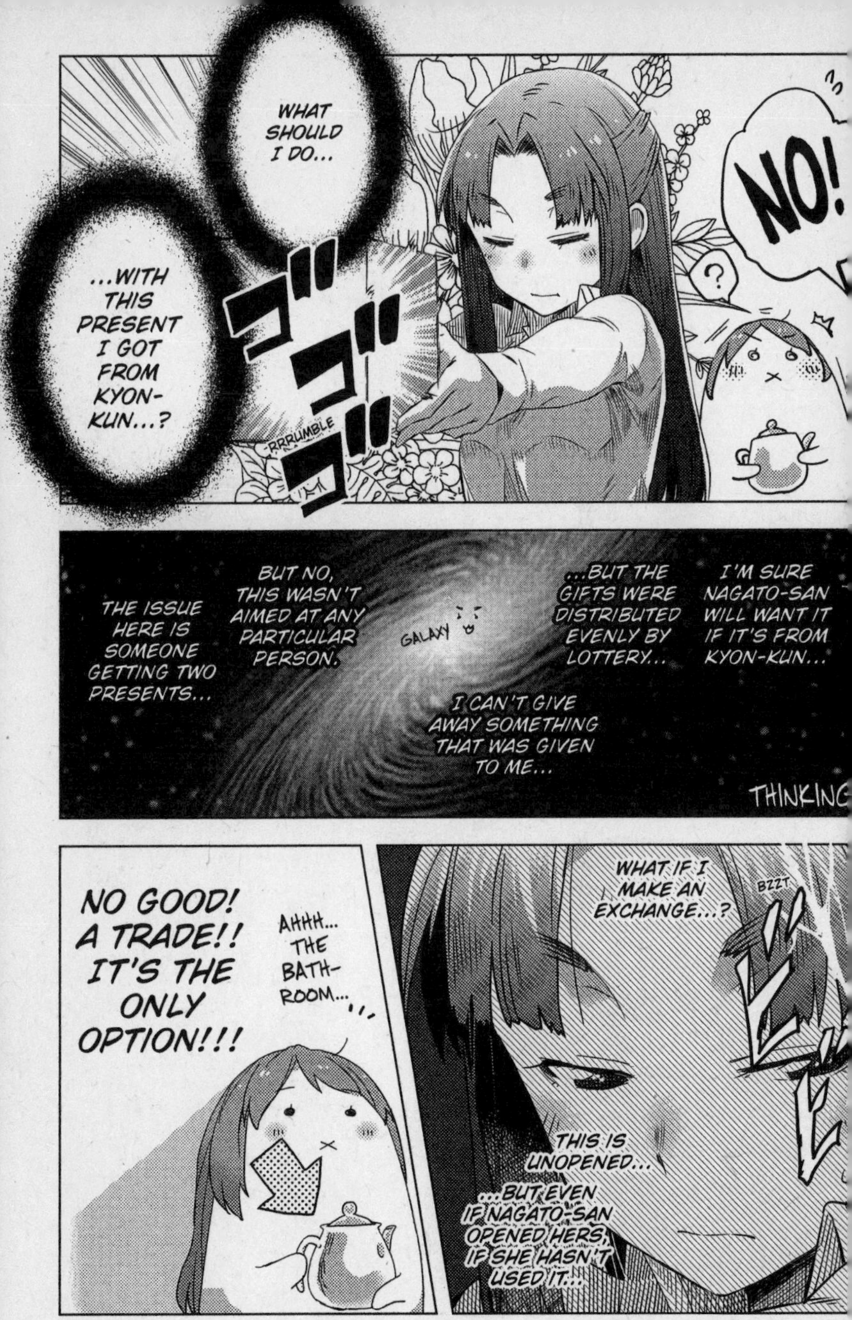
NO!
?
WHAT SHOULD I DO...
RRRUMBLE
...WITH THIS PRESENT I GOT FROM KYON-KUN...?
I'M SURE NAGATO-SAN WILL WANT IT IF IT'S FROM KYON-KUN...
...BUT THE GIFTS WERE DISTRIBUTED EVENLY BY LOTTERY...
GALAXY
BUT NO, THIS WASN'T AIMED AT ANY PARTICULAR PERSON.
THE ISSUE HERE IS SOMEONE GETTING TWO PRESENTS...
I CAN'T GIVE AWAY SOMETHING THAT WAS GIVEN TO ME...
THINKING
BZZT
WHAT IF I MAKE AN EXCHANGE...?
THIS IS UNOPENED...
...BUT EVEN IF NAGATO-SAN OPENED HERS, IF SHE HASN'T USED IT...
AHHH... THE BATH-ROOM...
NO GOOD! A TRADE!! IT'S THE ONLY OPTION!!!

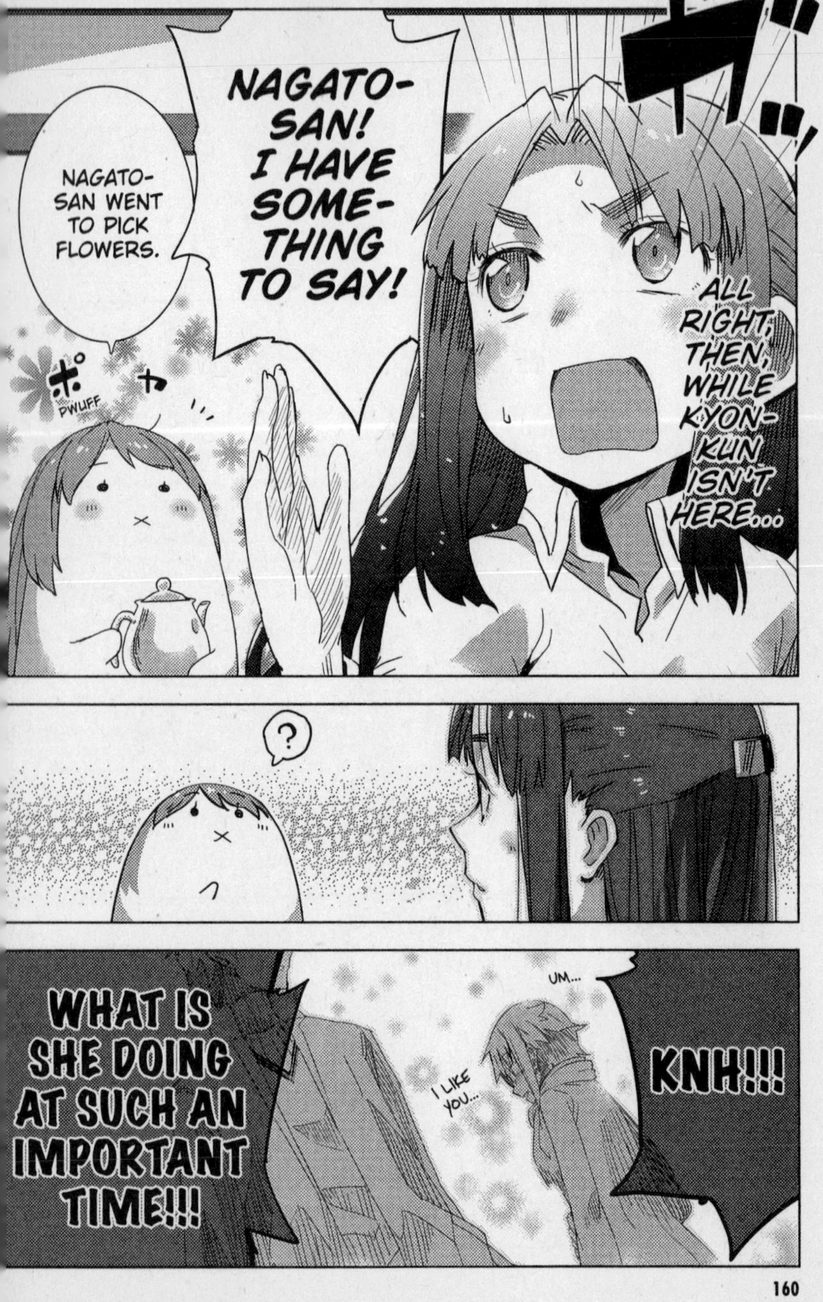
BAM
ALL RIGHT, THEN, WHILE KYON-KUN ISN'T HERE...
NAGATO-SAN! I HAVE SOMETHING TO SAY!
NAGATO-SAN WENT TO PICK FLOWERS.
PWUFF
?
KNH!!!
UM...
I LIKE YOU...
WHAT IS SHE DOING AT SUCH AN IMPORTANT TIME!!!

ASAKURA-SAN IS TAKING THIS
VERY SERIOUSLY, BUT THERE'S
JUST A REINDEER MASK INSIDE.

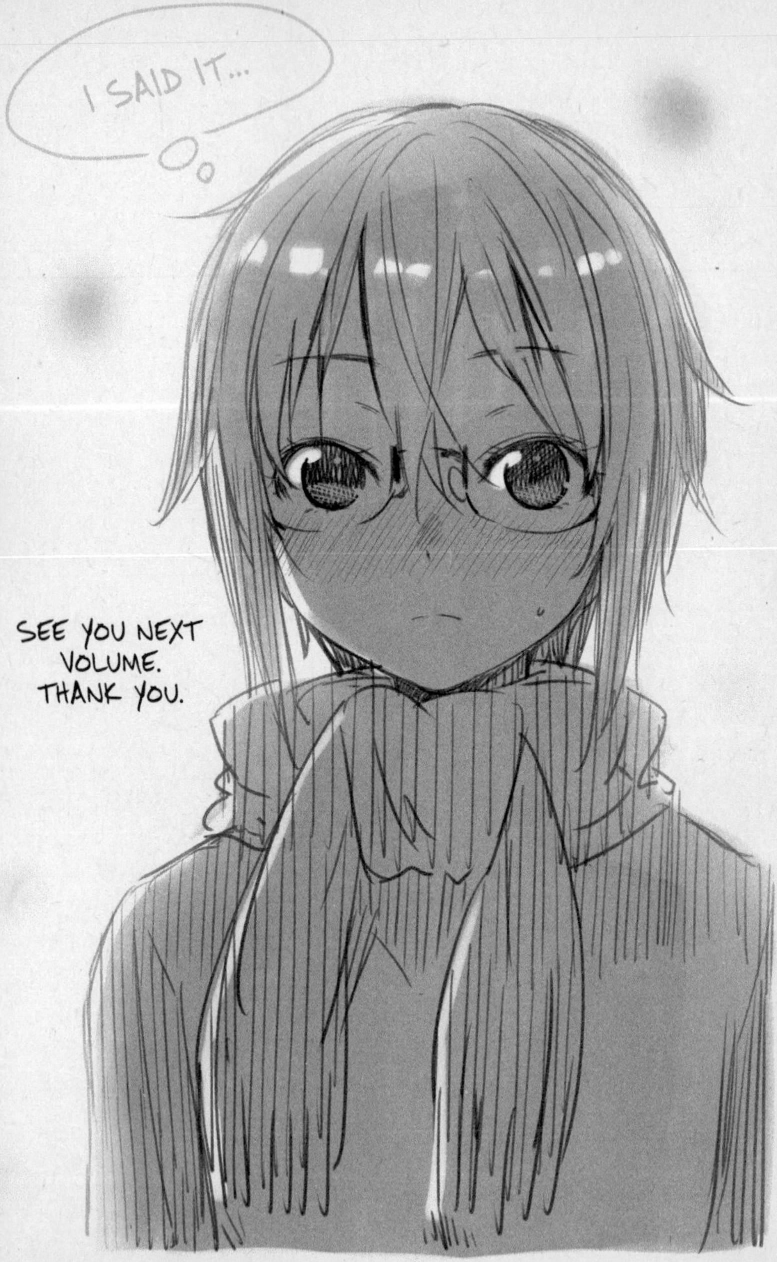
I SAID IT...
SEE YOU NEXT VOLUME. THANK YOU.

# THE DISAPPEARANCE OF NAGATO
# YUKI-CHAN

**7**

WITHDRAWN FROM COLLECTION OF SACRAMENTO PUBLIC LIBRARY

SACRAMENTO PUBLIC LIBRARY
828 "I" Street
Sacramento, CA 95814
04/15

Original Story: Nagaru Tanigawa
Manga: PUYO
Character Design: Noizi Ito

Translation: Yoshito Hinton
Lettering: Abigail Blackman

This book is a work of fiction. Names, characters, places, and incidents are the product of the author's imagination or are used fictitiously. Any resemblance to actual events, locales, or persons, living or dead, is coincidental.

NAGATO YUKI CHAN NO SHOSHITSU Volume 7 © Nagaru TANIGAWA • Noizi ITO 2014 © PUYO 2014. Edited by KADOKAWA SHOTEN. First published in Japan in 2014 by KADOKAWA CORPORATION, Tokyo. English translation rights arranged with KADOKAWA CORPORATION, Tokyo, through TUTTLE-MORI AGENCY, INC., Tokyo.

English translation © 2015 by Hachette Book Group, Inc.

All rights reserved. In accordance with the U.S. Copyright Act of 1976, the scanning, uploading, and electronic sharing of any part of this book without the permission of the publisher is unlawful piracy and theft of the author's intellectual property. If you would like to use material from the book (other than for review purposes), prior written permission must be obtained by contacting the publisher at permissions@hbgusa.com. Thank you for your support of the author's rights.

Yen Press
Hachette Book Group
1290 Avenue of the Americas
New York, NY 10104
www.hachettebookgroup.com
www.yenpress.com

Yen Press is an imprint of Hachette Book Group, Inc.
The Yen Press name and logo are trademarks of Hachette Book Group, Inc.

The publisher is not responsible for websites (or their content) that are not owned by the publisher.

First Yen Press Edition: March 2015

ISBN: 978-0-316-38374-5

10 9 8 7 6 5 4 3 2 1

BVG

Printed in the United States of America